A Music Biography

by
Sid Griffin

Sierra Records & Books
Pasadena, California 91107-0853

Dedicated to all of history's musicians who every played straight from the heart.
–Sid Griffin

Printed in the United States of America
First Edition

Library of Congress Catalog Card Number: 85-50827
ISBN: 0-916003-00-0
ISBN: 0-916003-01-9 (pbk.)

Publisher: John M. Delgatto
Art Direction: Heather Harris
Editor: Sid Griffin
Asst. Editor: Dennis Cooper

Not so long ago but, oh, it seems so far away, there was country music without Willie, Waylon and Alabama. When their time came, Waylon and Willie were called outlaws because of their music and appearance. Yet there was a time, before most of us had even heard of those so-called outlaws, when long-haired young men were experimenting with a sound they called "country-rock."

My personal thoughts race back to those January nights in 1973 at the old Calabasas Saloon north of L.A. where the jam sessions of guitar virtuoso Clarence White, the Country Gazette, various others of the contemporary music scene and a guy named Gram Parsons were setting the hills on fire. Hearing Gram and Roger McGuinn duet on their "Drug Store Truck Drivin' Man" while sharing a pitcher of beer with Clarence will never fade from my memory. A lot of progressive country music was being played for the first time at those jams and we all felt that we were on the threshold of something big. Only Gram Parsons seemed to realize how big.

With some of our Sierra releases such as NASHVILLE WEST, KENTUCKY COLONELS – LIVING IN THE PAST and GRAM PARSONS AND THE FALLEN ANGELS – LIVE, 1973, we have tried to recapture that time and share it with those who weren't fortunate enough to have been there. Through recordings we have been able to spread the magic of those times and those people to thousands who have turned on to the fact that something new and wonderful was happening right under our noses. It took too many years and too many claims of being "the first" for us to realize it.

This is a book about the music of only one of those persons – Gram Parsons. Yet as you read the words of those who interacted with him on a musical basis you will quickly see that Gram was a catalyst for a unique group of pickers and players and the development of a blend of music that has kept us rockin' even in today's jaded world. And, it is a music that will be heard for a long, long time to come.

There can be no definitive Gram Parsons story. No one but Gram Parsons could have lived it and no one but Gram Parsons could have told it. Sid Griffin, through his compilation of these interviews, has attempted to represent phases of Gram's musical life that have never before been brought together in one place to examine. The recollections and musings of these people who knew Gram and whose lives were touched by his musical genius give us, for the first time, more than just a glimpse into the very special music he staked his life on.

In conversations with my close friends Marley Brant and Paul Surratt, we often verbalize the belief that the rock and country music of the past decade and a half has been fragmented. If Gram's music and the innovations that he and his musical colleagues had started to develop had continued they could well have re-established the type of mainstream consensus that was associated with the rise of Elvis and the Beatles.

Hopefully, this book will provide insights into what was and what might have been. All in all, the magic was real and Gram Parsons lives on in threads of musical styles and presentations that even he could never have imagined.

John Delgatto
Pasadena, 1985

Table of Contents

1963

Introduction

Gram Parsons: A Music Biography is a literary montage consisting of essays, interviews, rare photographs, more interviews and a complete discography of one of America's great unsung musical heroes. It should serve as an introduction to Parsons' music for the newcomer and it should help the more experienced Parsons fan who simply wants to know more about Cosmic American Music.

Essays written both for this book and for other publications are interspersed with interviews of musicians who worked closely with Gram Parsons during his short career, many of whom went on to greater fame in no small part because of what they learned from Gram himself. In addition three previously unpublished interviews with Gram Parsons are printed here in order that Gram might "tell you how it all went down" from a Waycross, Georgia standpoint.

Throughout the book rare photographs of Gram at various stages of his career are used to illustrate certain themes, and if one picture is worth a thousand words then we are truly blessed by the generosity of Gram Parsons' friends, because these photographs are amazing. As a capstone to our work, Mark Holland of the Gram Parsons Memorial Foundation has allowed us to reprint his discography of the Grievous

1970

Angel and its completeness is the end product of many hours of hard work.

All too often a person's contributions are overlooked by others in favor of someone else's work, not that anyone was cruel or thoughtless, but that one person got the breaks and the other did not. It really boils down to the unfairness of life in general. Some people seem to be destined to labor just out of the limelight while another gets credit for a lesser effort.

Indeed life can be very difficult or even out and out painful and we sometimes wonder why we keep moving on. It's then I hear a Delta blues played by some sharecropper's son who never had a chance, a bluegrass lick which could be traced to the Scottish hills of three hundred years ago or some kid in a garage pounding away on a guitar because it's the most immediate avenue of expression available to him and his friends. And I no longer want to watch the parade, I want to get in there and pound away with the rest of them.

I hope there's a feeling which can do that to you too.

Sid Griffin
Los Angeles, California
July, 1985

The Outcast Southerner:

GP, 1973

©1973 KIM GOTTLIEB

Gram Parsons as Iconoclast

"A guy moved into town
I ain't seen you around
I feel a brand new heartache coming on..."
(Boudleaux and Felice Bryant)

"The South is America's Sicily."
Marshall Frady

Circa 1969

As a native Southerner I have a lot of owning up to do. Less than a decade ago I didn't consider myself a Southerner nor did I know what it meant to be one. I never thought of myself in regionalistic terms at all. When high school civic teachers asked me how I viewed myself politically I said I was a humanist, after which I would turn beet red.

Few people from the South with what could be called liberal politics wanted to raise the Confederate flag in those days. The South had been through its worst decade since Reconstruction and that's saying a great deal. Racial and political turmoil were compounded by radical economic changes and vilification at the hands of more than one social carpetbagger who needed to prove he was holier than us. Looking back I guess most of the nation was a lot less backward but it still didn't feel too good to have dirt flung on us from all corners.

I was born and raised along the banks of the Ohio River, the western border of the Mason–Dixon line. This gave me and my fellow Kentuckians some comfort since we felt we were authentic Dixiecrats yet far enough north to be removed a bit and therefore relatively blameless of the Deep South's racial troubles. Whenever the eleven states of the old Confederacy had another confrontation with the federal government we could turn our backs and tsk, tsk with the rest of the Yankees.

I now realize how wrong I was and I'm sorry, completely sorry I was ever such a fool. Years of being told how poor your schools are, how bad your health care is, how passé your values are, how backward your lifestyle is and how plain ignorant you are have a way of taking their toll on you. My brothers and I put up a pretty good front though we sure were hurting on the inside.

Marshall Frady was right. While the rest of the nation needs the South for its textiles, natural resources, cheap labor and unspoiled beauty, they don't really enjoy our company. They just want us near enough so they can use us and far enough away so we won't embarrass them by our backporch mannerisms. Most of all they need us for our Culture, for it gives America its scope. Only the West can come close to matching us in vastness and breadth of vision. The Central North is unimaginative, the Northeast is polluted and overcrowded, the Pacific Northwest is unpublicized and the worth of Alaska and Hawaii is still being gauged.

The South gave America its music for both jazz and rock'n'roll originated there. Southern lifestyle, while mocked when it is the sharecropper of Mississippi, is widely imitated as being extremely genteel and of good graces when it is the manor lords of aristocratic Virginia. Most regions have one city they can point to as a citadel of sophistication like San Francisco in the West and Boston in the Northeast. The South has three, those being Charleston, Atlanta and New Orleans. Everyone knows about grits, black–eyed peas and ham hocks but what do we know of the cuisine of other regions of the U.S.?

It is very difficult for me to look back because while the South's racial history is disgraceful, it has often been the region to lead the nation in many ways. Today it is the first in economic and population growth and is certainly no worse in race relations than South Boston, Pontiac, Michigan or Skokie, Illinois.

It is not my purpose here to go into the economic reasons behind the South's politics other than to say they were cause and effect. Nor am I writing a eulogy or paen to Dixie living. I'm writing to tell you why I now realize I am a Southerner. I'm writing to say Gram Parsons was a primary reason behind my discovery and a similar discovery by many of my friends.

My first exposure to the music of Gram Parsons remains my strongest. The song was "Hickory Wind" and with that lovely, evocative title I decided to attend the University of South Carolina upon high school graduation. I told my parents and they were delighted, probably because they figured I would be less exposed to so-called Northern radical thought. I said South Carolina had the courses I wanted to take but I really wanted to see if there were "many tall pines".

I had always enjoyed the Byrds; they were possibly my favorite group. My whole life had been dominated by rock'n'roll. It's been about the only thing that hasn't let me down in some way or another. "Sweetheart of the Rodeo" was a departure for the Byrds and it was also the beginning of a departure for me.

Sweetheart did not set forth any specifics or lay out any thought to the Movement in detail but the album showed guidance by example. Here, the songs seemed to be saying, country music ("redneck" music to all too many of us) isn't to be looked down on; it is your nation's heritage and you should be proud of it. C'mon, there's nothing wrong with the Christian Life or Life in Prison for that matter. It's all the same and we are all of one kin. That's right; you, me, rockers, rednecks, reactionaries, radicals...we're all flowers in God's bouquet, as Little Richard is so fond of saying. And if we don't stop bickering amongst ourselves we're gonna blow it and lose the planet.

Needless to say the catalyst behind the musical change and the reasoning behind it was Gram Parsons, a man who didn't want the Byrds to "write their own ersatz Dylan tunes". It's a fairly cruel statement to make around Roger McGuinn or Chris Hillman but at least all of them realized it was time for a change, time for a challenge. "We set out to hire a piano player and good God! It's George Jones in a sequin suit," said McGuinn.

In the Byrds, and later with the Burritos and as a solo artist Gram Parsons continually tried to unite the country and rock audiences. In retrospect he failed because neither side was willing to drop their petty prejudices about each other, but the Georgia Peach certainly gave it his best shot before calling it a day. He failed like all true romantics but only because his mission was doomed from the start.

The Gilded Palace of Sin was where Gram Parsons moved to the city and confronted its myriad evils for the first time. Women and infidelity, personal courage or lack of it, insecurity, simple loneliness or even the city itself were sung about with conviction and an inner strength that seemed to be saying everything would be all right if you have a little faith in yourself. Of special note is "Hot Burrito #1", a song which moves me to tears to this day. Parsons sounds like a white Otis Redding and they called the Big O "Mr. Pitiful". They both ended up gone before their public really knew what talents they were.

Upon arriving in Columbia to attend the University I recognized how so much of what I'd heard was true. The South has an infinite number of Chambers of Commerce who all declare their area to be a "Land of Contrasts". If there ever was a true statement that's got to be it. South Carolina has rednecks, a growing radical population, Holy Rollers, high rollers, WCTU clubs, moonshiners, the Silent Majority leading their lives of quiet desperation and good ole boys raising hell. Usually in the same family.

"One Hundred Years From Now": the Southerner's much–heralded sense of tradition shows up in rock'n'roll. You don't hit the rock community over the head with anything to get your message through, especially a peaceful one. Gram knew this and he lead by example in a Christ–like way. A wonderful mix of country, rock and Deep South sincerity.

Gram Parsons was a relatively well–known singer in the Deep South. He had his pockets of fans throughout the country and indeed throughout the world but with the possible exception of the Troubadour bar there was no place he was more loved than in the South. Young Southerners, for the first time flexing their considerable political muscle and realizing the need for a break with tradition, saw a kindred soul and a trusted spokesperson in Gram Parsons. The "poor little rich boy", as Buddy Scoppa wrote, was one of the crowd. Gram encapsulated the fears and expectations of the South's young in his music. He knew he loved the South yet he knew, like Walker Percy before him, he had to leave to get the necessary perspective. He loved tradition but knew it was time for a break with the past. He lost his accent and felt guilty about it. The one–time Harvard Theology major ran from one end of shunning vices to the other extreme of searching them out. He knew enough to know he didn't know enough to figure out why life, which has so much potential, is so wickedly awful.

I see Gram Parsons as a musician not worried or concerned about what others thought of his own life but concerned about lessening the burdens of others with a few plaintive tunes. I remember buying a *Zoo World* magazine for a review of a Fallen Angels concert and being shocked when the reviewer hardly mentioned the show; instead he attacked (there is no other word) Parsons for having several Confederate flags onstage as props. In a bizarre misconception of Marshall McLuhan the writer called the flags "symbols of Southern repression and racism" and all but labeled Parsons and Emmylou Harris as Klan members.

It was a watershed for me. You might say I took sides on the issue. My first reaction was to counterattack but I felt this was a simple case of ego needing to be curbed. Rather I found it in my liberal bleeding heart to see the writer didn't know what he was talking about and that you "don't criticize what you can't understand".

Gram Parsons' music, and that of the Byrds, is a universe knowing no boundaries, be they political, social or geographical. He is popular down South. He is popular in Norway, in France, in England, in Japan, in Manhattan, in Los Angeles and he is a superstar to the Dutch. He belongs to all of us.

The September 2, 1979 Los Angeles *Times* carried a story by Art Fein proclaiming rockabilly tops with England's teens. Bored with the Led Zeppelins of stadium fame, under 21's in Britain have turned to the music of the South for their release. "Do they really rock'n'bop all night down South?" asked one rockabilly fan of Fein.

WOPA radio interview, Burrito tour, 1970

Since the rise of Jimmy Carter the South has become popular in a unique way: sort of a curiosity to the rest of the nation. As Carter lost popularity, a great deal of the public has gone back to their former way of thinking. It's too bad in a way, I thought things were opening up. New York City has the Lone Star Cafe, a wildly popular C&W nightspot in mid–Manhattan. Laurel Canyon cowboys are are all over L.A. and Emmylou Harris continues to keep Gram's music in front of the public. Even the *Village Voice*, which in 1974 delivered a scathing attack on Lynyrd Skynyrd for "Sweet Home Alabama", has come around. Where they once thought "Sweet Home Alabama" was somehow pro-Wallace, a recent issue declared "it's too bad W.E.B. DuBois didn't didn't live to see the Allman Bros." I agree. I think the racial harmony in the Allmans would have done him a lot of good. Recently Joe Ely, considered by many to be Gram's heir, jammed with British punk–rockers The Clash at a Northern California concert.

Dizzy Gillespie, who refused to go down South for years, once told me he felt the South was destined to lead America in race relations. Gillespie is a native of South Carolina and I told him about Parsons. "Sounds like such a nice white boy," Dizzy said, "I hope everything works out for him."

Otis Redding and Steve Cropper worked together like hand in glove because they were two slightly different reflections of the same thing; because they shared the same Southern hardships in so many ways. Parsons refused to go to South Africa with the Byrds because he'd "seen enough prejudice to last a lifetime."

First Burrito lineup - Jon Corneal, Sneeky, Hillman, friend, GP, Ethridge, 1968

It's unfortunate how a superficial thing like a Confederate flag or a rural accent can turn people against you. It's an awful prejudice yet I'd never return the hate of those who held such beliefs because it would only make me as sanctimonious as they. There was once a time when long hair was considered either a mark of a homosexual or a Communist or both. Judgements based on extraneous images are absurd.

We are what we are and Gram Parsons forced me to own up to many things about myself. Nik Cohn wrote these words about The Band and I submit to you that they apply to Gram Parsons as well, "...their evocations were indistinct but they were the whole American past and all its space. Small towns in the Civil War, at the turn of the century, during the Depression; saloons with cracked windows and dance halls with leaky ceilings and hotel rooms with naked light bulbs; highways, deserts, great rivers, mountains; girls glimpsed once or left behind and revisited many times, for a few night's shelter; Saturday afternoon outings downstream or to the races, or over country roads in fourth–hand cars, with a bottle passed from hand to hand; truck stops, railroads, three–cell jails; gold rushes and oil strikes, eternal dreams of wealth; bad debts, hangovers; and movement, always movement– forever that sense of traveling back and forth across the land, trapped by its immensity and infinite change."

Take "Hot Burrito #1" again. Stanley Booth said it could have been written and recorded by the Platters in 1956 and he's right. Moreover it could be recorded by George Jones today or Sam Cooke in 1963, the song is so warm and stylized. Stylized not to a particular musical genre but to a musical feel, a Southern musical feel that Parsons called "white soul". Honesty and passion are the two hallmarks of the music of the South and it does not matter what kind of music you are refering to. Blues, country and western, rock'n'roll and jazz all originated down South and were carried to New York, Kansas City, Chicago and the West Coast by Southern musicians. Soul, believability, commitment, whatever you wish to call it, all these styles weighted aesthetically by their honesty and passion. Doug Sahm once sang, "you just can't live in Texas if you don't have a lotta soul," and Gram would have known exactly what he meant.

Columbia is the capital of South Carolina and the Statehouse is only a block and a half away from the University. But the block and a half can seem painfully long to the youth of South Carolina as they try to convince the elders who habitate the Statehouse nuclear energy is dangerous, that predominately Black schools are going without sufficient funds and textile plants are just this side of hell for workers. "Good luck to you all, I'm never coming South again," said Gram to the rest of the Shilos the day they broke up. Hell, the guy never left. He was with us when Jane Fonda spoke right after Kent State and the Army had a helicopter hovering over her head so you couldn't hear anything she said. He was with us when we pleaded not to have the Congaree Swamp (until recently practically untouched by man) sold to businesses and he threw up his hands when the State Legislature voted to have Barnwell become the nation's depository of nuclear waste if the Federal government would only send the state a little more money.

Anyone born since the outbreak of World War II has had some growing up to do, has had to come of age sooner or later if he or she did not wish to be an empty–headed tuna for the rest of their lives. Some people lost innocence with the firing of an assassin's bullets, others after the Democratic Convention of 1968, some after Kent State or Orangeburg. Others came of age in more personal, less dramatic ways. I lost my innocence, my naivete if you will, when I first heard Gram Parsons sing, for I knew then that there was more to life than what met the eye and that all of it was not going to be happy. The sense of movement Nik Cohn wrote about, the loss of a national purpose Jimmy Carter spoke of and the Sin Cities and Devils in Disguise Gram Parsons sang of are all related. I'm like Gram Parsons in a way, because I know enough to know I don't know enough. Parsons always said he really didn't know what the hell was going on in L.A. even after four years in town. "Man, when you been here as long as I have you'll know what I mean."

It was never the object or goal of this book to resurrect a fallen hero or clean up and clear out the facts behind Parsons' often unhappy life. Rather this book is about the music of Gram Parsons and how it affects the listener and those who were near him. This article, this book, Gram's music are about all of us in a way, about all of our experiences. Experiences we shared together, experiences we went through on our own and experiences we all felt but didn't know were enjoined. Gram Parsons was one hell of a smart but confused country boy and that is not a put down. It is a compliment. He gave us all the gift of his music so we could enjoy all styles without prejudice. And when you learn about others, when you begin to feel what they feel and think about what they think about, you gain a knowledge of yourself. Often this knowledge is so obvious you didn't even think about it. That is the way it was with me and the South.

A lot of my friends and I owe Gram a lot for teaching us about ourselves. We learned who we were and, equally important, we learned who we were not and who we could never be. I know now I take a lot of pride in what I am. Merle Haggard would understand. Jerry Lee would grin. The Devil would walk away knowing he couldn't have me and Socrates would say I was on the first plane to great self–awareness. Thanks to Gram Parsons and his music.

In Otis Redding's "Tramp" duet with Carla Thomas she admonishes him, "Otis, you're straight from the Georgia woods!" "That's *good*," Redding fires back. You're goddman right it is. And it's also good to be from Maine, Oregon or New Mexico. Or Japan or Egypt for that matter, as long as you're hung up on helping and not hurting. "Sometimes I wish I was a bird flying high above the Joshua Tree, circling and circling," Gram often said.

I'm getting carried away with my preaching now. I know that. I always do when it's something that matters. It's a great Southern tradition to reach for the hellfire and brimstone at the drop of a cause. I just wanted Gram and James Dickey and everybody to know I figured it's okay to own up to myself.

LeRoi Jones and Bob Dylan both have been quoted as saying the Beatles' main contribution to music was "making it alright to be white". In the same vein it could be said Gram Parsons made it all right to be a Southerner. Not that he gave validity to a stance, but he did show the trendies of the Sunset Strip the validity that was always present, the sanctity which sometimes gets obscured by regional hangups. If you've ever been to an LSU–Ole Miss game, if you've ever drunk too much Jack Daniels, if you've ever seen a horse give birth to a wide–eyed colt, if you've ever told a tall tale and kept a child enraptured, if you've ever stood alone in a field of tobacco you probably know Gram Parsons; you don't really owe him anything. But if you've never been out with the truckers and the kickers and the cowboy angels and recognized you're one of them then you don't know Gram at all. And you owe yourself a whole lot.

–Sid Griffin

BARRY FEINSTEIN

From a photo session for the first Burritos' LP, Joshua Tree, 1969

GP, 1969,

The Pacers, 1959, GP at far right

A Brief Look at Gram Parsons' Career

Gram Parsons' career was a hodgepodge of styles and groups ranging from the somewhat offbeat bands of his youth to the popular rock groups he was a member of in later years. Parsons' main musics were rock and country but it should be remembered he had a strong affinity for folk, blues and gospel.

To go back to the very beginning, Gram Parsons' first group might be the ensembles he led on the Parsons' front porch down South. His sister Avis and he would recruit a neighbor or two to make sure there was a sizable crowd before performing. Then Gram would put a Sun record on the family record player (usually a Presley selection) and imitate the singer while Avis and the neighbors acted like they were his backup band. Avis remembers how she pretended to play a toy piano Gram had set in front of her and if she actually did strike a key Gram would turn around and glare at her. "This was very serious business to him," she would later recall.

Perhaps Gram's first real group, if only in an amateur sense, was the Pacers. Formed in the late Fifties with teenage friends, the Pacers were a four piece of guitar, bass guitar, drums and Gram on another guitar and vocals. The Pacers played the hits of the day along with one or two country things. Somewhere around this time the very young Parsons attempted to write his first song. Gram then formed a Peter, Paul and Mary styled group called the Village Vanguards, but nothing ever came of it.

In his later teens Gram formed The Legends, a group that actually gave birth to three future recording stars, Gram, Jim Stafford and "Lobo" (Kent LaVoie). The Legends were another four piece, yet oddly enough they had no permanent bass player, just drums and three guitars. They were primarily a rock band and Stafford remembers they had some problems as to agreeing on which direction to go. Stafford, who later became a country star with several novelty hits, remembers telling Gram, "stick with country, you got country roots so you should stick with country."

Avis and Gram Parsons, 1956

BUS DIAL 239-9063 CODE 803 RES DIAL 244-3335

The Shilos

FEATURING ORIGINAL AND TRADITIONAL

Folk Music

LEWIS D. FREEMAN
MANAGER

P. O. BOX 6425
GREENVILLE, S. C.

The Shilos, 1963

Gram fronting the Shilos, 1963

The Legends were stopped by Gram's high school education. He attended the Bolles School in Jacksonville, Florida. Occasionally Parsons sang at school assemblies but he was really just biding his time until he heard Paul Surratt and Joe Kelly sing at a talent contest where he was the judge. Adding George Wrigley, who was in their group but sick the night of the show, Gram Parsons and the Shilos were born.

Sierra/Briar Records recently released a Shilos album (a review of the album appears in this book). They were a folk, Kingston Trio-type group and their music shows it. The group did well throughout the South, even appearing at the Bitter End in New York City where they rubbed elbows with acts later to become quite famous. Their manager turned down a chance for them to be on the Ed Sullivan Show, claiming they weren't ready, and there were other problems.

While the Shilos were Gram Parsons' first professional group, they were swimming against the tide. In January of 1964 The Beatles hit and to a large extent the folk sound was tossed out the window. The group had arguments over image and material. Parsons wanted to flirt more with C&W and rock while the others hated those sounds passionately and were against any deviation from the folk sound. In June of 1965 the group played its last show in Garden City, South Carolina. Gram then headed north to Harvard University and furthering his career. He said he wanted to be a novelist "but I really wanted to figure out what the hell Alpert and Leary were up to."

At Harvard Gram formed the International Submarine Band (the name was Ian Dunlop's idea). Gram and Harvard were compatible for only a little over a semester and a half. Then the band moved down to New York City and did some session work. Living in the Bronx was hell to country boy Parsons so he persuaded the group to move to California.

In Los Angeles the group found the going tough. After all, 1967 was not a big year for country–influenced music in the rock world. The band scored the theme for *The Russians Are Coming, The Russians Are Coming* film and were in the Peter Fonda movie *The Trip* where they appear onstage miming to an Electric Flag song on the soundtrack. Just before the group broke up Lee Hazelwood of LHI Records recorded an album of the group's music called *Safe at Home* (also reviewed later in this book). Parsons dominates the album and it is the first real country–rock album ever released.

Issued in April, 1968, after the band had broken up, the record sold poorly but did establish the name of Gram Parsons in certain music business circles. Without the group around to promote it, *Safe at Home* died a quick death.

Gram was extremely disappointed the album had not sold better. He complained to actor Brandon deWilde, a close friend, how he needed to get his affairs in order. Parsons was then introduced to deWilde's business manager who in turn introduced him to another of his clients, Roger McGuinn.

In April of 1968, the same month *Safe at Home* was released, Gram Parsons joined the Byrds. The Byrds hired Gram as a piano player, probably not envisioning his steering them so strongly into country. It's hard to believe that one of the main things Gram Parsons is remembered for is being a Byrd. He spent less than 3% of his life as a member of the group. But the Byrds were a distinctive, important and highly influential rock band and Parsons was directly responsible for some of their biggest changes. The most noticeable one was the switch toward country, but Gram also lessened the Byrds' reliance on Bob Dylan material and took the group a few steps away from the twelve–string Rickenbacker sound that dominated their early work.

Sweetheart of the Rodeo was the only Byrds album where Gram Parsons appeared as a full–fledged member (he had a song on *Dr. Byrds and Mr. Hyde* and sang on one cut on *Untitled*). The album, an acknowledged classic as well as a ground–breaker, had two of his compositions on it, "Hickory Wind" and "One Hundred Years From Now." "Hickory Wind" has subsequently been covered by several other artists, including Parsons himself on the *Grievous Angel* album. Written with Bob Buchanan of the ISB while that group was on its last legs, "Hickory Wind" is a testament to the peculiar Southern qualities of faith, traditional surroundings and a love for the land of your birth. Parsons' other composition on the LP, "One Hundred Years From Now" is more of a rocker, and speaks somewhat elliptically of a search for peace of mind. It is similar in thought to "Nothing Was Delivered", the excellent Dylan number closing out the album.

Because the Byrds meant so much to so many people and because country music was alien to the rock audience of the day *Sweetheart of the Rodeo* was a poor selling album by Byrds standards. After *The Notorious Byrd Brothers*, an album heavily laced with electronics and containing only a hint of country, many Byrd fans were surprised the new album was so straightforwardly C&W. *Sweetheart* was radically different, and Byrds fans were confused. McGuinn had originally envisioned the album as two records, starting off with traditional mountain music and ending up with modern electronic rock material like *Notorious* so the album would make a logical chronological progression. Columbia lost interest somewhere and the album was released with the country numbers given the limelight.

Byrds before GP - Hillman, Clarke, Crosby, McGuinn in their official Columbia Records' publicity pic

Byrds after GP - Parsons, Hillman, Kelley, McGuinn at the Troubadour, 1968

BARRY FEINSTEIN

Flying Burrito Brothers in front of the "the Gilded Palace of Sin," for eponymous album

Parsons sings on only a few songs. He sang lead on several others originally but his vocals were erased and replaced by McGuinn's (see Chris Hillman interview). Gram was greatly disappointed again. Then South African folk singer Miriam Makeba told McGuinn he should see what it's like to live in a segregated country and the lead Byrd was enthralled by the idea. Parsons, however, was used to segregation down South and saw no good at all in going to South Africa.

The Byrds were in London to play a benefit at the Royal Albert Hall. On the morning after the show Parsons told McGuinn, Chris Hillman and then–Byrds drummer Kevin Kelley he was not going to go to South Africa under any circumstances. Parsons left the group and stayed in London while the Byrds flew to South Africa where road manager Carlos Bernal, who only knew a few chords, took Gram's place. To say the least, Hillman and McGuinn were upset with Gram.

Gram met Keith Richards in London and stayed with him for a spell, turning the Stones onto country music. Suddenly songs like "Dear Doctor", "Country Honk" and "Dead Flowers" became part of the Stones' repertoire as Gram brought out the country in Keith and Mick Jagger, who before had admitted they thought of country as "something of a joke". "Country Honk", the Rolling Stones' C&W of their own "Honky Tonk Women", is Parsons' version of the song. Burritos roadies heard Parsons play it at the piano and asked him why he didn't get arrangement credit on *Let It Bleed*. "I didn't ask. It was an honor bestowed on me," said Parsons.

Parsons flew back to Los Angeles. He had patched up any differences with Chris Hillman, who had left the Byrds not too long after South Africa. Parsons had been jamming in the honky tonks of the San Fernando Valley with Leon Russell, Barry Tashian, Delaney and Bonnie Bramlett and a host of others, playing country music. He talked with Hillman about forming a group to play rock and country, thinking the time was right.

In late 1968 they formed the Flying Burrito Brothers, a name Ian Dunlop thought up to describe the jam sessions in the Valley. Chris Ethridge was on bass, Sneeky Pete on pedal steel and Eddie Hoh on drums. Hoh split during the recording of their first album, *Gilded Palace of Sin* and was replaced first with Jon Corneal and later with Michael Clarke from the original Byrds.

The Gilded Palace of Sin is another classic Parsons' effort. He wrote or co–wrote all but two of the songs and sang lead on all but one. It is undeniably one of the great rock recordings of all time. With the possible exception of *Grievous Angel*, Parsons never performed with such conviction on record. His writing with Hillman and with Ethridge is an impressive and moving display of talent, emotion and drive tempered by a subtle warmth and light humor. His singing is so emotional it transports the listener to agony and despair, then to amusement and celebration with disarming ease. The vocals are on a parallel with Otis Redding, Solomon Burke, early Rod Stewart or even (dare I say it?) Ray Charles doing "Georgia On My Mind".

None of this praise is meant to belittle the other Burritos. Hillman plays and sings with his usual exciting and seemingly effortless grace and Sneeky Pete merges steel guitar with fuzz for a true synthesis between rock and country. All in all a fine album. Unfortunately, the Burritos were a bit lacking in their early live performances and the album broke no hit single so *Gilded Palace* didn't get the exposure it might have.

Most of the public's enthusiasm for country–rock befell Poco, a band that had asked Parsons to join them when they started and who later showed they weren't in the Burritos' class. In Europe the Burritos were better received and the band began lengthy tours to get things off the ground. In late 1969 the group assembled to record a second album, *Burrito Deluxe*, which was not only a comedown from the first but a departure. The country influences were toned down a great deal for a more mainstream, R&B–styled rock feel. Parsons' group was still the "all things to all people" vision he had of Cosmic American Music but things were slipping fast. He begged the Stones to have the Burritos tour with them. After a Spring tour of Europe with the Stones fell through, the Stones relented once, and that was Altamont.

Gram was losing interest in the group and his personal life was not the most stable. In June, 1970, he used a motorcycle crack–up as an excuse to leave the group. In all fairness to the Burritos, particularly Chris Hillman, they hung on for two more fine albums before breaking up. Gram moved in with Terry Melcher, son of Doris Day as well as the Byrds' original producer. Rumors of a solo album in the works never amounted to anything.

All during the Burritos Gram Parsons had maintained his friendship with the Rolling Stones and influence was a two–way street. Whereas Gram had the Stones fiddling with country music, the Stones' lifestyle rubbed off on Gram. The Byrds made an offer to have Gram rejoin and Poco made another overture but Gram was not interested in joining either. He spent most of 1971 and early 1972 hanging out with the Stones in L.A. and the South of France. He lived at Keith's in the southern region of France and accompanied the Stones on tour. He hung out at the

Burritos, 1969 edition - Clarke, Parsons, Leadon, Hillman, Sneeky

Exile On Main Street sessions and sang on "Sweet Virginia". "Dead Flowers" was written about some roses sent Gram and the group, roses which froze and died while in air transit. There was talk of Richards producing a Parsons solo album for Rolling Stones Records but Keith could not find the time. In mid–1972 Parsons returned to the States, moved into a home in Laurel Canyon and accepted a contract from Warner Bros. Records to become a solo artist. It had been more than a two–year retirement from recording for him and other than singing on a Fred Neil album.

Chris Hillman introduced Gram to Emmylou Harris, a singer he and Rick Roberts had stumbled onto in Washington, D.C. Parsons was forming a backup band and he decided he and Emmylou would be great for doing country duets. Merle Haggard was scheduled to produce Parsons but he pulled out at the last minute. Hugh Davies, Haggard's engineer, stepped in to record the sound with Parsons' good friend Rick Grech getting formal producers' credits.

GP was the album they made. Elvis Presley's longtime sessionmen Glen D. Hardin, James Burton and Ronnie Tutt flew into L.A. to participate. Barry Tashian Buddy Emmons, Bryon Berline and Al Perkins all contributed licks and Gram, for once, was pleased about the results of his recorded efforts. *GP* is not as accessible as *Grievous Angel* but its rewards are many. His writing was as good as ever and his voice showed little signs of the neglect he had been giving it. Emmylou Harris' appearances on the album added much to Gram's vocals and it was obvious to all they had a very special musical relationship.

It is apparent *GP* was the beginning of a new era for Parsons, a new twist to the old objectives. His country had a new urbanized feel to it and the sophistication and depth to material like "The New Soft Shoe" and "Kiss the Children" came to light after several playings. *GP* was a marvelously easy and seductive display of a master trying out several styles, readying for a masterpiece.

In February and March Gram Parsons and the Fallen Angels went on tour. It was a good tour for Parsons, helping to whip his voice into shape and giving him and Emmylou the needed time to acclimate their voices. Last year saw the release of Gram's one live album, recorded on this tour.

Around the middle of 1973 Parsons began work on his second solo album, using many of the same musicians who appeared on *GP*. He produced it himself this time and things were going well. Emmylou Harris recalled "every night we would get rough mixes of what we had done, the rough vocal and we'd take them back and listen to them over and over again. We'd get so excited we would be dancin' up and down."

Parsons was in better spirits than he had been in a long time and his cheery demeanor proved it. He was looking forward to a fall tour and to a massive Byrds reunion scheduled for October in Holland where every musician who was ever in the Byrds would gather to rehearse for a special show as a treat to the country that loved their sound the most. Then Clarence White was killed in July while he was loading his guitars into his car , hit by a drunk driver . Gram was deeply shocked.

Clarence White was one of the few people who really understood Gram Parsons. Gram knew this and felt close to him. The two had a strong affinity for each other. White was called into the *Grievous* sessions when things got sticky, not as a player but as a stable sounding board for Gram to relate to and be near. White was in excellent health at the time of his death and his extraordinary flatpicking guitar style was finally being recognized by a wider audience. The funeral was a quiet gathering of musicians until Gram and Bernie Leadon of the Burritos began an impromptu duet on "Farther Along."

Grievous Angel was finished in late Summer of 1973. Gram was proud of it, as well he should have been. In September he went out to Joshua Tree in the California desert to relax with friends. On the morning of September 19, 1973, Gram Parsons was found dead in his room at the Joshua Tree Inn, a favorite motel of his. The San Bernardino County coroner's office reported Gram Parsons died of heart failure due to "natural causes". For once Parsons was in the headlines, if only briefly; the next day Jim Croce died and as he had had some AM exposure he proceeded to get whatever headlines Parsons' passing on might have snagged.

Warner Bros. held up *Grievous Angel* until January of 1974 to avoid being accused of trying to cash in on Parsons' death, and due to a dispute over the LP's cover. When the album was released it was to unanimous critical acclaim. The *Village Voice* polled some two dozen music critics to attain a consensus of the year's best rock albums. *Grievous Angel* placed in the top fifteen. Musicians as diverse as Elvis Costello and Johnny Cash praised the album's tenor and scope. Tom Petty calls *Grievous Angel* "my favorite album". Emmylou Harris modestly enough claimed it was a fine album except for her singing; she said she wanted a copy with herself erased so she could hear Parsons better.

Grievous Angel contained two songs in particular that will surely go down as chief examples of Gram Parsons' massive talent, "Return of the Grievous Angel" and "$1,000 Wedding". "Return of the Grievous Angel" uses haunting imagery and a wonderful rolling rhythm to weave the tale of a search for contentment that not only takes the singer across the land but across his own life as well. "$1,000 Wedding" ranks with "Hot Burrito #1" as Parsons' best bittersweet love story and with the Shilo's "Zah's Blues" as his most touching vocal performance.

Since his death there has been a tremendous awakening of interest in the music of Gram Parsons. The Shilos album was released in 1979 after years of frustrated effort on the part of Gram's friend Paul Surratt. The widely bootlegged International Submarine Band album has been reissued and two Gram Parsons/Flying Burrito Bros. compilations have been released by A&M Records. The first came out in 1974 and is called *Close Up the Honky Tonks*. It is a two record set with excellent liner notes and some interesting photos. The first disc is a Burritos' "Best Of" affair featuring cuts from their first two albums with Gram and the seldom heard "Train Song' single. The second disc contains previously unreleased cuts with Gram and several unreleased Burrito cuts after Gram had left the group. The record is a must for the Parsons devotee. The second compilation came out in 1976 and is called *Sleepless Nights* by Gram Parsons and the Flying Burrito Brothers. The Burrito cuts, which repeat two cuts from *Close Up the Honky Tonks*, are also unreleased and show the band in a somewhat disoriented stance. Yet the album contains three gems left over from the *Grievous Angel* sessions that are topnotch, "Brand New Heartache", "Sleepless Nights" and "The Angels Rejoiced in Heaven Last Night". They are well worth the price of the album.

In addition to appearing on several other albums as a sideman (see Discography) a bootleg EP of four International Submarine Band songs is making the rounds in Southern California, complete with picture sleeve. It is unfortunate that death is the best advertisement of a sensitive artist's work, yet one cannot help agreeing with Roger McGuinn of the Byrds who said, "Gram sure would have dug it if he'd known he was gonna be so hot after passing on." As is all too often the case we do not really know what we have until it is taken from us.

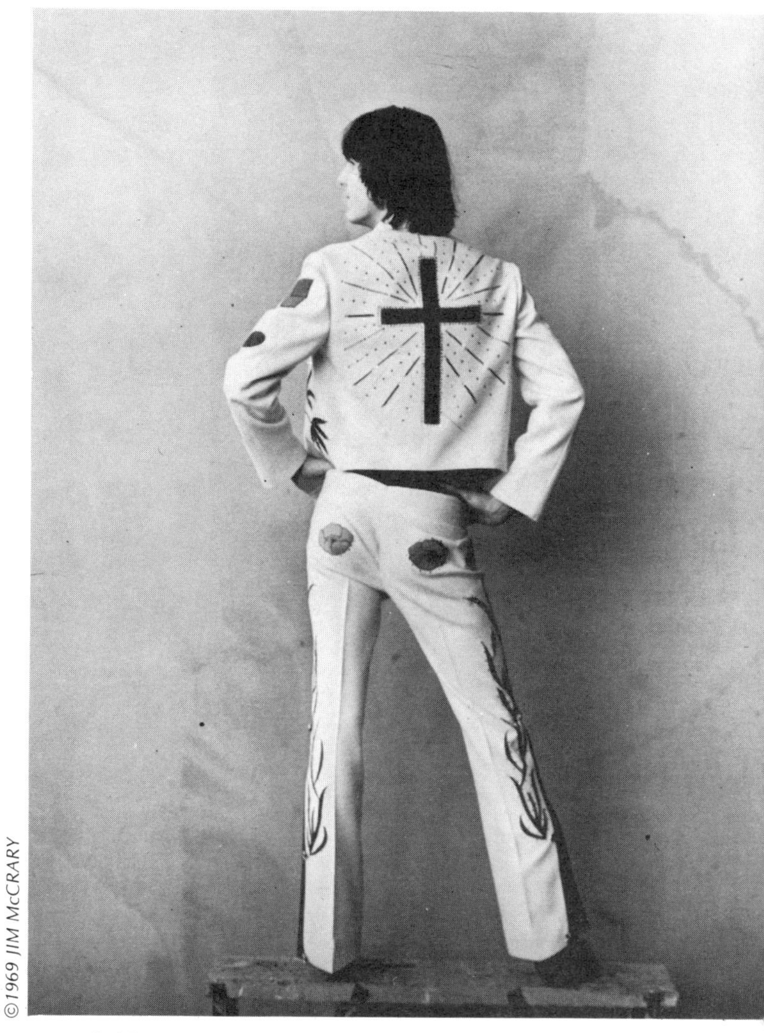

©1969 JIM McCRARY

Gram in his Nudie suit, 1969

John Delgatto

Clarence White with the Muleskinner band, February 1973

1962

Gram Parsons' Musical Validity

If you ever go to London you might want to visit Stiff Records, the New Wave label. When you enter the lobby you'll see the usual photos of the label's artists on the wall. Behind the receptionist with the doleful eyes you will see a big photograph of Gram Parsons, a country–oriented rocker who is not even on the label. The late Gram Parsons. From Waycross, Georgia.

With ethnic music occupying a larger and larger share of popular music and country–influenced rock coming out of the woodwork, many people are wondering where, why and how. As if on cue two releases by Gram Parsons may well be the answer. *Gram Parsons* (Shiloh 4088) and *Gram Parsons: The Early Years, Vol. 1* (Sierra 8702) were released within days of each other in April and both are on small local labels. They are the very definition of the term "labor of love".

While Parsons never became a commercial giant in today's mega–platinum sense of the term his music was always well–known and respected amongst musicians and is a thematic cornerstone of the Eagles–Ronstadt Southern California coalition. Mixing traditional American musics (that's hillbilly to you nouveau hip) with rock'n'roll Parsons created what he called "Cosmic American Music". His vivid images of sin, revenge and redemption became a major influence on many New Wave acts (see corresponding article). He is the Edgar Allan Poe of rock.

Born into a wealthy Southern family Parsons always knew a lot more than he would let on. Musicians and friends alike were staggered by the amount of talent and ambition he possessed. Possessed is the right word. His tragic tales of love lost and his achingly pretty singing made his music exceptionally emotional, almost frightening. If Robert Johnson were alive today he'd call up Gram to go drinking. They'd have a lot to talk about.

In the end it is the music he made that will stand as his final testimony. *Gram Parsons* is deceptively titled; in reality it is an album called *Safe at Home* by Parsons' first big–time rock group, the International Submarine Band. Gram formed the group after dropping out of Harvard. The band also did the score for *The Russians Are Coming, the Russians Are Coming.* While Parsons does dominate the proceedings it is hardly a solo effort as the title implies.

The album starts off with "Blue Eyes", a Parsons original in a very melodic commercial form. The song has been an onstage favorite of the Nitty Gritty Dirt Band for years. The imagery is pure Parsons with one exception. The singer actually gets the girl he is pursuing instead of Parsons' usual ending of rejection and cruelty.

The album then moves through several country standards, composed by the likes of Merle Haggard and Jack Clement, before two more Parsons originals. "Strong Boy" is a country song with stock changes, but what's interesting about this material (particularly in light of rock's then—notorious attitude about country) is not how well the numbers are performed but that they are being performed at all. 1967 was not a good year for country—rock, since the genre didn't exist then. Certainly anyone who can perform the music admirably in addition to overcoming his peer group's considerable prejudice against country and western, is not only an artist but a politician of some note.

"Luxury Liner" is the next original. Yes, the same one Emmylou Harris recorded. Here the fast maturing Parsons is coming to grips with the dark spectre of death as a metaphor and as a song catalyst. The song is a tale of a typical lonesome boy pining away for his girl. In most pop songs the singer simply complains about the distance between him and his girl. Parsons' protagonist admits to infidelity and implies he knows how to get revenge. Sink the luxury liner, hell, that'll teach her. This is right in line with Faulkner. Dickey, Poe or any one of a number of Southern writers. Vengeance, if done neatly, is not a wicked thing at all but a necessary part of saving one's face and self—respect.

A cover of Johnny Cash's "I Still Miss Someone" shows the Submarine Band were able to play straight country as well. The song has been covered by countless singers and Parsons' is the best version I have ever heard. I'm sure it brings a wider audience to the song as many young people have a biological aversion to Cash's bullfrog voice.

"Do You Know How It Feels To Be Lonesome" also appeared on the Flying Burrito Brothers' *Gilded Palace of Sin*. If anyone could write and sing a heartbreak song it was Parsons. Charlie Parker stretched jazz boundaries not only because of his musical ability but because he translated his emotions into heartbreaking sax riffs and breaks. Parsons sang well not only because he was technically proficient and well—versed but because he put his emotion right into his voice. He would let it get close to the breaking point and then pull it back time and time again. What sounded like an untrained, love—struck young man on first listen was really a trained singer who went one—on—one with pain so often he could seemingly translate emotion into song effortlessly.

His singing was a very personal affair. Besides occasionally coming close to cracking altogether, his voice also half—talked passages, almost recited the words. It was an oddly intimate method that worked well. He gave the impression something was going on

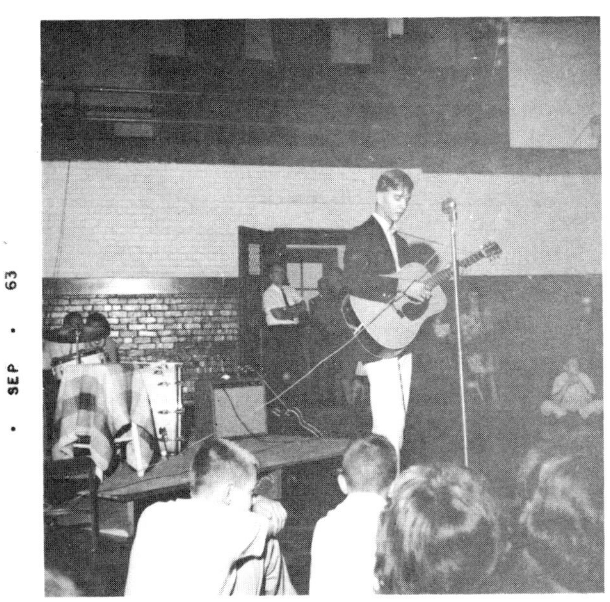

Gram fronting the Shilos, Greenville, S.C., 1963

besides the main story the song was conveying and he was trying to let the listener in on this dark secret without anybody else overhearing.

Emmylou Harris has been quoted to the effect it is easier to make love to someone than to sing with them. It must have been an ecstatic sort of hell with Gram Parsons, whose final two solo albums were chiefly duets with Harris. Parsons, like any other master, learned the rules of his trade and then proceeded to break them one by one.

The final song on the *Gram Parsons* album is a medley of "Folsom Prison Blues" and "That's Alright Mama". In the grand tradition of Sun Records, Parsons juxtaposed a blues with a country song, knowing they are the same in content and theme if not racial origin. By that I mean the only difference is in a subtle musical way and in the color of their authors. Down South the economics force the two races into a similar fate while putting them at each others' throats politically. Yet the two poor white sharecroppers are in the same boat with the black farmer down the road; they just don't know it or want to know it. Steve Cropper and Otis Redding worked closer than any Northern soul duo you can think of and the reason is because they shared not only the same economic cruelties but also the same musical heritage of eliminating pain through song. Parsons was much the same way.

"That's Alright Mama" was in fact the first Presley release, backed with "Blue Moon of Kentucky". Unlike the Presley sides, which did the blues number in a country style and vice versa, Parsons meshed the two styles together so white and black man's blues were indistinguishable.

The Shiloh Records release proudly touts "rare photos" of Parsons on the jacket inner liner. Indeed, there are five black–and–white shots I have never seen before but, while interesting, they are hardly worth the price of the album to those who already own either the bootleg version or the original *Safe at Home.*

I presume Shiloh Records got its name from Gram's first group since I had never heard of the label before the Parsons reissue. Sierra/Briar has issued, for the first time, an album of Gram Parsons *with* the Shilos to add to the confusion. *The Early Years, Vol. 1* documents Parsons' stay with the group, his first professional band. Recorded in March, 1965, at Bob Jones University in Greenville, South Carolina, the record is a fascinating piece to thrill the Parsons faithful and puzzle the newcomer to the legend.

There are only two Parsons originals on the album but they are excellent. The rest of the material is divided up between Gram's friends' work and traditional folk music. The group sounds a bit like the Kingston Trio and shows little of the country and rock proclivities which later shocked the popular music scene.

Stand–up bass, banjo and an acoustic guitar or two provide the instrumentation and all the Shilos sing. Parsons, of course, takes the lead vocal. It is interesting to note how his voice is more sure and professional than on the later recording, *Gram Parsons.* This proves the theory Parsons used the heartache–filled voice to get his message across since on the earlier record his voice is as sure as possible.

"Zah's Blues" was written during a Shilo's stay in Greenwich Village, where Parsons met a singer named Zah. Strumming a blues chord progression on an acoustic guitar, with a bass for back–up, Parsons movingly sang a cryptic tale of love lost and love regained. Interestingly enough the song seems more in line with Parsons' later work as opposed to the *Safe at Home* album, which was recorded two years after "Zah's Blues".

The words to "Zah's Blues" are beautiful but they are eclipsed by Gram's unbelievably moving vocal. His voice actually breaks once but this only adds to its charm. I can honestly say the affection shown for Zah makes the song so real that not only is emotion transmitted to the listener but a sprituality as well. It's the sound and feeling of a young man putting his heart (through this voice) right on the line. Parsons was to master this technique later.

Besides scoring *The Russians Are Coming* Parsons wrote the Cypress Gardens theme. Little wonder how he got the job; it used to be his mother's property. "Surfinanny" is the song, recorded in one of the Shilo's living rooms in Greenville. Parsons wrote the song on the spot, and as an insight into his methods it is a valuable piece as it shows Parsons able to come up with more ideas in a short time than most writers. Elvis Costello writes with similar proficiency and his own motives reflect infatuation with Parsons' themes of movement and unwanted loneliness.

The eight other songs on the album mirror the folk boom of the day. "The Bells of Rhymney" compares favorably with the Byrds' more rock–oriented version, and "Oh Didn't They Crucify My Lord" will bring back memories of a Southern Baptist church service to anyone who has been to one. Parsons' charismatic singing brings life to the most mundane arrangements of those early sixties chestnuts and is quite moving in places even if the material sounds dated today.

Admittedly this is a young Parsons. He reminds me of O.J. Simpson at USC – a young man not yet matured in his field who, nonetheless, is a spellbinding performer because he uses his heart to get him to places where his lack of experience would slow him down. And he plunges ahead come hell or high water.

To be sure, the albums might be little more than curios to the outsider. Yet Parsons has a knack for attracting followers out of the most unlikely prospects. Outside of the South both Manhattan and Los Angeles have sizable Parsons cults. Stiff Records is a haven of Parsons fans like Elvis Costello. Parsons was an ambassador for country in some ways; he had the amazing ability to make fans out of those who distrusted anything remotely country, remotely down–home.

You can count on the fingers of one hand the musicians who knew or saw rhythm and blues and country as glorious American pop music. Even fewer is the number of musicians who successfully wed the two genres together to form a unique synthesis, a stunning rock sound. Elvis did it at Sun, the Everly Brothers knew about it, and so did the Lovin' Spoonful at times. Gram Parsons not only realized it; he could never get over it.

Like Otis Redding he took his version of blues and proceeded to wed the style to pure Sixties rock'n'roll. Redding was cutting Dylan in Stax–Volt's Memphis studios before his plane crashed; Parsons was moving country and rock ever closer and blurring the edges until his own candle went out.

Gram Parsons tried and succeeded in marrying rock, gospel, country and blues on one album. He did it three times: *Sweetheart of the Rodeo* with the Byrds, *Gilded Palace of Sin* with the Flying Burrito Brothers, and his own *Grievous Angel*. These two early albums show the young artist testing each form before deciding he'd be the one to put them all together.

That these discs are now available is a tribute not only to Parsons and his fans but also to the labels themselves. While both are selling better than expected one must admire the fortitude of small independents to go up against the mega–bucks of the Sunset Strip.

Parsons is still reaching new audiences today. His close friend Keith Richards shows a grievous influence on "Country Honk" and more recently on "Faraway Eyes". Emmylou Harris continues his legacy with textbook detail while British New Wavers marvel at his country Southernness, Gram's bravado showing up in their own uneasiness and social displacement.

Parsons lived life with bravado and when life ended at 26 a lot of us felt like part of us went with him. The Byrds once sang a song that I'm sure Gram knew, maybe too well. It went "Though I never met him I knew him just the same." I never met Gram Parsons but I knew him just the same. C'mon and I'll tell you all about Sin City....

–Sid Griffin

Los Angeles Arts Review

Gram, 1963

SEP 63

The Legends, (left to right) - Jim Stafford, Kent LaVoie (Lobo), Gerald Chambers and Gram, 1960

Jim Stafford today

Big Country: Jim Stafford

Jim Stafford has had a string of successful recordings starting around the time Gram Parsons passed away and in addition to those hits he has successfully branched into television and other showbusiness ventures. What is not widely known about his career is that as a teenager he was in a group called the Legends with Gram Parsons and the effect they had on each other was enormous. Backstage at the Palomino during one of his recent appearances there Jim Stafford talked at length about Gram for the first time in a long, long while.

J.S.: Gram had just gone through this sort of Greenwich Village thing when I met him. He always seemed to be going through styles for a time. When he first started playing the guitar he was less than thirteen and when I met him he'd just gotten a Stratocaster and was trying to learn rock n' roll. I was a real student of the guitar at the time and I was doing almost eight hours a day on the guitar by the time I was sixteen.

I really was working hard and we'd get together and we'd have sessions, just kids you know, and I'd spend the night over at his place a few times doing whatever you do when you're a teenager and Gram... he was a very mature fellow. When he was in his early teens he was already dating and I don't think I ever saw him date a girl his own age, they were always older women. He was a romantic and would fall in love with everybody. He was learning rock stuff and leaning toward folk, kind of getting away from the electric stuff.

After all that high school rock 'n' roll, "At the Hop" period passed Gram got interested in folk, Hootenanny type stuff. He went to New York and hung out in Greenwich Village and then got involved with the Shilos. He came back into town once and was talking real discouraged and he said he'd tried rock n'roll and he'd tried folk and he really didn't know what else to try to play. We had a talk and I said to him, "you've got country roots, folk's a craze anyway, why don't you sing some C&W as a longhaired young guy?" Gram seemed to really like the idea.

Now this is not to say he hadn't aleady thought of it. I'm telling you this not because I want it to be my idea, on the record, to have Gram pioneer this form, but right after that he got involved in country-styled rock and then a little later the Byrds and *Sweetheart of the Rodeo*, which is probably pretty close to the first longhaired country stuff. I don't know if Gram would have a particular song or point you could point to as the start of country-rock 'cause you have to remember years before Elvis was doing "Blue Moon of Kentucky" in a rockabilly form and all of that stuff going on, it's just that you didn't have a Nitty Gritty Dirt Band or any of that stuff. I was real proud, I must say, when he did start doing this type material and I must honestly admit I don't know how much of it he would have done anyhow. I'm not saying that trying to get any kind of credit cause I don't know what I'd do with any kind of credit.

S.G.: You can't bank it.

J.S.: No, you can't bank it and not only that it don't much matter now.

S.G.: Yeah, unfortunately. Could you tell me about the Legends a bit?

J.S.: One of the fellows in the Legends was Jim Carlton and there was a guy named Bill Walter, who is also no longer with us. He was building a homemade helicopter and was decapitated. Gram had big money, you know. There's a guy in Florida

Gram with his parents, Winter Haven, Florida, 1948

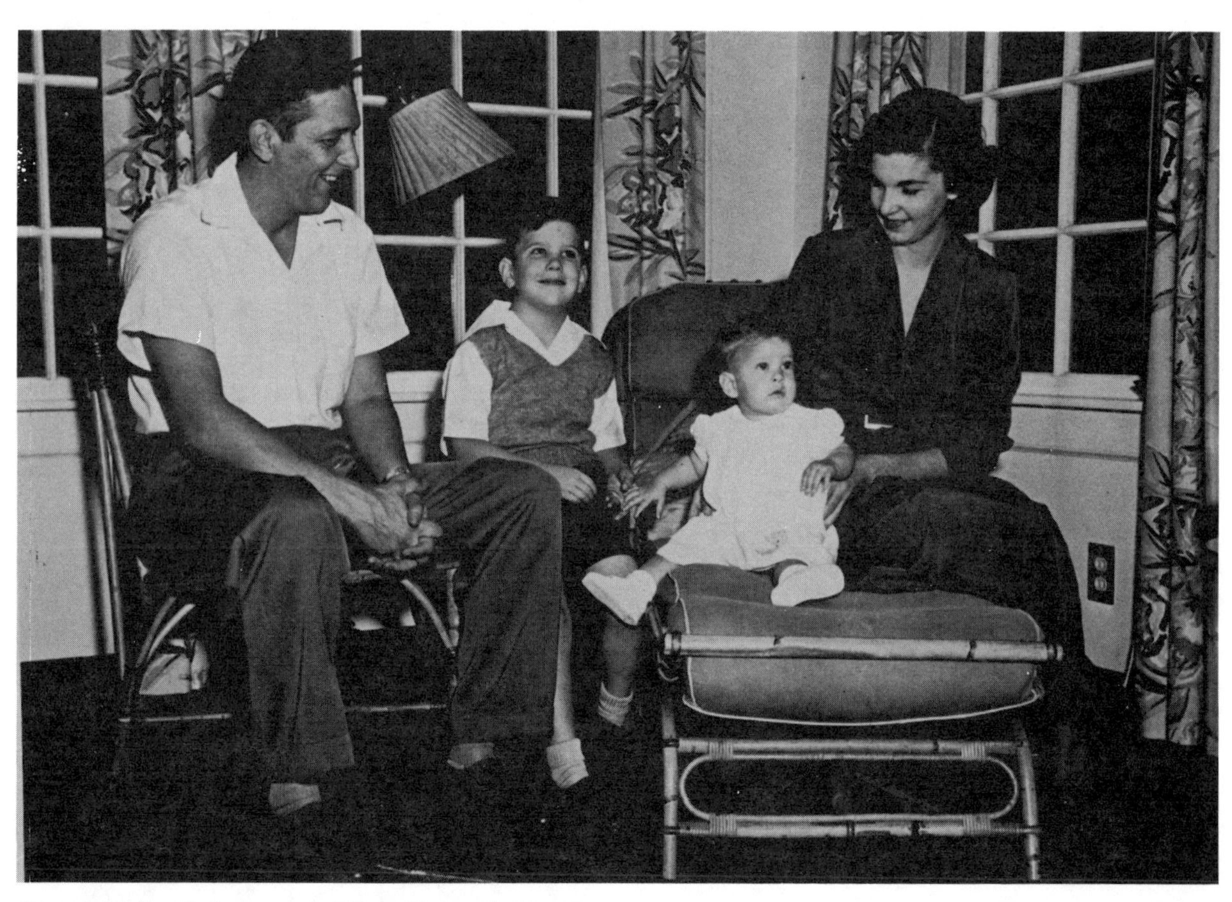

Gram and Avis with their parents, Winter Haven, Florida, 1953

Gram out hunting with his father, grandfather and family friend in 1957

named Big John Snively who started that whole clan. I was born and raised in a place called Eloise which was there because of Snively's big citrus plant. When he died the kids divided it up and started hating each other and trying to get each other's money and the whole thing fell apart. The last time I saw the Snively Packing plant it was a great huge rusting hull. Gram's mother was a Snively.

Gram was outfitted with whatever he needed. Guitars, they even bought him a Volkswagon bus in which he hit a cow one night on his way to playing a club called the something or other in Cape Canaveral. Only two or three of us made it all the way through the Legends. We were never any good at all, the band was never any good. We didn't rehearse much and none of us knew how to play very well. We just did the tunes of the day and as a matter of fact I don't believe we did any original tunes at all. I think Gram would write them occasionally and we'd record them but I don't think we performed any of them at all.

There was Kent LaVoie who was Lobo, Gram, myself, Jim Carlton on bass... Carlton's father had come south to Florida to play bass on a radio show and they'd stayed on. I'm not sure who else was in it. We mostly played teen centers and dances, things like that. That's about all we ever played. Strictly a rock group of the time, we did "Johnny B. Goode", "Sleepwalk", and Gram would do "Ebb Tide" sitting at the piano.

S.G.: Did you sing?

J.S.: No, I didn't sing at all. Gram sang but I didn't sing anything.

S.G.: Carlton said he had tapes.

J.S.: He's got tapes of the Shilos, tapes of the Legends... Bobby Braddock of Urbandale, Florida, about three or four miles from where we were, was involved in the tapes and so were the Chambers Brothers who now play backup for the Bellamy Bros. Bobby Braddock is in Nashville and a writer and wrote "Divorce" for Tammy Wynette.

S.G.: I always heard Carlton taped bands he thought had potential and if your band had you, Gram and Lobo he was right.
J.S.: I don't think he had any plan at all in mind, I think he was just making them to make them. He's a very good friend of mine. He was married at one time and had a son whom he named after me, Justin Stafford Carlton. I just saw him last week. He's just a real good fellow making some tapes. We'd all get together and he would roll a tape and I don't feel he had any eye on the future at the time at all.
S.G.: This wasn't any professional type deal then.
J.S.: No, he was the same age as Gram, just a sixteen year old boy making tapes. The thing about Carlton is he's like an information center and retains a lot of facts, even today when I talk to him he knows which groups are doing this and which groups are doing that and he enjoys statistics and this type of thing. Now he's into videotape. I don't know how many tapes he has.
S.G.: Is he the guy who has the videotape of Gram and wants whatever for it?
J.S.: I don't know. I do know he couldn't be very difficult to deal with on anything he has. He is not the kind of guy who has all this foresight and then tries to cash in on what he has. I obviously don't mean to speak for him but he's really a good guy.
S.G.: When did you and Gram realize country was the thing for you both to do?
J.S.: There was a conversation in my living room when he came back from Greenwich Village when I told him what he ought to sing as I mentioned earlier, because Gram was confused about what to do.
S.G.: When was this, about 1965?
J.S.: If you checked on when *Sweetheart of the Rodeo* came out I believe the conversation was about two years earlier than that, or close to it. He was always hanging out with real heavy duty people, Gram. He died at 26 but he'd lived the life of a guy at least in his mid-fifties because Gram had truly seen and done a lot. I think he knew he had the talent and the ability way beyond what many people seemed to be interested in and I think something like that can really help do a fellow in.

Funny thing was I came out to California and tried to get in touch with Gram and I never could, never could get ahold of him. I believe my first record was about to take off about the time he died. I don't think he ever knew I was here. I was never able to speak to him, couldn't get in touch with him. I don't think I could have done any good by then, but I heard he was in trouble and I was trying to find him.

I got a friend knows a lot about him, a drummer named Jon Corneal. A drummer from back then.
S.G.: Yeah, I know the guy.
J.S.: Jon told me the story about his death, what a tragedy.
S.G.: What did you guys listen to as kids in the Legends?
J.S.: At the time I met him, strangely enough, Gram was nuts over Peter Nero. Because Gram was still playing piano then, He owned *Music for the Nero Minded*, some Ray Stevens album he was crazy over, a Smothers Brothers record, he loved Jonathan Winters, loved Brother Dave Gardner... I can't remember any of the groups he listened to since we mostly performed rock standards in the Legends, by that I mean no particular groups jumped out.
S.G.: Why did the Legends break up?
JS.: I believe it was because Gram was going off to some boarding school. One of the last things I ever worked with Gram was a gig he booked at a boys' school he attended in Jacksonville. I drove up but they cancelled it for some reason. There was a Legends playing there, I think maybe the Triumphs were playing that day. I was in both groups.
S.G.: Seeing how you realized Gram had so much talent and you were practicing so hard it seems odd you didn't try to form another group with him.
J.S.: He moved and I was stuck where I was. Gram left town. Gram was then away at Bolles School. The family seemed to be moving apart then.
S.G.: Looking back on all this what do you remember him for? As a writer, a singer or what?
J.S.: I remember a real nice goodhearted guy who, like a lot of us in this business, was desperate for attention. I don't think

IN KIWANIS SHOW—"The Village Vanguards," a Winter Haven musical trio, will be one of the acts in the Polk County Kiwanis Talent Show Friday night, March 29 at Nora Mayo Hall. (1963)

L–R, Dick McNear, Patty Johnson and Gram in another group Gram had during the Legends period

he got a lot of attention from his mom, from his dad or the family as a whole. And like a lot of us he saw what you had to do was to show off to be noticed and I think this is what Gram wanted. He was a guy who would have liked to be loved, or even noticed. I think this is what he spent what little of this life he had doing, trying to be noticed, trying to get people to say he was something, he was special. Because he'd try anything in a performance. He'd try sunglasses, any old thing if he thought it'd get him noticed. If he thought it would make him look neat. He was a real ambitious guy but the thing he wanted was the thing which killed him.

S.G.: *When you guys were younger did you think you'd get this famous?*

J.S.: Gram was the only dreamer then out of all the guys. Gram was into making it. I was into my guitar, the drummer was into girls, Gram wanted to be a star. I think Gram wanted to be a star when he first discovered music. I think he wanted to be a star like these little girls who sing in talent shows at ten years old and know what they want. Definitely.

The Shilos, l–r Paul Surratt, Joe Kelly, GP and George Wrigley at a photo session, Greenville, S.C., 1964

Surfinanny! : Paul Surratt

Paul Surratt was a teenager when he sang with Gram Parsons in the Shilos, the first professional band for both of them. While the Shilos never made it big they did lay important foundations for Gram Parsons and they recently provided us with *Gram Parsons, the Early Years Vol. 1*, a fascinating look at Gram's early singing and musical influences.

The interview took place on a lazy Sunday afternoon in the San Fernando Valley, a very warm talk about Gram and music and the kind of person he was before he came to Los Angeles and cultish fame. Throughout this and other interviews in this book two things emerge: first, Gram Parsons was a highly complex individual and second, Gram Parsons was a man truly loved by his friends and fellow musicians.

SG: Paul, what are your earliest recollections of Gram Parsons?

PS: The first time I ever met him was at a talent show that was in the magazine that comes with the Shilos album. We were doing a talent show for Coca–Cola's Hi–Fi Club talent show, I'm not sure of the date. We met Gram there. There were three guys in the group (the Shilos) and one was in the hospital; George Wrigley was in the hospital for some reason. So Joe Kelly and I were going to do the talent show anyway. This guy was singing that night...I can still see Gram up there singing. He was singing "You Know My Voice, I've Heard Your Name", the New Christy Minstels song. He was wearing a purple shirt and a gold piece and he had such a great voice we couldn't believe it, so when we came down off the stage we ended up talking for a while. It ended up he was going to be one of the judges of the show. We didn't know that. But we found out he liked the Journeymen

Coca Cola Hi Fi Hootenanny starring Gram Parsons, Greenville, S.C., 1963

A commemoration of same saved from Gram's own scrapbook

WHITE SPRINGS — The FSU Madrigal Singers, a folk singer and an ... str... featu... day at ... Stephen ... on Pa... sonville and ... and Mrs. Clara ... Blocker of Lake City ... join Walter James and the Madrigal Singers in the variety program scheduled in the Tower Auditorium. Mrs. Blocker will also be featured in a program of incidental piano and melodeon music in the Foster Museum.

PARSONS, A senior at the Bolles School, is recognized as one of the outstanding folk artists in the South and has sung in clubs and on other programs in New York, Charleston, and throughout the Jacksonville area. He has made one recording and plans another in the near future.

The young singer, who composes much of his material, will be heard in "Far Side of the Hill," "3:10 to Yuma," "Spanish Is a Lovin' Tongue," "Soft ... the Summer Winds" and "You've Heard My Voice."

Two pages from Gram's own scrapbook circa 1964

as much as we did so we started singing. I don't even remember how or why we started singing but we started singing and we all knew the Journeymen's songs so we could harmonize right away. I'll never forget the first time we sang. We probably sang "Pullin' Away" or "Run, Maggie, Run", which was Journeymen stuff. Probably "Run, Maggie, Run" because it was two chords.

SG: *John Phillips' material?*

PS: Yeah, John Phillips and Dick Weissman and Scott McKenzie stuff. Right away, it was unbelievable, we instantly harmonized. We all went "whoa" and went to work up some songs to play for the talent show. The next night they had the talent show finals and we won...it was really weird because Gram was one of the judges. After we won we got up and sang some songs together. Nobody ever said anything about it or anything. It was really odd 'cause we won $150 and then Gram and all of us got onstage and played together. It was crazy as hell.

SG: *What did Gram look and act like in those early days?*

PS: Well, I'll tell you how I saw him though that may not necessarily be right. Before I got to know him he was sixteen and he had been groomed for show business all his life. He had been groomed well and moved well. He was a great liar, like he said he wrote "You Know My Voice" and he had us snowed under. A tremendous singer and an unbelievable talent, great voice that he could just mesmerize you with. For a sixteen year old boy to be able to do that...I never thought he was that great a writer at the time although as he got older his stuff got better and better. As a singer he could kill anybody. He was unbelievable, just unbelievable. And he...I was spell bound. I remember the first time in my life I was unable to sleep. After the talent show he was to come over and see us the next day and I was so afraid he wouldn't call that I didn't sleep all night. I was so excited about meeting this guy. I had visions of us being the next Kingston Trio. We almost did, it was odd. I found out later that Gram's manager Buddy Freeman did not want Gram to get in touch with us. He thought Gram was too far above us. He tried to talk Gram out of it. Gram said No, how he was gonna call us and how he wanted to sing with us. The next day he came over.

SG: How did he act around you?

He seemed worldly, whether he was or not. Talk to Jim Stafford, who was in the Legends with Gram. He had complete control. It was like nothing bothered him. Whether it did or not inside I didn't know at the time. He had a way with women. He'd act like he didn't care and they'd fall all over him. I never saw a woman that didn't like Gram. Even our mothers were all crazy about him. When he came to play with us at my high school there was a little girl who was stuck–up, who really had her nose in the air. Well, she skipped class all day long just to follow Gram around. He changed my life, some of my attitudes and things like that.

SG: So then you had the first Shilo rehearsals after he called?

PS: We got together the next day, made contact and got to singin' I recall. I don't remember exactly but right away there was contact and connections. For a long time I was afraid we would never see Gram again because he was so strong, so great.

SG: That whole folk sound the Shilos did is steeped in liberal politics. How did that go over in the South in 1965?

PS: We never knew anything about politics back then. All the four of us knew is we were doing great songs about fun things. George was political but as kids... you just make money making records and live happily ever after. I was only sixteen...The big folk boom was on. Folk was everywhere back then and as it is the South's cultural heritage it went over real well.

SG: Name some of the places the Shilos played.

PS: We started off playing fashion shows, teen dances, coffee houses, school assemblys, college concerts and TV shows.

SG: Any TV shows still around of you and Gram?

PS: No, they have all been erased. We used to do one local show called "Shindy". It was a takeoff on "Hootenanny". We never did any major shows although we almost did an Ed Sullivan Show. We had...we were very close to it but we had a falling out with our manager.

SG: Why didn't you appear on Ed Sullivan?

PS: He said he didn't think we were ready. Buddy Freeman always had the concept of the group as the New Christy

JOE F. JORDON

Kathy Fowler, one of the vocalists from the Shilos Revue that Buddy Freeman concocted, and Gram, Greenville, S.C., 1963

Minstrels. That was his idea of the Shilos. He wanted to have two girls, and have a self–contained show where we would come out and do songs and leave and then Gram would come out and sing solo, then the two girls, then one girl would duet with Gram and then bring the whole group on for an encore. Freeman was really into Vegas shows which the four of us were certainly not. But he was booking us fairly well so we went along on some things.

SG: What towns did you play?

PS: I got a lot of them written down. Greenwood, Charleston, Myrtle Beach, Jacksonville in Florida, coffee houses in New York City. We played in Georgia right after Kennedy's death. A small auditorium in this little town.

SG: Was Buddy Freeman booking the gigs?

PS: Yes, and you know back then it wasn't so hard to book the gigs. We were getting quite a following and Buddy said, last time I talked to him, he *still* has

Shilos rehearsal, l–r Paul Surratt, George Wrigley, GP, Joe Kelly, Greenville, S.C., 1963

people come up to him and ask him if he is still working with groups like he was in the Shilos days. They still remember Gram and us from that long ago.

Was Buddy still booking the gigs by the time the Shilos went to Greenwich Village?

PS: No.

What year was this?

PS: 1964.

Where did the Shilos play in the Village?

PS: We played at a place called the Cafe Wha'. We played at a place called the Bitter End. We played the Bitter End's hoot night and we got an encore and came back the next week. We did so well...you see nobody could believe Gram and us could sing so well, young as we looked...they couldn't believe sixteen year olds could do it. We got the gig because Gram went to New York and saw what was happening and then came back and got us. He said, "We gotta go." Actually it must have been 1965 'cause the Byrds were playing in the Village, too.

At that time Jimi Hendrix was a regular at the Cafe Wha'.

PS: Well, the Byrds were playing right across the street at the Cafe A Go–Go. And it's funny 'cause John Phillips and John Stewart came walking down the street while we were there, and we knew Phillips at the time because of the Journeymen. And I was so into the Journeymen I would go see them play every time I possibly could. John Phillips and I met in Greenville when my father had driven us to their show. So John comes walking down the street and George saw him and John Stewart outside one of the clubs, the Cafe Rafael. We had played there almost every free night. Anyway George recognized them and said hello. He told them he was playing in a group with Gram Parsons and Paul Surratt. "Surratt," says Phillips, "is he here?" "Where is he?" And I had gone out to get a pizza. I missed him. So the next day we went to John's apartment and met Michelle. They were living together. Dick Weissman was there. He's a really fine person; he's still around. He just put a book out. John took us to see Grossman's people who wanted to book us at the Bitter End at Christmas, but the group fell apart before that.

What was Buddy Freeman's influence on Gram?

PS: Buddy was close to the Parsons family. Gram called Buddy up and just told him "Buddy, you're my manager." 'Cause people had been calling him saying Gram Parsons was playing such and such a place and telling people you're his manager. Buddy had no idea.

How many Gram Parsons' originals did the Shilos record?

PS: "Surfinanny" was not all Gram's. Part of that was George's. There was a song called "Raise A Ruckus Tonight"...George wrote the music to that and Gram wrote the words.

Are there any Gram Parsons' Shilo originals that did not make the Sierra/Briar release?

PS: I don't think so. Gram wasn't writing very much in those days. Almost all the stuff was friends' material or George's. George loved doing original arrangements of old stuff.

Anything left on the tape from your living room of Gram doing "Surfinanny"?

PS: Yeah, there is. There's one song, you're right. It's called "Great Silky."
Is it original?
PS: No, it's an old song Gram rearranged. I have an entire live album of the Shilos from Florida. We did that on tape...we left one good tape of us in the back of a car. I don't know what happened to it. I mean...the Shilos and Gram...we had no conception of not being together for the rest of our lives. We were all so young we didn't know any better. Anyway, I put the tape of us on at a friend's house and we were listening to Gram sing. And he gives the date and it's sixteen years and two days later than the date we recorded it.
Is that your wolf whistle on "Surfinanny"?
PS: Gram does that himself. It's not on the original tape of that song that we recorded in Chicago, for Cypress Gardens. Unless Avis (GP's sister) can find it. Mark Holland went there and they told him it was destroyed, but perhaps they said that just because they didn't know him. I'd love to hear those tapes. We had drums backing us up... professional bass player.
How did the breakup of the Shilos affect you?
PS: That's when I first finally realized what depression was all about. I saw my whole life crumbling. I couldn't comprehend it happening and the Vietnam war was getting close. Everything fell apart for me at one time. We broke up because...Avis said Gram said he was tired of doing folk material. I think we could have stuck together. If we'd have latched onto folk–rock we'd have been giants with him. But we were not open enough to see it at that time. George had to go to college, as did Joe.
How did the breakup of the group affect Gram?
PS: There was no doubt in Gram's mind he would make it in the music world. He just used us as a stepping stone. He went on into another style of music. I'll bet it affected him but I'll never know how bad.
Why didn't you follow Gram up North?
PS: I was seventeen and my father died at the time. The service was closing in on me too. I was so crazy about Gram and

Gram and George Wrigley, Sept. 1963

The Shilos with manager Buddy Freeman, second from right, 1963

SEP 63

Gentlemen:

We would greatly appreciate your giving the enclosed tapes your most careful consideration. We believe we have the newest and freshest style to come along in the folk field for many years.

As performers, we have won tremendous acclaim in night clubs, coffee houses, college campuses, radio and television. Youth is on our side since no one in our group exceeds eighteen years of age.

Regretfully, our tapes are not of the highest quality. We had no time to achieve proper balance through reverb and possible overdub.

We feel that we could be of significant value to your company.

Sincerely yours,

THE SHILOS

REF ~~Enclosure~~s

WFBC	Andy Scott	Greenville, S. C.
Club Jamarta	Mr. Posey	Greenville, S. C.
Ivey's Fashion Show	Ed Wickliff	Greenville, S. C.
WCSC	Carol Godwin	Charleston, S. C.
The Citadel		Charleston, S. C.
Derry Down	Helen Page	Winterhaven, Fla.
Cafe Rafio	Ed Gordan	
	Bleaker St., Greenwich, New York, N.Y.	

Charlestown/Fort Caroline, Mr. Herbert Cannon, Myrtle Beach, S.C.

taken with him I was thinking I would have to spend my life near him, maybe being his valet. I know this sounds pretty corny to you but he had such a power over me I figured if I wasn't going to be singing with him I would at least be with him in some part of his life.

SG: *But you didn't go to Boston with Gram?*

PS: I was chickenshit. I was seventeen years old. I later moved to New York on my own.

SG: *Let's talk about the ten years it took to get the Shilos album out. Are there any near misses?*

PS: I've got letters of us being turned down. "I'm sorry Mr. Stratton this is not what we are looking for." I went to Nashville myself...my father put up $100 in 1965, good money in those days in the South, when he was making $2.80 an hour. He believed in Gram too. So in 1965 here I was in Nashville trying to put out the tape. Everyone let me do what I could with the tape. Once I took them to Gram and he borrowed them but I got 'em back quick 'cause he had a habit of losing things. They were the only tapes I had. I almost got a bootleg of it out but then...I met this couple at the Icehouse and they introduced me to John Delgatto of Sierra/Briar. John had already done a couple of albums with great effort and expense. He'd done an album with Doc Watson. John heard the tapes and said, "I'll put this out. I'll get the money and I'll release it." It took us a solid year from that point. Real nice fellow. Company worked hard on this. First record they did real well with, Gram's Shilo stuff. I went on vacation and I interviewed Buddy and Avis. Avis and I stayed up all night talking. I hadn't seen her in ten years. I got permission from everybody. Gram is what sold this album. We are lucky to have it out.

SG: *You've said how you like Gram's singing better in the early days than in the Grievous Angel days.*

PS: The reason is that back then he was new. His voice still had a fresh quality to it. He somehow got to believe in country music in that...well, he started country rock, at least I believe he started it...Stephen Stills says he did, I think...but either way...Gram deliberately started copying some of the old singers. You've heard him sing. He had a great voice. I think he had a few too many binges

Shilos rehearsal, George, Gram, Joe and Paul, 1963

Gram and Joe Kelly rehearsing, 1963

The actual gig - a high school hootenanny, Greenville, S.C., 1963

where he started to screw up his voice because I played that tape of the Shilos for Chris Ethridge just before he joined Willie Nelson, and Chris called his wife and said "Come here, come here, you won't believe this. It's Gram before he ever joined us...listen to that guy sing!" Chris said he never knew Gram could sing that good.

SG: *Well, he wasn't any slouch later.*

PS: Aw, he wasn't...I mean compare the two voices. Did you know Gram was asked to be in the original Poco? I can't confirm that but I heard he was asked and he turned it down so they asked Jimmy Messina. That's what I've heard. I don't know if it's true. The Eagles had a great song called "My Man", about Gram. And Poco had a great song about Gram called "Crazy Eyes". Gosh, that's a great song. "Crazy Eyes".

SG: *You moved to Los Angeles around 1970, right?*

PS: I left New York. I left South Carolina in 1966 and moved to New York and then I got this litle letter in the mail "we request your presence at Fort Jackson, South Carolina". They wanted to see how I looked, if you know what I'm saying. So I went down and my whole life fell apart. I was stationed in California for four years. San Diego, San Francisco, coast of Viet Nam for three years and back and forth, back and forth from Nam. Discharged, went straight to L.A.

SG: *Was the last anybody saw of Mike Bixel, the Shilos' biggest fan, when he went to Viet Nam?*

PS: Mike Bixel was one of the last few casualties of the Viet Nam war. He was one of the last shot down. I even read it in the paper and I didn't know if it was Michael.I was so sick of reading about the whole thing. I didn't pay much attention and then a few weeks later somebody said it was Mike, that he was one of the last few casualties. While flying over Viet Nam Mike used to have a tape deck in his plane playing the Shilos...while he was doing his missions. He loved the Shilos, by gosh. He had tapes of Gram and us with his old lady but they are unmarked. I don't know where the original Shilo tapes are. All I have is a copy. I think George's folks used one of them.

The Shilos onstage, 1964

SG: By the time you'd moved out here you had kept in touch with Gram, hadn't you? Did he know Paul Surratt was coming to town? Did you see him?

PS: No, I had to find him. I saw him once when he was in the Burritos. I remember I saw him and Chris Hillman somewhere in town. Then I went to his place, his home. I got in touch with Gram through John Phillips this one time, when he lived in Bel Air little bit after the Mamas and the Papas. It's funny about Gram. He was always vice or versa.

SG: Do you think the Stephen Stills, the John Phillips, the Jackson Brownes, the Nitty Gritty Dirt Band recognize Gram Parsons? Do they appreciate Gram? Do they see him as a rival?

PS: John Phillips liked Gram. I have no idea what the others think of him, but surely they must have some idea since they knew him. Richie Furay is all positive about Gram Parsons.

SG: About Gram?

PS: I think part of it is he is such a Christian he won't say anything but the best about anyone.

SG: Furay talked with Gram a lot. He lived across the street from him in Greenwich Village.

PS: We should get in touch with him.

Between 1970 and 1973 did you see

SG: Gram? Did you talk with him or socialize with him? Did you ever see the Fallen Angels?

PS: After he left the Burritos I went to Gram's home in the Chateau Marmont on Sunset. I used to go over there all the time and see him . And I went there one time...I never felt in place with those people because I wasn't in the rock'n'roll echelon. I was in Gram's past and he kind of looked down on me a bit. At least I felt like he did. Perhaps

may 27, jacksonville

dear bear-

the pictures are tremendous. whoever took them really xxx knew how to capture the spirit of the group.
i've been thinking. if we want to make it as a x group we're going to have to do some serious rearranging. the people want a really different sound, and ours isn't different enough yet. of course, we might not like all the changes but i do think they're necessary. for one thing i think we should sing all new music with a few exceptions. i think we should work on my material. i know it will sell. music, believe it or not, is turning towards a more xxxxxxxxx intellectual vein. we should go into serious rehersals, now i know we've said that before but now it <u>is</u> a necessity. i'm sure that my music is going to be as big as dylans, and after my album we will have the advantage of owning my music plus dicks. we are going to have to cash in on this thing dylan's started, and like it or not we'll be associated with him. i still want very much to make it with the shilos. i always have.

there is a bigger chance for us than i imagined, even at spring. don't get too excited though. <u>it is going to take a tremendous effort</u> on our parts.
write me as soon as you get this and tell me what joe and george think.

sound as ever,

[signature]

g. parsons
bolles
jax, fla.
32207

paul surratt jr.
44 n. garden circle

it was my own insecurities. He was always nice to me but I didn't visit as much as I should have. I didn't know the rock'n'roll rules. I didn't know the rules of hanging out. He told me one time... I was very depressed...I said how do you get on a label? And Gram looked at me and said Paul, I don't know what the hell is going on. He was with the Burritos at this time. I said but Gram, you're on a label. And Gram said after you've been in this town three or four years you will know exactly what I'm talking about. And I thought what is he talking about? I was so confused at the time. Now I know exactly what he was talking about. He even came out to see my band when we were rehearsing one time.

SG: *Did he like it? What was the name of the band?*

PS: Gram was doing a lot of this and that by then. When I first met him he was (speaks energetically) "Okay men, let's go!" Then it was like (speaks slowly) "Well, come in...good...to...see you."

SG: *What happened in the two years or so between leaving the Burritos and the GP album?*

PS: He did an interview where he talks about hanging out with the Rolling Stones. He sings on "Sweet Virginia". They did some songs together. The Rolling Stones got a lot from Gram Parsons. They learned a lot from him.

SG: *What are the possibilities of a good Gram Parsons biographical motion picture ever coming out?*

PS: A lot of people have given me scripts and they tell me they have ideas but the only possibility is if one of his albums gets real big and his legend grows even more. And you know how that can happen. All the people who love Gram Parsons are hardcore fans but none of the general public are really aware.

SG: *What were the final sales figures of the Sierra/Briar album?*

PS: At this point around 10,000. That's the kind of album that can go on selling for years. We can sell it for five years breaking it out in small markets.

SG: *I told you about the time in Lexington, Kentucky, where this guy had a Gram Parsons Memorial Festival at the University of Kentucky. This was the Summer of 1975. At the old basketball arena he had two nights with Chuck Berry, the Nitty Gritty Dirt Band and the next night was the Band, Roger McGuinn and Ray Charles. Ray Charles refused to play because the guy's checks were bouncing. I saw the Band and McGuinn and they mentioned Gram. The final night was someone and Emmylou Harris. Emmylou went to the arena and saw this banner that said "Gram Parsons" and nothing else on it and she split. Actually it read "Welcome Gram Parsons".*

SG: *I want you to tell me what Gram Parsons' favorite singers and influences were.*

PS: The Journeymen and the Kingston Trio. George Jones. The Beatles. The Rolling Stones. The Beatles killed every kind of music for awhile. That's all people wanted to hear. Gram really got into Country later. When we played at Fort Caroline amusement park he told me, "Paul, someday Country is going to be as big as Folk or Rock, I'll tell you." It never quite did. The Eagles are doing close to it.

SG: *I've often heard that Gram thought bubblegum music was the pits.*

PS: I don't really know about that. He liked Dylan a lot. Maybe the Byrds.

SG: *When you look back on Gram Parsons as a person, through all these years, what do you remember?*

PS: I remember the good parts. I always loved Gram. He was very nice to me. He used to say to me "I don't care what anybody says, you are a musician so accept that and enjoy it." He felt that we were different from other people, special. He had a lot of hard family problems. They hurt him, the problems did. I always loved Gram very dearly. I miss him, and I still miss him a lot right now. I wish he was still around. He'd have been a lot of fun today.

CARON

Sum Up Broke: John Nuese

John Nuese knew Gram Parsons for eight years, from September of 1965 until Parsons' death in September of 1973. During those eight years John Nuese saw Gram Parsons grow both as an artist striving to meet his potential and as an individual adapting to the changes brought about by increasing notoriety. Nuese knew Parsons as a fellow musician and as a friend, forming the International Submarine Band with Gram (and playing lead guitar on the ISB's only album) in the mid–Sixties, and came full circle by forming a touring group for Gram and Emmylou Harris in late 1973. The latter group never got off the ground – a fine band silenced by Gram's untimely death.

This is by far the most comprehensive interview ever given by John Nuese or anyone else concerning the International Submarine Band. It also sheds light on Gram Parsons' plans upon the completion of the *Grievous Angel* recording sessions. It's a fascinating story that needs to be heard.

SG: Where and when did you first meet Gram Parsons and how did he strike you at the time?

JN: I first met Gram in Cambridge, Massachusetts, in mid–September of 1965. He had just enrolled in Harvard after coming up from New York where he was doing the folk circuit in Greenwich Village, singing solo on one of those stools in the clubs, accompanying himself on acoustic guitar. He had been in Harvard a short while and he came to an antique shop where the gal working was the sister of the gal I was staying with. She invited him to come by sometime and he showed up late one night. I got back from a gig – I was playing with a group called the Trolls in Cambridge, the nucleus of which later became the Youngbloods behind Jesse Colin Young. I walked in about twelve–thirty at night and Gram was sitting in the living room with the two girls. I met him then and there. He seemed like a very straightforward, down to earth individual, a very nice guy. He had an acoustic guitar there. He whipped it out, played a tune or two. Then the two of us proceeded to play and the magic thing happened right there, just fell in because he was very easy to play with. Right from then I just fell in. I had a very good musical rapport with him from the very outset, and bang! He played very well and he had a very easy, flowing style that was easy for me to get into. Very straightforward.

SG: How did the rest of the ISB get together and could you tell me about the various personnel over the years?

JN: After getting together with Gram informally since meeting him in September...oh, a few weeks later he expressed an interest in getting together and starting some kind of a band. Also living in Cambridge at this time was an old friend of mine – Ian Dunlop, a bass and saxophone player whom I had worked with in a couple of bands over the years in Cambridge. Happy Pantaloon and the Buckles was one of them. Ian was also there on the scene. Ian expressed an interest in doing things with Gram too. Shortly thereafter I went with some friends to Boston's downtown area sailor bars to hear this band Roger Paice, a group from Baltimore who were a white soul thing, to listen to its drummer. We got him over to Cambridge and recruited him for this new band with Gram. Slowly we were coming together. At this same time a Berkeley School of Music piano playing friend of Gram's by the name of Tom Snow – who was playing jazz – came on the scene. We started, I think, as five people or so. We started formally rehearsing a couple of Gram's tunes. One of the ones I remember was called

n at the Cafe Express in Florida, 1964, solo

"November Nights". This was the initial Submarine Band, but we were only five for a few months. Gram, myself, Ian Dunlop and Mickey Gauvin stayed on. Tom Snow was only with us for a few months in the fall, as he was primarily a jazz player. We all went home around Christmas time and he stayed in that scene in Cambridge. The four of us moved to New York. Gram had a connection in New York, having lived there for a summer with Marty Ehrlichman who was Barbara Streisand's manager at the time. He offered to do some demos of us for RCA. There was a session. I think he did a couple of things. We went down to New York to do those informal sessions and also to play with Brandon deWilde, who was a good friend of Gram's. Brandon figures very heavily in the history of this band. He was very close to all of the people in the band throughout its history. He was the unofficial fifth member. We were one large family.

SG: What was the Cambridge music scene like at that time?

JN: The Cambridge scene at that time was very nice. A lot of music going on, a lot of players around, lots of places to play. The whole vibration, the whole feel, the entire atmosphere was good times and nice people.

SG: How did you guys get on Ascot and Columbia for those two singles and who played what on them?

JN: When we got to New York we became involved with a couple of managers by the names of Monte Kay and Jack Lewis. Jack Lewis handled the Modern Jazz Quartet and Flip Wilson at that time, and some other black acts. We were primarily involved with him. His partner was our producer and first landed us a contract with Ascot Records to do something simultaneously with the movie "The Russians Are Coming, the Russians Are Coming". One side of the single which resulted was an instrumental of the Johnny Mandel theme from the movie and the other side was a Buck Owens song called "Truck Driving Man". Just four people played on the two singles we did for Ascot and Columbia. I should say right now that a very important fact is that when this band got together I was the only one with experience playing and listening to a lot of country music. Mickey was a black soul kind of drummer. Ian was familiar with some country but was primarily a rock'n'roller and Gram, who had been exposed to country music during his formative years, was doing commerical folk music. It was my influence that turned this band onto country music. For instance, Gram didn't know what was going on in country music. He knew no Buck Owens or, say no Merle Haggard. Nor had other members of the band. When I turned them on to these singers they all liked it very much and were caught up, totally hooked by the music. After we did the Ascot single for the "Russians Are Coming" movie nothing really seemed to happen. We couldn't get too much action on the record. Our managers then terminated the contract and we were signed to Columbia. We did one single for Columbia. The "A" side was called "Sum Up Broke" and Gram and I did it together. He wrote the words and I wrote the music. The second side was one of his songs called "One Day Week". We recorded this with the same personnel as the earlier single and we put it out. We found that we had become like a computer card in the great huge file at Columbia Records. And although they had us signed and had something in the can they really didn't do anything with it. So nothing really came of the Columbia single. We lived in New York from about January of 1966 to around March of 1967. During that time we played a lot of the clubs in the city like Trude Heller's, the Night Owl...a lot down there on West Fourth Street. We did various gigs around at discotechques, did some television stuff in New Jersey. We did one of the Zacherly television shows out of New Jersey. We actually did quite a bit of work in that year and a half or so. In the spring of 1967 Brandon was in California and Gram went out there to pay a visit. He got hooked on California. We talked to him and it was decided at that time that the band would move out to Los Angeles.

ST 5908

MUSIC FROM "THE TRIP"

Original Sound Track Album Composed and Performed by

THE ELECTRIC FLAG, AN AMERICAN MUSIC BAND"

The Electric Flag, An American Music Band:
Mike Bloomfield: *Leader and Lead Guitar*
Harvey Brooks: *Bass*
Barry Goldberg: *Organ, Piano, Harpsichord*
Buddy Miles: *Percussion*
Nick Gravenites: *Vocal, Guitar*
Mark Doubleday: *Trumpet, Flugelhorn*
Peter Strazza: *Tenor Sax*

Paul Beaver: *Moog Synthesizer*
Bob Notkoff: *Electric Violin*

SIDE A

1. Peter's Trip
2. Joint Passing
3. Psyche Soap
4. M-23
5. Synesthesia
6. A Little Head
7. Hobbit
8. Inner Pocket
9. Fewghh
10. Green and Gold
11. The Other Ed Norton
12. Flash, Bam, Pow

SIDE B

1. Home Room
2. Peter Gets Off
3. Practice Music
4. Fine Jung Thing
5. Senior Citizen
6. Gettin' Hard

Prouuced by JOHN COURT
A GROSCOURT Production

SG: Tell me about appearing in The Trip, the sixties youth movie. Why did they dub the Electric Flag over you guys?
JN: Brandon, who was a friend of Peter Fonda's, got us this contract to work in this film of Peter's called *The Trip*. We recorded some things to do in the film and we appeared in some scenes in the movie. The reason they overdubbed us was probably due to a decision of the film's producers. It was nothing we had anything to do with. The Electric Flag had just formed and they were pretty well known. As a matter of fact they were rehearsing up at our house in Laurel Canyon, the Burrito Manor.

SG: How did Lee Hazelwood and his record company enter the picture?
JN: When we got to California and assembled in the Spring of 1967 we became involved with a manager by the name of Steve Aldsberg. He was an L.A. person and through his friends and so on we eventually got a hold of a gal by the name of Suzi Jane Holkom who was working for Lee Hazelwood. She came to Burrito Manor and we played for her as sort of an audition for the record company. She liked us very much and it was through her we were signed with Lee Hazelwood. At this time there was a

split in the band and the second Submarine Band comes into being. Everything split. Gram and I went in one direction to do primarily country music while Ian and Mickey went to R&B and got together with Barry Tashian, Bill Briggs, Junior Markham and Bob Keyes to form, in the spring or early Summer of 1967, the original Flying Burrito Brothers. At the same time Gram and I formed the band that made the ISB album. In June of 1967 Gram went to Florida for a brief visit where he happened to run into Jon Corneal whom he'd worked with before in a previous band. He asked if he was interested in coming out to Hollywood and doing this album with us and Jon was happy to. In mid or late July we recorded "Blue Eyes" and "Luxury Liner", two of the tunes that are on the album. It wasn't until around Thanksgiving 1967 that we went in to finish the rest of the album.

SG: Tell me about making the ISB album with Gram?

JN: We had a basic style where we would get in a circle and play flattop guitars. Gram and I had developed a very good rapport doing this kind of thing. This was the basic style in which we would review what we were to record. When we did this album the method worked in part but not on the whole, because of problems with Suzi Jane. She and I disagreed on how to do things. She was into piecemeal recording, doing basic tracks then building stuff over them. I was into a thing, as Gram was, of recording the whole thing live. But we did this album in two separate recording stints. Suzi Jane was producing in the studio. Gram played rhythm guitar. I played rhythm guitar and lead guitar. Corneal was playing drums. Chris Ethridge was playing bass. A chap by the name of Bob Buchanan also did some singing in the November sessions. J.D. Maness, a very fine steel player, played steel. Earl Ball, a very good piano player, did keyboard work on the album. Gram did the lead singing and backup singing was by Jon Corneal, Bob Buchanan, Suzi Jane and a chap by the name of Virgil Warner did a little.

SG: What do you know about Hazelwood objecting to Gram singing on the Sweetheart of the Rodeo album?

Chris Ethridge, circa 1969

ISB

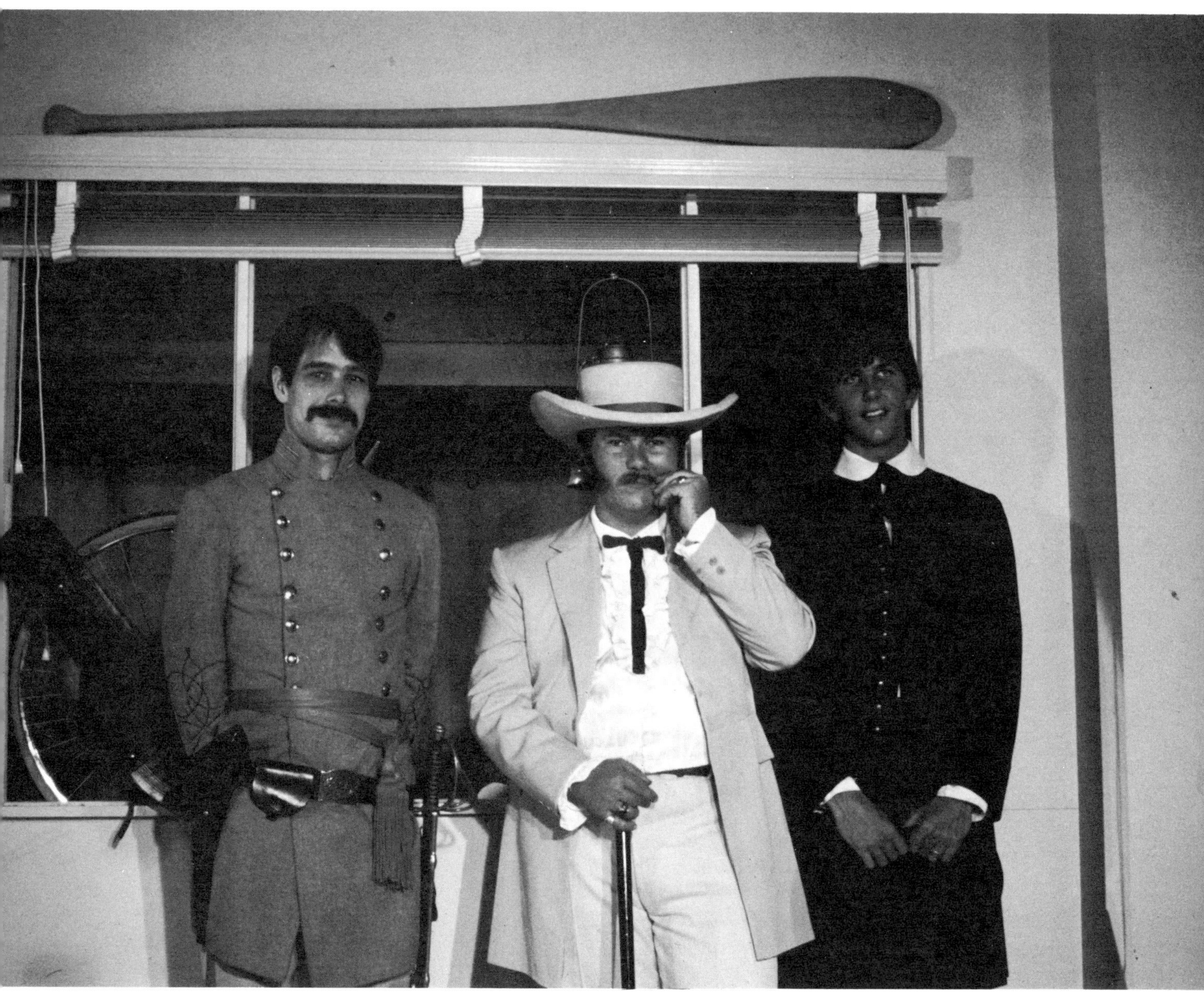

The International Submarine Band in full regalia, l–r John Nuese, Jon Corneal and GP

JN: Gram was under exclusive contract, as were all of the ISB – a contract covering everything. Hazelwood didn't want him doing anything with anybody except the Submarine Band and he was... when he found out Gram was doing a recording thing and dabbling with the Byrds he objected. And it was because of Gram being under exclusive contract that this came about. This also was a factor or *the* factor which legally brought the end of the band, because the Submarine Band broke up only under legal pressure.

The scene was that Lee Hazelwood had a lawsuit pending against Gram. He said that if Gram didn't stop recording with the Byrds he was going to press the lawsuit. Gram was offered a choice which was his but which reflected on all of us. What it was was this. Hazelwood said that Gram could either record with the Byrds and give him (Hazelwood) the royalties or else give up the rights to the name "International Submarine Band". And that's eventually what happened. Gram came and talked to us and we

Official ISB publicity photo

decided that was the thing to do. We didn't have the bucks to free ourselves from Hazelwood so our choice really only was give him the name International Submarine Band lock, stock and barrel. He owned the tape anyway. Gram was the root of this thing being under contract to Hazelwood so when Hazelwood found out about Gram playing with someone else he understandably became very mad.

SG: *Describe the music of the ISB. At first it seemed very "1966" and suddenly things became more country oriented. Why? Was it hard to find country players your own age?*

JN: We started playing country music just about at the onset of the ISB, around the end of 1965 or the begining of 1966. We were interested in and listened to a lot of the black R&B scene. Our drummer Mickey and Ian were both from that scene. We played a lot of black stuff and a lot of country stuff and some regular rock n' roll. As far as other players playing country music around the various music scenes we were in, well, there were just none. We were the only guys playing country music. We would have liked to recruit steel players but in 1966 it would have to had been from among country studio musicians or country bar bands, who were really divided at that time from rock music. The whole thing of that time boils down to that country music is white blues. It's the same expression of pain and suffering through music — the music of hard times. The expressions are identical but at that time no one was hip to that kind of correlative. People were primarily thinking or just playing in the black blues idiom. The idea of younger white musicians playing country music hadn't dawned on many people yet. But we pulled it off. The crowds we played for liked it very much and we knew, especially Gram and I, that it was something which was going to work and was a coming thing in music.

SG: *What was Gram Parsons like in those later days just before the group broke up?*

JN: That was a very heavy, emotional period for Gram. He was involved with this beautiful, high-strung gal by the name of Nancy Lee Ross and they lived together. She became pregnant and had a child. That was the heaviest emotional scene we had seen Gram go through. It was tearing him up constantly during that period, which was the Summer of 1967 on into the fall and winter. We had stopped playing regularly together. Also after Jon Corneal came out in the Summer of 1967 Gram had some second thoughts about his coming. It was a heavy period, all in all.

SG: *What kinds of records did Gram Parsons enjoy?*

JN: Mainly just modern country music and some other modern things. Maybe some Ray Charles or current rhythm and blues but mostly the country sounds of that period.

SG: *Tell me about the breakup of the International Submarine Band and how you parted ways with Gram.*

JN: In March or so of 1968 we terminated this thing. Gram was working with the Byrds and going through the emotional thing with Nancy. Also he had some second thoughts about working with

Jon Corneal. We were sitting down with Gram one time in March of 1968 and our rapport was fine and he just said he wanted to work with these other fellows. My relationship with him then was fine. He just sort of eased out of contact with me. Corneal and I continued for several months to try to find a replacement for Gram. We were still involved with Chris Ethridge on bass. We couldn't find anyone in the L.A. scene of that time who could cut it so in the late Summer of 1968 we just called it quits and folded up the whole thing. We had already given up the name to Hazelwood and then we just couldn't find anyone to replace Gram.

SG: Did you have any later contact with Gram? When was the last time you saw Gram Parsons?

JN: I had periodic contact with him when he was back East with the Flying Burrito Brothers during their first tour. I had gotten in touch with him in the L.A. area off and on when I was in California from 1969 to 1972 or whatever. My real return to Gram's graces was in late 1972 and throughout 1973. In later Winter of 1973 Gram was in the East finishing up his tour for the *GP* album with his Fallen Angel band. We got together and started to make plans for the future. What I set up with Gram was, in short, a new band for him to tour with after his second album in the Fall of 1973. Gram had gone through a lot of heavy stuff and had been very indulgent, perhaps, but it seemed this band was a return for him to playing with some of the more down–to–earth old friends that he had worked with before. I think, in truth, that Gram wanted to cool it with the whole Hollywood scene and get into a more relaxed and easier thing like he had experienced with the ISB. He wanted to get into a situation which was less intense and less pressured. The makeup of this band was to be as follows. Gram, of course, was to sing and play rhythm guitar. Emmylou Harris was to sing and play guitar. I would play electric lead guitar. Barry Tashian would play electric rhythm guitar, piano and do some backup vocals. Mickey Gauvin was the old ISB drummer and he would play drums. A banjo and steel player from Woodstock named Bill Keith would cover us there and everything was set except for the position of bass guitar. The last time I actually saw Gram was when he was finishing up the tour in the East in 1973, in the Boston area. We had had a lot of telephone contact over the spring and summer getting this band together. I believe he had just finished the album and was with Phil Kaufman at his little guest cottage when Phil said Gram was going out to the desert for the weekend, to relax after the album, you know. That was the weekend Gram died.

SG: What do you remember Gram Parsons for the most? His singing, his stage performance or his writing?

JN: The main thing about Gram was his feel for country music – the way he played it and the way he sang it. His guitar playing was very much in tune with the mainstream country method of recording and playing, mainly out of Nashville. Coming from the South he understood the pattern very naturally, that four count where the bass is counting on one and the drummer's side stick is on three and you use this repetitious pattern of playing which sets up a very even and flowing solid rhythm with a front and back beat. He sang very much in accordance with the way he played, and it gave his whole musical thing an overall power and sense of being able to play and express music. He was the easiest person to play with that I had ever met and, as I mentioned earlier, it was something that immediately clicked in and fell together beautifully. But let me elaborate on the issue of the ISB and their introduction to country music. Gram had grown up in the South and had listened to a good bit of country music over the course of his life, had played country music with earlier bands but had gotten out of touch with the country music scene. For him the ISB was a reintroduction, a reawakening in him of the emotional thing which produces country music. No doubt a lot of the things from his youth came back to him and he brought these things into play when he returned to the music that was largely a part of his tradition. Mickey, for instance, was from the R&B scene. Ian was from the rock'n'roll and R&B scenes. Tom Snow was strictly jazz. I myself had been listening to country music since being introduced to it in 1948. I'd been playing it for years, using these tools and so on. And the hand of fate, as it were, cast me as the catalyst who would reintroduce Gram to country and give the others their first taste of it. Once that was done, I guess we just carried it on into the work that we did.

Gram Parsons Interview: From Safe At Home to Sin City

"There is no Gram Parsons.
Yours truly,
Anonymous"
—Gram Parsons

"I think the mystique built up around me is the creation of the press and fans," says Gram Parsons, G.P., the mysterious prophet of country rock who has spent the last two years, in his own words, "learning how to be invisible." "But I'm willing to share responsibility for whatever comes next," he adds.

What comes next is hopefully the vindication of Gram's painstaking odyssey in search of a workable amalgamation of musical forms to bridge the gap which regrettably still exists between the pop and country music markets. That says something about what the man and his work are all about; just how he has reached the current point in his life and career ain't a bad story at all.

Gram Parsons was born in Florida and raised in Waycross, Georgia. His childhood was quite literally filled with the South's very special personality... the cultural in-breeding and introversion, the Dixie provincialism. Country, gospel and Black spiritual musics decorated the radio at the same time that people like Elvis Presley were picking up local followings with a hybrid style combining all three.

"I listened to whatever stations my parents would have on," remembers Gram, "as far back as 1954."

Parsons picked up guitar in his early teens after having played piano for several years.

"I just wanted to play guitar because Elvis played one," he says. A succession of local bands with guys the same age followed. One, the Legends, playing lots of Everly Brothers and Chuck Berry material, did well enough to make the club circuit and do a TV show or two.

"I really hated what I heard on the radio at this time," says Gram. "Bobby Vee, Bobby Vinton and that whole bit. It was negative inspiration."

"On the other hand," he continues, "local dance promoters used to hire these incredible black R&B bands, and book 'em into dance halls in small towns during the early sixties. They figured to make a killing since kids in these towns hardly ever heard live music played by a

m's official publicity photo for CBS, 1968

Gram's Ivy League "extra-curricular interest" surfaced earlier on this page from his own scrapbook, circa 1964, depicting poppies and cartoonist Rodrigues' offbeat humor

real show group. These bands had names like, oh, Big Jake and the Soul Twisters and so on, with big robes and turbans and jewels on their foreheads. But it backfired when a lot of parents wouldn't let their kids go to *that* kind of show. They either had to stay home or sneak over, and only the local musicians were always in the audience. I imagine these bands didn't even get paid if the show bombed. Hundreds of incredible bands like those never got national recognition for various reasons, and they never will."

Along about 1965, Gram moved on to college.

"I did a back-dive into Harvard," he says. "They were looking to break out of their traditional mold of choosing students, and I was way out of the mold. I was also ready to start thumbing to get out of Waycross. There's an old saying about it; as soon as you learn to walk, you start walkin' out of town."

Seriously, Parsons did have an interest in writing and literature which initially didn't seem too out of place in Cambridge.

"I think I was there about four hours and fifteen minutes," he laughs. "At Harvard, you don't major, you concentrate. One thing I was hellbound to concentrate on was what Alpert and Leary were up to with LSD. But they'd left. Mainly I was turned off by the fact that I had to study all these things I didn't understand. I lasted four or five months by playing music and having good times."

In Cambridge, Parsons met some other young musicians through what he recalls as a series of bizarre occurrences. Besides Gram, there was an English psychiatrist's son, a Connecticut judge's son and some kind of anarchist from Baltimore ("he was very artistic but kept getting busted for blowing up draft boards"). They were the legendary International Submarine Band, the world's first-ditch country rock and roll band. New England in early 1966 was hardly the place for them.

"Country music formed the basis for what we played," explains Parsons, "but we experimented with some noises. We wuz keepin' up with the times. It was one of those bands that rehearsed a lot more than it gigged. We moved down to the Bronx and lived in a big old house. There wasn't much of a country scene there either. Plum nearly starved, too!"

Some people did hear the Sub band in the Big Old Apple. Gram got to know a lot of the famous Village folkies, almost even got a chance to work with David Merrick on a musical, did some country music for the soundtrack of a comedy film and met the late actor, Brandon de Wilde, who dug all kinds of music, among them country.

"de Wilde encouraged us," remembers Gram, "and got us a job pretending to play in a Peter Fonda movie in L.A. So we went to California and got out of the cold, next door to Bakersfield and near some good country radio stations."

In L.A., another place where country music was not really happening in rock and roll, the Submariners struggled to become known but ended up in disarray.

"The International Submarine Band split in two," Parsons explains. "The bass player and drummer began using the name 'Flying Burrito Brothers,' or sometimes 'The Remains of the International Main Street Flying Burrito Brothers Blues Band,' depending on who played. They jammed a lot in clubs with people who wound up becoming strongly identified with Delaney and Bonnie, Barry Tashian from the Remains and occasionally myself. The ISB guitarist and I did the ISB album for Lee Hazelwood with some help from other musicians we literally had to scrounge from the woodwork. Most of 'em are known now, but then, there weren't many country musicians in Hollywood. We wanted to get something out of the ISB after all that time and effort, but it didn't happen."

The album, *Safe at Home*, is an obscure classic, and was essentially the first full-blown country-rock LP. It was also the official obituary for the Sub band. Gram's abilities as a musician, songwriter and singer had already brought him to the attention of both the press and the Byrds.

"I'd met Chris Hillman in a bank," says Parsons. "We had on the same kind of jeans and the same looks on our faces. At a session of theirs later on, I mentioned the name 'Flying Burrito Brothers' and they wanted to use it as the title of the album that was eventually called *Notorious Byrd Brothers*. I wouldn't let 'em have it. But I joined the group a little after that."

Parsons made his auspicious "big-time" debut in the Spring of 1968. While it can be said that the Byrds had always had some country leanings in their collective personality, it can also be said that rarely has the addition of one musician had such a drastic effect on the music of a major rock and roll band as did the Byrds' acquisition of Gram Parsons. He took "folk-rock" right to the heart of Nashville, the Grand Ol' Opry, recorded on one of the group's most acclaimed albums (*Sweetheart of the Rodeo*, which included two Parsons vocal performances until contractual problems brought about their deletion) and toured both in American and Europe. He left at the end of that summer when the Byrds were scheduled to tour South Africa and Gram refused to accompany them.

"At first, Chris Hillman wouldn't speak to me because of the rough time they had on tour after I quit," says Gram, "but later, when he left the band, we eventually got back together and began jamming at country bars. We picked up Sneeky Pete Kleinow and Chris Ethridge and resurrected the Flying Burrito Brothers. We stole the name."

The Flying Burritos certainly left some kind of a mark, though they never found the audience they deserved. Gram initially took the band out to Nudie's Rodeo Tailors in North Hollywood, California and dressed everyone up in amazing outfits. He then set out to find that elusive sythesis of pop and country music he had begun to contemplate pretty seriously.

"Things were always going wrong with the Burritos," Gram recalls. "At first, we toured before our album was out, so audiences didn't know what to expect. And the group didn't evolve like I'd hoped it would. I was looking for some kind of total thing, almost like a revue, but it didn't grow that way. The Burritos were a group of good musicians, but collectively, they weren't what I was looking for in the long run."

In early 1970, Gram had a motorcycle mishap and was forced into a welcome period of recouperation. Most of the next two years was spent traveling, writing music, and contemplating his goals and intentions. The time was divided between L.A., Louisiana, England and France. Though there was always talk circulating about a Gram Parsons solo album, the only studio work Gram did was to sing background on one cut of the Byrds' *Untitled* LP. The Burritos, who continued on without him for over a year and a half, saw him again briefly in late 1971 when he guested with them at two concerts. But basically, Gram for awhile was one of the phantoms of rock.

"I began getting ready for a solo album in earnest about eight months before I went into a studio," he says. "It took a lot of mental preparation. When the time came, I was lucky enough to get good people to help, like four people from Elvis' band, and my old friend, Rick Grech (a young British musician Gram met on tour with the Byrds; also an ex-member of Family, Blind Faith and Traffic) and Byron Berline. There's also a great new female singer from Alabama named Emmylou Harris, originally found by Chris Hillman."

Which more or less brings things up to date. But G.P. doesn't leave it all up to chronologies.

"I should mention that some strange people have really been helpful," he says. "There's Brandon de Wilde. And the guys in the ISB were important; they always had their ears open and they actually reintroduced me to country music after I'd forgotten about it for ten years. And the country singers like George Jones, Ray Price and Merle Haggard. They're great performers, but I had to *learn* to dig them, and that taught me a lot."

"The people I've written songs with," he continues, "especially Chris Hillman and Chris Ethridge, have also been helpful. When we can sit down and take the time we need, it's really worked out well."

"I've never really had the freedom I needed to let my music go in the direction I have in my head," concludes Parsons. "That's why I'm no longer in a band. I believe in music that can reach anybody, regardless of the labels. Either you like it or you don't. Rock and Roll has probably contributed to the creation of more musical prejudices than it has broken down and I hope what I do helps to destroy those and other prejudices. As long as I can keep trying with my music, I'll be okay."

December 1972

LINDA EASTMAN

The Byrds before GP, l–r Chris Hillman, David Crosby and Roger McGuinn, 1967

The Byrds after GP playing The Troubadour, Los Angeles, l–r Parsons, Hillman, Kelley, McGuinn, 1968

Gram Parsons Vs. The Density of Sound

"I think the difference is in the mechanical sounds of our time. Like the sound of the airplane in the Forties was a rrrrrrrroooooaaaaaaaaaaahhhhhhhhhh sound and Sinatra and other people sang like that with those sort of overtones. Now we've got the krrriiiiissssssssss-hhhhhhhhhhhh jet sound, and the kids are singing up in there now. It's the mechanical sounds of the era: the sounds are different and so the music is different." Jim McGuinn, 1965.

When Gram Parsons joined the Byrds he completely changed the direction the band was headed. David Crosby, Gene Clark and Mike Clarke had all left by this time and with those three original Byrds went much if not all of the Byrds sound described above. McGuinn's 12-string became less prominent with Gram in the group (coming back to the fore when Gram left, significantly enough) and the traditional Byrds three-part harmony vocals stayed, changing slightly into a more Appalachian sound than the rock harmonies of the first Byrd album.

Perhaps the first inkling of change occured before Gram Parsons moved to Los Angeles, much less joined the Byrds. On the Byrds' second album, *Turn, Turn, Turn!*, the group sang Porter Wagoner's hit "A Satisfied Mind", using their always-indebted-to-country vocals as a pivot while changing the rhythm, beat and instrumentation to a lighter, more C&W sound. In essence this is what Gram Parsons had the group do when he joined in the Spring of 1968.

"A Satisfied Mind" gives you some idea of what would happen if the Byrds wanted to play straight C&W as opposed to crossing their own Byrdsongs with country and coming out with "Mr. Spaceman" on *5D*, "Time Between" and "The Girl with No Name" on *Younger Than Yesterday*, or "Wasn't Born to Follow" and "Old John Robertson" on *The Notorious Byrd Brothers*. While "Wasn't Born to Follow" has the lighter, obviously C&W feel of "A Satisfied Mind" this is largely due to production, so I include it with the other tunes, which are obviously Byrdsongs first and C&W second, unlike "A Satisfied Mind" which is country first and not very Byrdsy at all. The other tunes are all dominated by 12-strings and hard rock guitar in one way or another and it is the absence of the Rickenbacker 12-string which made *Sweetheart of the Rodeo* such a unique Byrds album (and perhaps why it was one of their poorest-selling).

Gram at the Troubadour gig, 1968

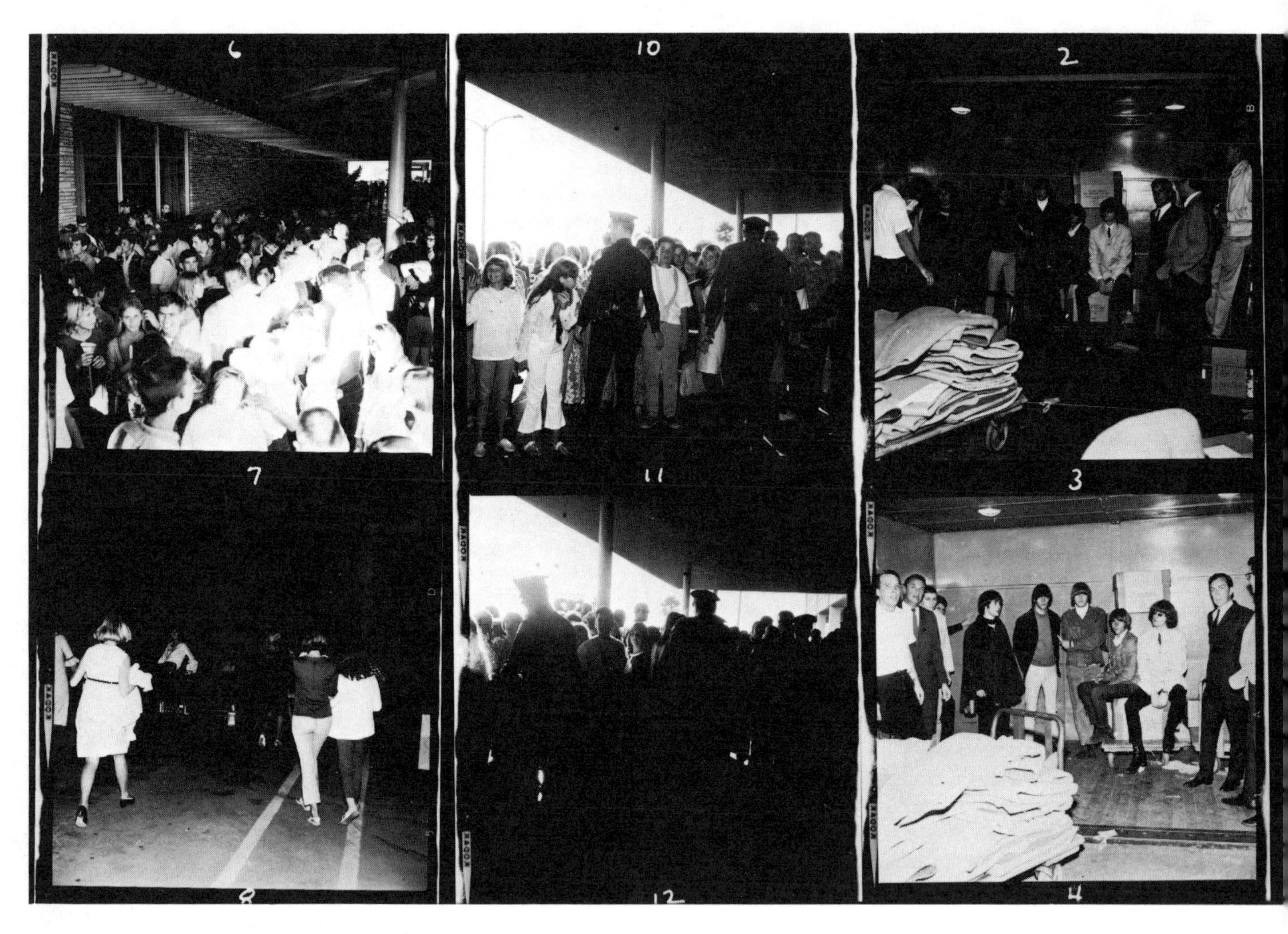

Byrdmania! Outside and backstage at the TNT show, Santa Monica Civic Auditorium, 1965

Before Gram Parsons joined the Byrds the band was in a rut. Their initial string of hits had started to taper off ever since Top Forty stations decided "Eight Miles High" was about drugs (McGuinn says it was about landing in the fog at London airport) and the bands live performances, always somewhat shakey, featured less and less new material, just the same hits being played unenthusiastically. Gene Clark left after the "Eight Miles High"/"Why" single (though he sang on Byrds LPs for years to come) and in 1968 David Crosby left during the recording of *The Notorious Byrd Brothers*. Then Drummer Michael Clarke left Los Angeles and Chris Hillman recruited his cousin Kevin Kelley, who was playing with Taj Mahal, to take his place. The Byrds were a trio in trouble.

Exactly how Gram Parsons became a Byrd is not our subject but it is generally accepted that his business manager, who also represented McGuinn and Hillman, introduced Gram to the group. The Byrds were then coming off of what many considered to be their best LP in *Notorious Byrd Brothers* but had no real band for touring. Nonetheless they appeared as a trio on *American Bandstand* and *9th Street West* miming "Eight Miles High" and "So You Want to be a Rock n'Roll Star?" looking somewhat ill at ease. McGuinn and Crosby had been heralded just a few short months earlier as raga-rock guitar pioneers, playing Indian (Shankar) influenced licks on ever-long widening songs. "Eight Miles High" had helped start a West Coast guitar fad that was all too brief and the Byrds themselves never got it on wax due to Crosby's leaving the group. Mike Bloomfield jammed with Crosby a lot about this time and the sound I'm referring to is found on the Butterfield Blues Band album *East-West* on the cuts "Work Song" and "East-West". While the Byrds were playing this music and looking like they did on the cover of *The Byrds' Greatest Hits*, Gram Parsons was looking sweet and innocent in the International Submarine Band and he was playing relatively straightforward C&W with a twist of R&B, what he would later call "Cosmic American Music".

Crosby left the Byrds in part because they didn't want to cut "Triad" for *The Notorious Byrd Brothers* and

MARTI COLE

The Byrds playing the "9th Street West" television show with Sam Riddle, l-r Parsons, Kelley, McGuinn, Hillman, 1968

John Delgatto

The Byrds onstage at The Grand Ole Opry, 1968

instead cut Goffin-King's "Goin' Back" and "Wasn't Born to Follow." The raga and synthesizer bit went out the window with him and the Byrds wondered what in the hell they would do next.

"Our albums are bi-annual, audio magazines dating from the time we first started recording. I think of myself as the editor of the magazine. Even Sweetheart of the Rodeo *fit. You don't think doing an all-country issue is in itself an editorial? It was a feature on country music, a close-up, a special issue."* Roger McGuinn in Los Angeles Herald Examiner, Nov. '69.

So Gram Parsons joined the group in April of 1968, after waiting to finish the ISB's album *Safe at Home*. A wonderful album, it was not promoted at all and it died a quiet death only to be reissued in 1979 (see discography). Almost immediately the four Byrds went to Nashville to record an album. "Gram thought we could win over the country audience," McGuinn later told Bud Scoppa, "he figured once they dig you they never let you go."

The Byrds became very clean-cut at this time (see photo). Everyone shaved and got a haircut as the band was on the bill at the Grand Ole Opry, becoming the first rock act to play there. Two songs and that's *it*, were their instructions from the Opry management. They went on and Parsons sang "Hickory Wind" but not before giving a long, spaced-out rap dedicating the song to his grandmother. They were not asked to return.

McGuinn never was a big C&W fan, much less a purist like Parsons. He always said out and out country was a bag Gram and Chris Hillman had gotten him into. "We hired a piano player and it turned out to be Parsons... George Jones in a sequined suit..." he told Scoppa.

As for Gram himself he said he was consciously trying to get the two last original Byrds away from their "imitation Dylan" into new music, a new music for longhairs anyway. What is important to remember here is how aghast many old Byrds followers were initially when their heros took up the music of a region they regarded with suspicion and hostility. Dylan had not recorded *Nashville Skyline* and except for the odd C&W-styled Beatles cut no major rock act had touched pure country. In England the Downliners Sect had cut *Country Sect*, the first true country-rock album — overlooked completely, probably because it was not all that terrific an artistic achievement and because it sold several dozen copies. For our purposes and to most people, the Byrds, with Gram Parsons leading the charge, were the first act to delve into country headlong and headfirst.

Once in Nashville several things went awry. CBS backed out of financing a two record album, asking the Byrds to give them one album instead. This ticked McGuinn off because he had envisioned a two record set starting with traditional mountain music working its way to Byrdsongs and then finishing up with moog synthesizers representing the music of the future. Past, present and future all in one bundle. Yet this massive shift in styles couldn't be done in just one long playing record's time so the band stuck with country and western. Cuts such as "Pretty Polly", "Sing Me Back Home", Gram's "Lazy Days" and "Reputation" were already cut but they were left in the can, squeezed off the album by lack of space.

I can't prove it but I'm fairly sure these are the tracks Parsons refers to when he makes his famous "there is another *Sweetheart* and I, uh... dig it" comments later in his career. Because these cuts were left off the album and because several of Gram's vocals were erased and replaced with McGuinn and Hillman's, Gram became very upset and these two reasons possibly contributed to his ease at deciding to leave the group before their planned visit to South Africa.

Actually it was Parsons' own fault as much as anyone's that his vocals had to be erased. Legal problems set in because the Byrds found out Lee Hazelwood and LHI Records still owned Parson's voice as a member of the International Submarine Band and the Byrds only had rights to his songs and instrumental talents (see Hillman interview). So McGuinn and Hillman reluctantly but grudgingly re-recorded the vocals on "The Christian Life" and "You Don't Miss Your Water", two songs Gram Parsons introduced to the group.

"Sweetheart *is a 15 or 20 years ago C&W album. It's not like country today. I really wanted to see if we could get that sound."* Roger McGuinn, *Rolling Stone*.

They did. "You Ain't Goin' Nowhere", the Bob Dylan song off the Basement Tapes sessions, is the only song other than "Nothing was Delivered" (another Dylan tune) that is anywhere near a Byrdsong. With it's loping, circular chorus which seems to go on and on it is close to the sweet monotony of the *Mr. Tambourine Man* album. Significantly the 12-string Rickenbacker is missing; had it been there and on other *Sweetheart* cuts the album would have sounded more Byrdsy.

It all goes back to "A Satisfied Mind" versus the other early Byrd attempts at country. Vocals stay much the same as they always were with three-part harmonies where one Byrd sings a relatively normal lead with a harmony added and a high, third harmony soaring over the top. Yet the beat has softened and the instrumentation has changed. For the most part electric rock instruments are removed from the traditional Byrds lineup and replaced with acoustic mandolins, guitars, banjos and so forth. It's interesting to note this change of instrumentation brings the Byrds full circle in many ways since McGuinn often said he was playing folk chords to a rock beat with electric instruments. Perhaps *Sweetheart* took him back to his early Old Town folk days in other ways too because he and Hillman contributed no original songs to the album but instead used old country and folk songs like Woody Guthrie's "Pretty Boy Floyd", a song McGuinn must have been familiar with for years.

Production is of course different. Without rock instruments and no hard backbeat things simply had to be changed. Ensemble vocals like those on "Turn, Turn, Turn!" are absent in favor of standard solo voice country vocals with harmonies on the chorus. Only "100 Years From Now" has the "All I Really Want to Do" harmonic approach. Drums are very muted if present at all. Piano appears occasionally, courtesy of Earl Ball, who also played on *Safe at Home*. Clarence White appears more often and more prominently than before (he played on Hillman's country cuts on *Younger than Yesterday*). When the band toured Europe in May and June of 1968 they took along Doug Dillard on banjo in order to get closer to the *Sweetheart* sound. While a fine instrumentalist in the C&W vein, Dillard's pickin' did sound out of place on "Feel A Whole Lot Better" and other early Byrds songs during the tour.

If singing stayed similar to before and instrumentation and production changed, then what of the songs themselves? I mentioned how the chords, structure and melodies of these songs were related to what the Byrds had played before and that's true. Lyrically however, things had done a complete turnaround.

Gram Parsons was the only Byrd with material on *Sweetheart*, the rest of the songs chosen by him, McGuinn and Hillman. They used material from Dylan, Woody Guthrie, Merle Haggard, Gene Autry and soul man William Bell; and other than Dylan, none of these songwriters wrote material Byrds fans had been used to their heroes singing. Metaphysical and spiritual values, spacial references and intergalactic ideas were dropped altogether in favor of more down to earth subject matter like unrequited love, respect for nature and the value of keeping one's health up.

Parsons and McGuinn at a Troubadour gig, 1968

The elder generation lyrically came in for their due after five albums of Byrds (and Dylan) lyrics where their values and institutions were questioned if not laughed at with amusement. Where the Byrds had been in many ways the ultimate Sunset Strip philosophers they now sang from a perspective almost the polar opposite of the albums of yesteryear. The group still used bluegrass vocal inflections while changing slightly the method of presenting Byrds harmonies, but one can still hear the irony in the vocals which the band, particularly McGuinn, was noted for. So instead of this great lyrical and philosophical about-face being too hard to swallow, McGuinn and Co. oiled their singin' with a little sarcastic phraseology in order to let everyone know they were only trying out a new musical style, not a new political order.

"Gram added a whole hunk of country. Gram's bag is country and we are going to let him do his thing and support him and work on other things." McGuinn to Jerry Hopkins, *Rolling Stone*, May 11, 1968.

Parsons and McGuinn, the Troubadour, 1968

Scottish Byrds fan Brian Hogg recently wrote how *Sweetheart of the Rodeo* was merely pleasant, "a new step perhaps, but without the fusion of contrasting ideas, certainly not 'real' Byrdsmusic." Indeed he is correct in many ways. The presence of Gram Parsons changed the Byrds and the music business in many ways and the argument could be made that GP helped sink the Byrds.

Before Gram Parsons the Byrds were an innovative, popular band playing rock music in many ways years (or at least albums) ahead of its competitors, including the Beatles and Dylan. George Harrison wrote "If I Needed Someone" off the changes of "Bells of Rhymney" and John Lennon's "Ticket to Ride" starts off with a vintage 12-string Byrd lick. But after Gram came and went, Roger McGuinn's efforts began to sell less and less in the marketplace. Except for a brief resurgence with *Untitled*, the rock audience slowly left the Byrds more and more. Yet this is not to say McGuinn and his charges didn't continue to do strong, even excellent, work. It is merely to point out Gram Parsons was never known for being a good luck streak when it came to record sales, be those sales that of the Byrds, the Burritos or Gram himself.

After *Sweetheart* and Gram's leaving the Byrds after only four months in the group (GP refused to tour segregated South Africa) McGuinn and Hillman made Clarence White a permanent member, first with Kevin Kelley on drums and later with Gene Parsons. This Byrds ensemble never got on wax.

Gram hung out in London with Keith Richards and late in 1968 formed the Burritos with Chris Hillman, the Burrito monicker coming from Ian Dunlop who had used it to describe the huge jam sessions they were having in L.A. with Barry Tashian, Leon Russell, J.J. Marks, Bobby Keyes, Jesse Ed Davis and the rest of creation.

Without Hillman or any of the original Byrds left to argue or debate McGuinn's plans, "the fusion of contrasting ideas" Brian Hogg wrote of was indeed missing for the most part. My point here is Gram Parsons did create, for all intents and musicological purposes, country-rock, but that country-rock never became so big that its practitioners and those chiefly dwelling in it were monster sellers in the record industry. They were too freaky for C&W straights and too straight for R&R freaks. Hence the explanation behind theories of Gram ending the Byrds and why the later Byrds, early Burritos and Gram-Emmylou albums never sold a great deal yet were artistically topnotch.

I agree *Sweetheart* was both a turning and a starting point for the Byrds and country and rock musics but I have a somewhat different perspective about it. In summary *Sweetheart* didn't end an era so much as start one. Byrds vocals adapted themselves slightly, but not too much, to the new sound. The group's playing, instrumentation and outlook did change the minute Gram Parsons stepped aboard the spaceship with his idea of Cosmic American Music. Production values were different due to the absence of the 12-string jet plane overtones and new found authenticity in acoustic instruments. The door was thrown open by the new country and rock crossing for a bigger country audience awaiting and an entire battalion of future country-rock performers who had stayed in either the C&W or the rock n'roll field with little or no crossover.

Sweetheart of the Rodeo is a fine album, no question. Whether or not it is a fine *Byrds* album depends how you feel about 12-strings, David Crosby and Lear jets. If you miss those things then you are missing out on a lot of what *Sweetheart* does have to offer. Without a Byrds or a Gram Parsons or somebody willing to take a chance on new artistic innovation of some sort, art gets stagnant pretty damn quick. Every single giant in the arts was considered something of an upstart at the beginning of his career and without these people beginning careers and risking their necks life becomes seductively safe and boring way too soon.

GP, Hillman and McGuinn, the Troubadour, 1968

Later McGuinn would go back to the 12-strings and space metaphors but it was never the same even when it was similar. He even used producer Terry Melcher again. What is interesting to note is later Byrds songs were magical in a different way from the great songs of the "Eight Miles High" era. "Chestnut Mare" and "Lover of the Bayou are fine examples. Both have the jingle-jangle of McGuinn's Rickenbacker, one of the truly glorious (in a spiritual/spacial manner) in all of rock. Yet neither is about quasars or space travel or love in the almost fairytale sense of the early Byrds material. In each the dominant Byrds/Rickenbacker/McGuinn sound is matched with what I dare call a Gram Parsons lyric, or at the very least a Gram Parsons subject matter.

Here the countryish theme matched with the 21st Century sound gives the numbers "the fusion of contrasting ideas" both Brian Hogg and I find so fascinating, so appealing. A country sung with NASA instruments instead of Fenders. Since the Burritos' were the major Byrds spinoff band was *Sweetheart* evident in their music? Certainly. "Do-Right Woman", off the *Gilded Palace of Sin* is a soul ballad given a C&W, Everly's styled vocal by Parsons and Hillman. "Hippie Boy" is a country ballad about a longhair subject. "My Uncle" is a bluegrass tune matched to a rock theme. These are all fusions and fusions are what make the best rock n'roll. Hell, rock n'roll *is* a fusion of country and blues (white man's blues vs. black man's blues) so *Sweetheart* is merely the culmination of a natural cycle and no group was more aware of cycles than the Byrds.

Without Gram the Byrds' country returned to electric instruments and the musical children of "A Satisfied Mind" are born. The mechanical sounds of the era were no longer tractors tilling soil but "Krrriiiiiiissssssss-hhhhhhhhhhhh". Gram took his vision with its myriad quirks elsewhere, having changed the Byrds' course and starting a genre represented today by Emmylou Harris, Linda Ronstadt, Eagles, Poco, Joe Ely, even Willie Nelson. (Burrito bassist Chris Ethridge plays with Nelson).

"The Byrds were formed in Los Angeles in August, 1964, and if they had a single aim it was to bring maturity into rock n'roll music." a 1967 Derek Taylor press release.

In terms of marrying country to rock, *Sweetheart of the Rodeo* was where it all started. And maybe even ended for some since the country-rock thing, like disco, never did become as big as the record industry or its practitioners imagined it would. If Gram Parsons had lived perhaps it would have been bigger. Through it all only the first two Burrito albums and Gram's two solo albums had the charm and magic of the country-rock wedding sound on *Sweetheart* (although the Dillard & Clark albums and Emmylou Harris' work sometimes comes close).

"The Byrds are one of the few groups with value, who relate to values beyond the sound of music. There are only a handful of those with the power to reach to the edge of the world and touch, just touch a human spirit and leave the touch to work and activate what it may. The Byrds are one of these groups and one cannot say why, because if it isn't felt, then it isn't to be explained in words." Derek Taylor's liner notes to *Untitled.*

PHOTO COURTESY OF 20TH CENTURY FOX TELEVISION

Peter Fonda in a recent publicity still

HEATHER HARRIS

Peter Fonda photographed by this book's Art Director, backstage at a Byrds' concert, Feb. 22, 19 Admission to this benefit for C.A.F.F. (source of acronym is long forgotten but it had something with Eliot Mintz) which featured the Byrds, Buffalo Springfield, The Doors, Peter, Paul & Mary and Hugh Masekela was all of one dollar: eat your heart out, concert-goers of today!

November Nights: Peter Fonda

Of all the people kind enough to share a few moments to talk about the work of Gram Parsons none is better known worldwide that Peter Fonda. Peter Fonda is primarily recognized for his fine acting but he is also a writer, director, producer and musician of note. His movies are almost always great successes aesthetically as well as at the box office, a recurring highlight being their wonderful use of popular music to heighten the visual effect of the shot taking place onscreen.

Peter Fonda met Gram Parsons when both were young men, at an age where music is more than just a soundtrack to a young man's life, at an age where a love of music can be representative of that person's life itself. He and Gram became close friends and for the first time ever Peter Fonda discusses what Gram Parsons meant to him.

In an effort to be realistic I confess this is the only interview done over the telephone, the rest were done in person while John Nuese was mailed his questions, answering them himself in a recording studio. Peter Fonda was on a farm in Montana when he called, stranded by the Summer of 1980's actor's strike, and to keep things honest I have transcribed this interview verbatim from word one as opposed to using a little creative editing to make it appear we actually met.

The actual advertisement for Peter's famous poster from "The Wild Angels"

Peter Fonda: Hello?

SG: *Peter, this is Sid Griffin.*

P.F.: Hello Sid, how are you?

SG: *I'm doing real good, how are you?*

P.F.: Just fine thank you. I'm in a very fine area here with clean air.

SG: *Yes, I wish I was. Let me get down to cases...I thought if we could only talk to Peter Fonda it would be another aspect of Gram's career no one's ever heard about.*

P.F.: That's for sure!

SG: *I need a little background on how you guys met. I know you were a huge fan of the Byrds.*

P.F.: I met Gram through Brandon deWilde and Gram was a young musician who had just arrived in Los Angeles and I don't really know how he connected with Brandon. But I met him at Brandon's house while Brandon and I were listening to him play with the International Submarine Band.

Gram was from Georgia, Waycross, I believe. What I knew about him was he'd come from a family of some means

stereo
Original Motion Picture Sound Track
SIDEWALK.
THE TRIP
THE TRIP
PETER FONDA · SUSAN STRASBERG
BRUCE DERN · DENNIS HOPPER
PSYCHEDELIC COLOR
JACK NICHOLSON · ROGER CORMAN
the Electric Flag, an American Music Band

The soundtrack album, 1967

but had decided to come to Los Angeles to become a musician because he was a good guitarist. That's all of his past as I know it, I didn't delve into it too much. When I met him that's what I found out from him right up front (laughter). So from then on it was a one on one thing whatever he was up to with his life, whatever he did with music.

SG: In The Trip *you and Bruce Dern went to a club and the ISB band were playing, at least onscreen but the music actually heard on the soundtrack was that of the Electric Flag. I've heard the ISB looked the part but didn't play freaky enough.*

P.F.: Yeah, I acted in that. Unfortunately Jack Nicholson wrote a great script which also was not used.

SG: That is unfortunate.

P.F.: Yes and if you'd read Jack Nicholson's script you would've understood why I thought this film could have been the greatest thing in my career, which it was not. Nevertheless one of the things you do with this type of film when you are shooting IA is the guys playing behind the band cannot be playing live.

Although the Submarine Band did a track for what the filmmaker's were up to they were turned down for the very reason that AIP and Roger Corman didn't think it was "acid" enough.

SG: For a quote unquote, acid movie.

P.F.: Yes, exactly.

SG: How did they get the job in the first place?

P.F.: I asked them to do it.

SG: Because you essentially dig the ISB?

P.F.: Hey I wanted to give them any exposure I could. John Nuese was a fine guitarist and Mickey Gauvin was a hell of a drummer. A fast foot, that boy had a fast foot.

SG: Yeah Nuese was real kind to me. Sent me photos for the book. Was what we saw in the movie an actual performance in a club in L.A. or was it staged for the movie?

P.F.: It was a real club in L.A. but it was used as a soundstage.

SG: Do you remember the name?

P.F.: Nah. Had to walk downstairs to get to it. I was an actor walking into a club. I could tell you the scene but I couldn't tell you the location, I wasn't thinking as a director anymore, it was blowing my mind what was happening. I was trying to do the best I could as an actor.

SG: Then there was nothing recorded of the ISB at that date?

P.F.: There was! They were playing but it was never released and I do not know what happened to the recordings as I did not own them. I did not grab them.

SG: I recently found the Chisa single of Gram's "November Nights" as done by you. He wrote it a few years before you recorded. When did that come out?

P.F.: It came out in 1967.

SG: How did this come about?

P.F.: I wanted to have "November Nights" as the A-side and have the Donovan song ("Catch the Wind") on the B-side. I heard it and said to Gram, "That's terrific." I recorded it and Gram said how thrilled he was. He taught me how to play it and I went and practiced it and practiced it and went out and cut it.

SG: Was GP at the sessions?

P.F.: No. he was with me while I was practicing it though. He was back in the East doing gigs with the Sub Band and doing things with the Stones.

SG: Was there ever a follow-up album on Chisa?

P.F.: No, just the single. Most of my experience with him, my direct experience with him musically, was he would drop by this house I rented on 3rd and San Vicente in Los Angeles and play. There was this darkroom where this character used to edit film of the Byrds and I'd edit film there and Gram would drop by when he had nothing to do and we'd do old Everly Brothers stuff, do the harmonies. Sit down with our guitars and do old Everly Brothers songs, Buddy Holly songs.

SG: So that's some of the Gram music which rubbed off on you.

P.F.: Yes. His whole attitude rubbed off on me in a way. I got along with the fellow real well, he was very nice. He had manners and he was not rude. That kind of thing.

SG: I was wondering what you were thinking when GP joined the Byrds. When Gram joined them it was a major change and while I love Gram it did cost the Byrds a certain part of their audience. The move into country, that is.

P.F.: Well I think an artist should be able to try anything. You can't tell Picasso not to paint green or whatever. I think if an artist wants to sing a ballad or if he is a country and blues singer...fine, go ahead. You have to do what you want to do. Now you are right about the commercial end of it but the Byrds were not thinking in commercial terms they were thinking of making good music. And they took the consequences for it but I admire that.

SG: I do too. I'm afraid to say I once wrote an essay in college where I claimed Wyatt and Billy were based on Roger McGuinn and David Crosby of the Byrds. Wyatt and Billy looked like those two guys and they acted in a similar fashion.

Now is it possible, if that's true, that the character in Outlaw Blues *who was a singer had a little of Gram in him?*

P.F.: No, I would like to say that but no. My life was certainly affected by Gram Parsons and I'll carry that with me always. I did not intercept the role through Gram in any way, however. I mean it was about why this guy got thrown in the slam.

And about Wyatt and Billy being Roger and David...they were friends of ours certainly but we had more interest in updating a Western in *Easy Rider*. The characters there were more like Mongomery Clift and John Wayne, *The Searchers* put into today's symbolic thing. But that doesn't mean they were not used in the film in any way because we had the two Byrds cuts. Had "Draft Morning" in the long version.

SG: You mean in the long version of the movie?

McGuinn's official publicity photo, when he was still Jim

P.F.: The long version of the movie.

SG: An uncut scene in Easy Rider?

P.F.: Yes in one of the cuts it was there. For a long time it was down to two hours and to get under two hours we cut this montage shot of them driving along the beach early in the morning with billboards behind them. "Draft Morning" was going on behind this.

SG: Do you think Gram and the Byrds' swing toward country had any effect on the music industry at all because that's certainly what they are doing today?

P.F.: Yes he had a lot of influence. He influenced a lot of people and a lot of things in a great many ways. For instance he brought a certain influence to the Rolling Stones when he played with them. And this is what we see, his influence not in the market but on the market indirectly, as filtered through other artists.

SG: What I was getting at is you say Gram affected you but what do you mean by that? A lot of people have said it.

P.F.: You can't articulate something like that.

SG: Yes but it's hard for someone reading this to understand what you mean. Is it some style of character or talent?

P.F: No, he had manners. He was kind and that's a rare quality. He had more influence on me as a person than any other way.

SG: What are you up to now that the actor's strike is over?

P.F.: Well right now I'm trying to get down to the river while there is still a little light left and cast a few flys (laughter).

SG: Sounds great. Thanks a lot.

P.F.: Good luck with your book, hope you have great success.

SG: Thanks again....

One

Elliot Gilbert

Jim Seiter in 1976

Hundred Years From Now: Jim Seiter

Artists need more than fans and managers to get by; they need road managers, drivers, soundmen and technicians too. Jim Seiter has done all of these jobs, even being an artist when he played guitar on a few sessions down through the years. Seiter started out "driving the Byrds to San Francisco" and seventeen years later finds himself still in the business.

Jim Seiter started working for the Byrds about a year before Gram Parsons joined the fold, leaving just days before Gram informed the group he wouldn't make the South African trip with them. Seiter then joined the Burritos' crew at the invitation of Chris Hillman and Michael Clarke, working for the group over two years, during Grams' stay with the band. Seiter returned to the Byrds for awhile and later worked with Roger McGuinn steadily passing through the ranks in each successive band.

He's been everything from roadie to manager of the entire group's affairs even if, to hear him tell it, he never got credit for much of his efforts. Today Jim Seiter manages Rocky Burnette and for one late fall day he stopped his busy schedule to reminisce about his trials and tribulations working for Gram Parsons.

SG: *How in the world did you get involved with Gram and this whole show business thing?*

J.S.: I was at a big party at Brandon deWilde's house, who was in the International Submarine Band with Gram, and we had a party at his house in Topanga. Chris (Hillman) was there and as far as I know they met there, I don't know if they knew each other before or not.

Gram had come around before, hanging around Byrd's sessions and before we went to play New York he was around. This is early in '68. He was only in the Byrds for four months or so too, quitting because he wanted to hang out with the Rolling Stones.

SG: *Lots of people have written about Gram not going to Africa because of the apartheid thing and some said it was just an excuse so he could hang out with the Stones. Do you think there is any truth to that?*

J.S.: I think it is mostly that Gram just wanted to hang out with the Stones, that's really where it was at. It's only my opinion of course because I wasn't there. I was up to this time working but at the time of the tour I had had an auto accident four days before South Africa so I couldn't go. I've also thought this might have had something to do with why Gram didn't go.

I left the Byrds when John York came on the scene because I wasn't too fond of his playing, he didn't fit. When Hillman left...well, Clarence White was great, Kevin Kelley didn't fit, Gene Parsons was fine and Skip was great. But when York was playing bass I didn't care for it so when Michael Clarke and Chris asked me to come and do the Burritos I went over there to do that. And I started working with Gram again.

You know the Rolling Stones thing got in the way tremendously because Gram was like a groupie to them. I'm sorry but that's where it was at. "Oh, sorry guys but I'm going over to hang out with the Stones now." The times I picked him up over at Keith Richard's were a little strange, they'd come out skipping like little kids.

I left mostly because we got in a huge argument over Altamont, which Gram insisted the Burritos play. I said no but Gram said "hey, there's gonna be a film," which they were in about a second and a half of. Not even enough

KURT INGHAM

The Altamont-era Rolling Stones, live at The Forum, Los Angeles, 1969

to see them. The guy running the show was a jerk, the Rolling Stones at that point had no one in control, they were just kind of ambling around.

SG: *Yeah, the film [*Gimme Shelter, *USA 1970] showed the back of Gram and Chris for about half a minute doing "Six Days on the Road."*

J.S.: Oh man, it was ridiculous. Between that and spending the night in jail with Gram I pretty much learned where it was at. So I went back to work for the Byrds then, only periodically staying in touch and involved with what Gram was doing.

SG: *Did he cut any records with Keith Richards? People tell me Gram and Keith made tapes but when they say that what does that mean, that they played around on cassettes in the living room or they went in the studio and cut stuff?*

J.S.: I don't know. See the Rolling Stones do a thing when they travel. They get a place like Stills' house where there was a recording studio or rehearsal room, nothing fancy and they'd invite people over to play.

"Gram, come over to play." And Gram played "Country Honk," his version of "Honky Tonk Women," one night. Ry Cooder, the same thing, they were inspired by his bottleneck virtuosity.

SG: *Yes, because all of a sudden after the creative impass of* Their Satanic Majesties' Royal Request *we get bottleneck, open tunings and country stuff like "Dear Doctor" and "Dead Flowers".*

J.S.: Exactly. The country influence was Gram Parsons. The Stones invited Sneeky Pete up there and he wouldn't go. Gram was up there all the time. The Burritos were working the Palomino and the Corral in Topanga and then a New York gig on the weekend, like Carnegie Hall. Every week the Pal and the Corral because this what we did then to keep alive. Gram would get his trust fund checks and he didn't care as much as the others about the importance of these gigs.

Sometimes it was pathetic, pathetic. He was showing up late for rehearsals and everyone was pissed off about it because these were grown-ups, professionals and this late stuff wasn't their scene. They needed to rehearse and go over new songs. Gram wanted to hang out with Keith all the time.

SG: *Did any Corral or Palomino shows get taped? Did any GP/Burritos shows get taped?*

J.S.: No.

SG: *Too bad, a pity.*

J.S.: Yes it is. I agree with you. We did a show in Philadelphia, like the second show I'd done with them, that was absolutely phenomenal. They had never worn their Burrito suits onstage, from the first album cover, and they decided to wear them that night. We were opening for Three Dog Night on a club tour. Three Dog Night were wasting their time going on, it was intense. Gram went out and bought turbans, silk turbans with stones on them, a different stone for each guy and Gram ended the set by falling off the organ stool. He was cool, when he played like that he was real fine. It's just this thing he had for the Stones I don't like.

You know Gram would always say the Stones were going to come see the Burritos perform and when the word would get out the place would be like a zoo.

SG: *You mean it's a zoo in that people would come to see the Stones?*

J.S.: Sure, though we had quite a following too, playing there every night trying to build a really L.A. following because A&M was trying to merchandise a country record and they never had before. They were gonna need help. This was the first growth of A&M from the original MOR label. Since then it's grown several times.

But Gram and them went in the studio with Johnny "Guitar" Watson...

SG: *What do you mean? To cut some tunes?*

J.S.: Watson produced a Burritos single, which I actually have a finished acetate of.

SG: *A finished acetate?*

J.S.: Yeah, maybe the "Train Song", I think.

SG: *What was the flip?*

J.S.: No, I can't remember. We were just about to do the first album when I left, that is the first album with me. The only recording I've been involved with Gram is...okay, there is a whole album I've recorded with Terry Melcher, right?

There is a whole album of unheard Gram Parsons, produced by Melcher, that A&M owns but doesn't know where the tapes are. They were like eight track or something. Melcher did it, doing Gram. It was ending up pretty silly with Gram trying to sing lying flat on the floor and Melcher asleep on the console. A&M canceled the project but they had the tapes and they were almost finished.

SG: *How many songs? An album's worth?*

J.S.: Sure, probably 12 or 15 songs and they are supposed to be great! Someone recently called me about them, asking me where they were and evidently A&M is just now realizing what they have but they don't know whe.e they are. Someone signed it out to Gram, meaning he signed them out of the A&M library and took them.

SG: *Paul Surratt was there [see Surratt interview] when the two of them tried to cut "White Line Fever" and he seemed to think it was a waste.*

Melcher and Gram are very much alike. They are both very talented but because they have their futures predicted (Melcher is the son of Doris Day) for them with money they have no real desire to be anything other than what they are. They just do things till it doesn't suit them any more and then they go do something else.

You know speaking of photographs as you did earlier, I think I have the consummate Burritos photo collection, for what it's worth. Phil Kaufman does too. Gram wanted Phil in on everything

SG: *I've often thought Hillman was Gram's opposite in some ways. Whether or not he's a star this week on the charts or that week doesn't matter to the guy, Hillman will still go out there and try hard, really work. It seems to me Gram and Melcher had a little of that incentive taken away by wealthy parents.*

J.S.: Gram got $50,000 twice a year and he knew how to spend it.

SG: *Did you help manage the Burritos for awhile?*

J.S.: Right. I did the road through Eddie Tickner, the first manager. I helped drive them (the Byrds) up to San Francisco, set up, the group came and stayed twenty minutes, did the show and split. I couldn't believe it. That's all there was to it. Rude? Man, none of them ever said a word to me.

Hillman and Parsons backstage at the Troubadour, 1968

GP and McGuinn, the Troubadour, 1968

John Phillips from a contemporary drawing, 1968

SG: *This is the Byrds?*

J.S.: Right. I was helping out. Then they asked me to go on tour with them, set them up here and there. Tickner told me "you deal with them." Later I met Larry Spector and he was their manager. Spector knew Gram and helped get him in the Byrds.

Anyway Spector didn't know much about rock n' roll itself so a lot of that part of it got passed down to me. I did all the day-to-day stuff. Then I left to be road manager with the Burritos. Remember Gram was in both groups while I'm doing all this—not at the same time.

The Burritos had a lot of guys screwing up over there so I told them "it's either me or those guys" and they put me in charge. Gram said fine but Kaufman has to be your partner. That was that.

SG: *Yeah, it's too bad the business end got away from the Burritos because they were a very special band, all the more special when Gram was singing with them.*

J.S.: I agree. Gram had a special gift, no doubt about it but he wouldn't use it enough and God punishes you if you don't use it. I know this. I've known other people who were the same way like Melcher, who also has a tremendous talent but won't use it, he's been punished too.

I don't understand people like that. I try and do as many things as I can, I like to. Gram had a way of really pleasing people but he never did all he could have done.

SG: *How serious was the motorcycle accident because wasn't this Gram's reason for leaving the Burritos, it wasn't just another riff was it?*

J.S.: The accident was very bad, a real bad accident. He was doing 50 miles an hour on the Coast Highway when the handbars came off, the front tire went off and the frame dug into the Coast Highway. Gram didn't keep up his cycle at all. You've got to get out there everyday and test those nuts and bolts and make sure they are tight. Musicians shouldn't ride bikes unless they are mechanically inclined.

SG: *Okay. Then Gram didn't do any work after the second Burritos L.P. He and Papa John Phillips heal from their bike accident (Papa John was riding with Gram), he sings back on a couple of albums and it is almost three years until he reappears with the "GP" record. Although he did do the Melcher sessions in 1971.*

J.S.: Gram always needed someone around him to motivate him which is one reason Hillman was so good to have around Gram because Chris could spark Gram. Hillman would just take hold of Gram and say "listen, wildman, this is what we have to do." But it started slipping away, as I said, when the Stones came to town.

Remember Hillman wanted to kill him anyway when Gram left the Byrds. I heard he was down at the motel banging on Gram's door saying he'd better not split the band. And after this one stage of their careers full of anger neither one wanted another. Cause they had had to work South Africa as a trio.

And I want to say it wasn't all that bad. Supposedly the South Africans didn't allow whites and blacks to congregate at the same place and Gram didn't want any of that. Said he'd seen enough of that growing up in the South. The Stones told him English musicians don't go down there and he used that as an excuse.

They told him English muscians don't go to South Africa and that's true but one of the other reasons English musicans don't go to South Africa is there is a huge war between the South African musician's union and the English musician's union. It's been going on for years. And they are not welcomed down there.

SG: *There was a rumor Richards was going to produce Gram for the Rolling Stones' record label.*

J.S.: I don't know the story there, Sid. I wasn't around. That would have been after the Burritos and I went back to the Byrds by this time. Next time I saw Gram was at the Sundance Saloon in Calabasas. After that the next time was with Emmylou.

SG: *Were you involved at all with the "GP" tour and those days?*

J.S.: No.

SG: *The reason I asked was because you were quoted as saying you were more comfortable with that particular Gram Parsons that the guy who mimicked the Rolling Stones.*

©1969 JIM McCRARY

The Flying Burrito Brothers resplendant in their Nudie suits, 1969

J.S.: Personally, I just disagreed with the Stones' attitude Gram affected, that's all I meant. When Gram was the best it was always as himself, it was as his own person. The best performances he'd do were at the Palomino on Talent Night on Thursdays where he'd come out and do a song or two. George Jones, thank you very much.

Gram had a phenomenal way of putting emotion in a song, he'd make people cry, I mean actually make people in the audience shed tears. He would do it. And it used to piss us off so bad when he wouldn't do it and we'd have to drag it out of him. 'Cause when he would do it....

This amazing series of photographs shows the Burritos playing for the inmates at the Atascadero Prison, 1969 during the first FBB tour

We played a prison up in Washington State, a men's prison and the way Gram sang for those convicts was unbelievable. They loved it, went nuts. Gram sang his ass off to those guys.

SG: *When was he doing the Palomino talent nights? During the Burritos?*

J.S.: Before, after, during. Just one song by himself and he did it at other clubs also.

This particular GP resurfaced with Emmylou Harris. He respected her so much and she respected him and so he was about as together as I had ever seen him. They sang like angels together. Emmylou has great talent and she was always there. If they had stayed together they'd have been incredible. Around her he put out to his potential, which was he could take any song and put so much emotion into it and you'd just go wild. He had a soulful quality about him.

Gram was one of those creative people who needed more input from people emotionally to keep going. He needed the challenge. He needed someone like Emmylou to keep him interested.

SG: *Is it possible Gram and Emmylou would have been big in the Outlaw thing where country music became respectable to the masses suddenly or perhaps been big in this Urban Cowboy thing?*

J.S.: Oh man! If they, either the Burritos or Emmylou, had caught fire or gotten a few breaks...like the Opry thing.

SG: *That was broadcast on WLS across the nation. Is there a tape somewhere?*

J.S.: Maybe at the station. The Byrds and Gram were the first longhaired band to play the Opry and all week long it was touch and go, touch and go. They'd cancel on us and then we were back on the bill. CBS did it while we were working at CBS at Nashville, you know, do the gig as the album wound up with a few of the local players who were on the album. We were using a lot of modern technology they hadn't seen yet and after a few days they got used to us and realized we were not such bad guys after all.

The album (*Sweetheart of the Rodeo*) was a classic because no one had gone to Nashville yet from the rock world. We

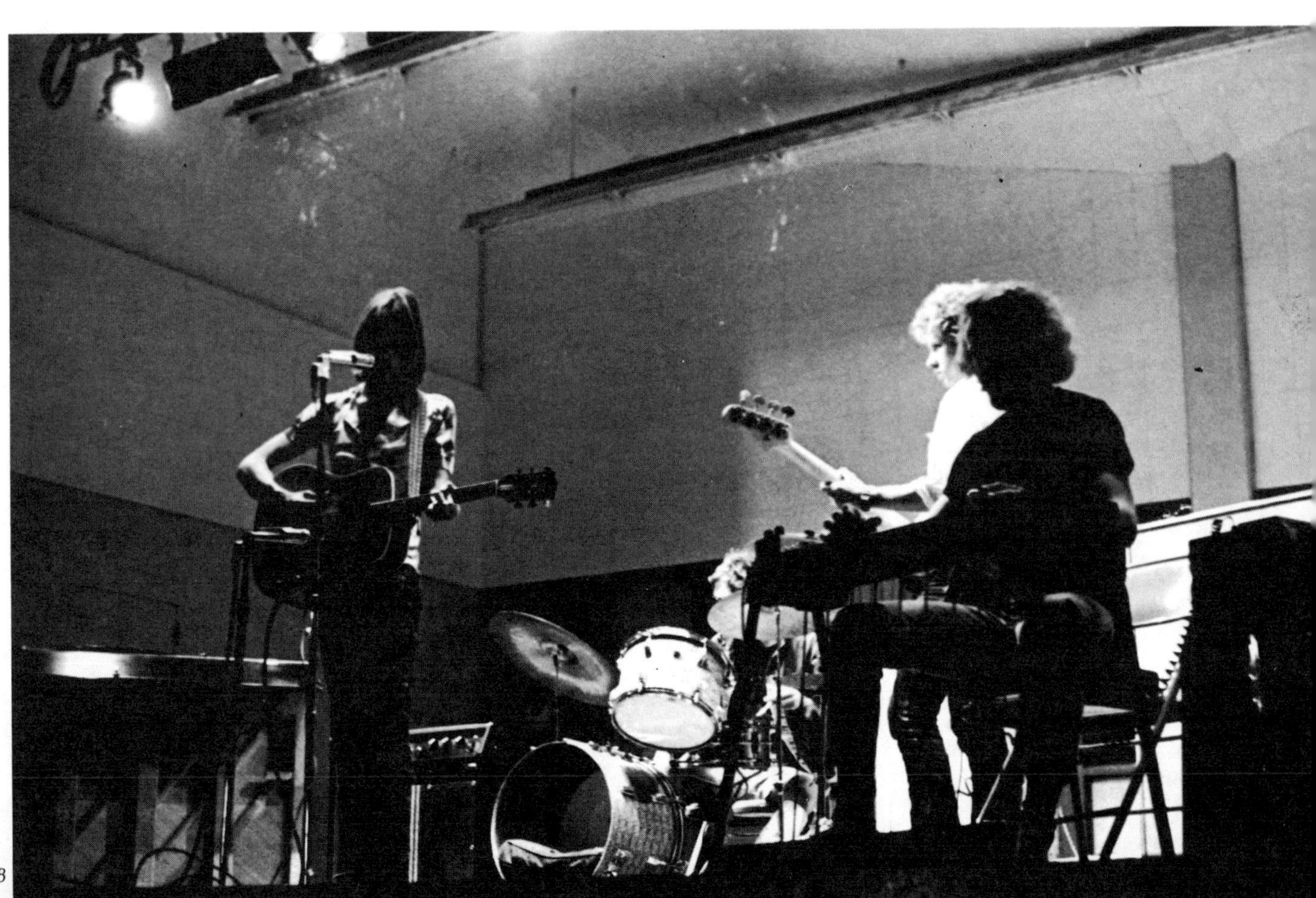

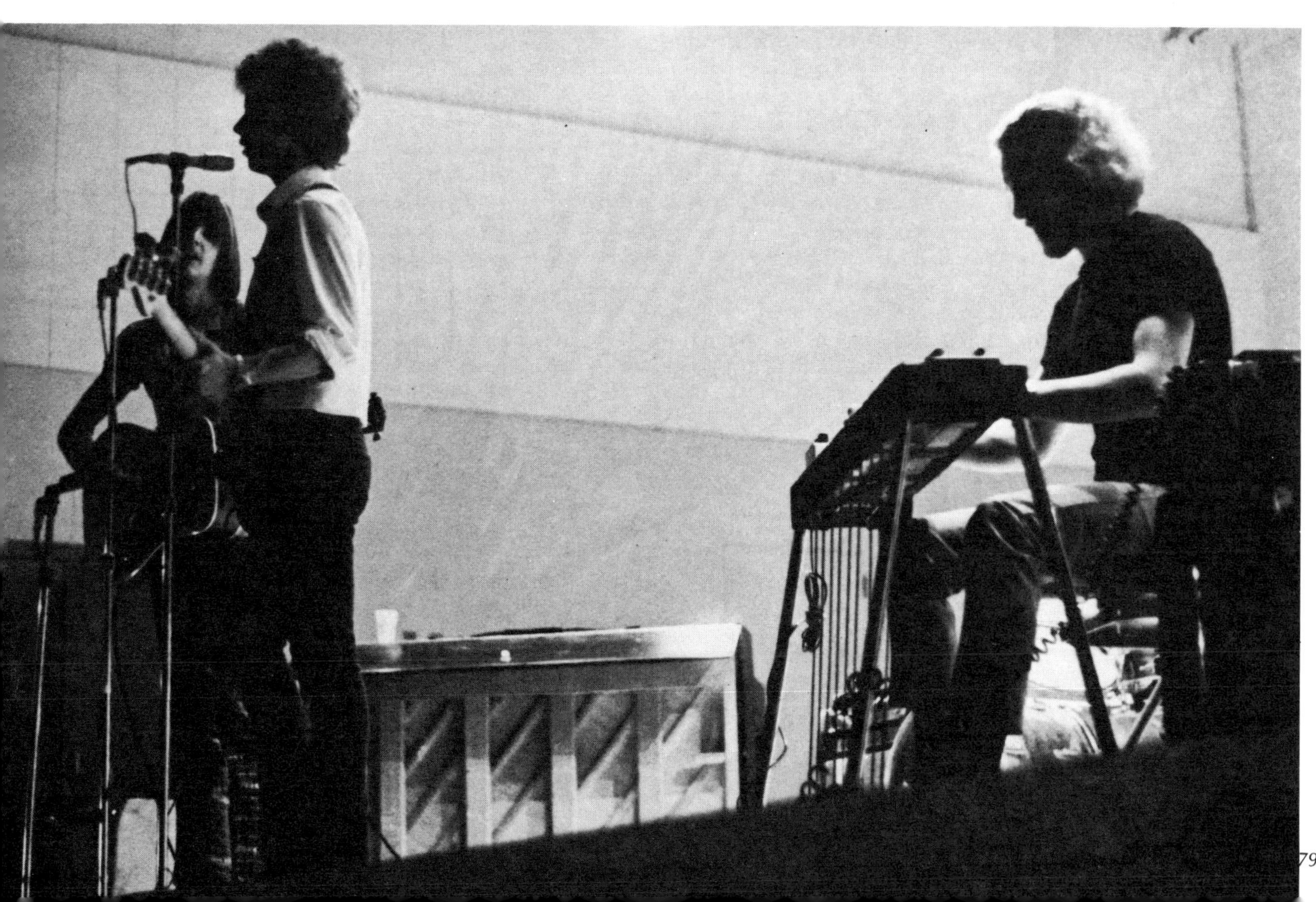

had two eight tracks plugged together and no one there had ever seen that before. All the players came from miles to look at our machines. Just to look at them.

The engineers were so straight too. They start at ten, eleven, twelve or one. Or nine.

SG: *At night?*

J.S.: No, this is Nashville! Nine in the morning, three hours till noon, an hour break and then an afternoon session. They do six tracks *every day*. That's what happens.

So I showed up at nine-thirty with the Byrds' equipment and started setting up. This took about two hours. The group didn't show up till one, that being the way we'd planned it. These Nashville engineers went crazy! I said, "Hey, don't worry about it, you don't want them here while we are getting the sound together."

I told the engineers let's just make sure everything works first. The band will be here when they get ready and by the way if we can get only a track a day that's fine. I mean I'm sorry, I don't care. That's our attitude.

And this was completely foreign to their attitude because they do six tracks a day, an album in two days. That's the way Nashville does things. We take three weeks, which is short for us but on *Sweetheart of the Rodeo* the Byrds were going for a feel anyway.

SG: *Gene Clark once said he was almost beaten up outside the Opry in 1966 for having long hair. How did the Opry react to Gram and company?*

J.S.: They had long hair but it wasn't real long. The Opry was very tense. They announced we were back on and then they told us, this is all being handled like...people who are on the Opry are on 26 weeks a year and they all know what to do. We go there and we didn't know what to do or anything near it. We walk in and there is no one there to tell you. Then a guy says "go on stage", and you go on with a snare drum and brushes, played standing up, no other drums, no drum kits on the Opry stage. Kevin Kelley played standing up. They announced the two songs and then Gram says he wants to do two other songs and he wants to dedicate them to his grandmother!

SG: *They don't allow dedications at the Opry.*

J.S.: I know [laughter].

They went crazy! I got such a hassle from the Opry officials 'cause we totally broke tradition, totally. We did "Hickory Wind" and I think they sang "You Ain't Goin' Nowhere" which came off really well, they got a great response from the people there. Man, when they went to commercial the guy on stage started screaming and yelling at us on stage. They just walked by like "forget you, man." These two country guys played with the Byrds and they got a lot of crap from their friends there for playing with us. Hell, two songs, we're out of there and like Gram says nobody got hurt by it so what the hey. Clarence White's brother Roland was there and he helped out. Kept things cool. Roland was with another band. I loved Clarence.

SG: *Did you hear the* Silver Meteor *album with Clarence on it? It has four finished cuts from his unfinished solo LP.*

J.S.: No, I didn't

SG: *I'll get you one, it's on* Sierra, *an L.A. company that did the Gram and the Shilos' album. It's really good. The Everly's are on it.*

J.S.: Yes, please send me one for certain.

SG: *How much of an influence did the Byrds and GP have on people in the industry like the Stones or whoever?*

J.S.: A lot. Look at "Faraway Eyes." "Sweet Virginia", which Gram sang on. The Byrds were the first professional band I'd worked with in the business and it was always a respectful thing in the industry. Especially from people in the business because they saw the Byrds as innovators. And they really were.

SG: *Because sales slipped after the first two records while quality got even better.*

J.S.: Well, *Untitled* and *Byrdmaniax* got them going again. McGuinn had to get it back to where it was done correctly. Gram had a great, great feel for country and I and some of the other Byrds people actually didn't feel things should go straight country. Roger McGuinn was not going to be able to play anything better than what he plays, you know? The 12 string sound.

SG: *No, McGuinn's not a country picker and he's said so.*

J.S.: No, not at all, which is what I mean. Clarence White was, though. Now Clarence and Gram got along great but they had the C&W thing. Clarence is on the album Gram did with Terry Melcher. Melcher love Clarence's feel for music. The Byrds were all "feel" players, if you know what I mean.

I have a tape of the OD's, by the way.

SG: *I've always wanted to hear that band.*

J.S.: It's Gram and Brandon deWilde and a couple of other people at a party doing old Byrds' things and it is a very interesting sound. Doing "Train Song". I should have recorded more shows in those days.

SG: *What was the story behind the Gram Parsons Music Festival in Lexington, Kentucky in 1976? I was there and it seemed like a good series of shows but who did all the work?*

J.S.: I don't know that either. We all got paid for it though. McGuinn and all of us. The Burritos were there too. We had a big party so it was really a fun gig, everybody knew each other from Los Angeles. The Band, McGuinn, the Dirt Band, Ray Charles, Chuck Berry, Emmylou, the Burritos...what a great night! Hung out with them all night. Wait a minute, I was with the Burritos then. Sorry. When did we play?

SG: *I think the Burritos were the last night.*

J.S.: It was a disaster in some sense, I mean no one knew what was going on backstage. but they did pay all our expenses. We wondered about it too because some of the acts were really good. We thought there might be millions of people there or something.

SG: *Is there anything you want to add?*

J.S.: Before I finish I would like to say Gram Parsons was a beautiful guy and I know one day he would have found the notoriety he sought because he was so talented. Too many people knew he played from the heart to keep him a secret.

"Hot Burrito #1"! That was the last song we did the night he fell off the organ stool opening for Three Dog Night. And it was incredible, there was no way anyone could have ever followed that show. It was something special, possibly the best show they ever played. His singing could give you chills.

The Burritos perform on a 1969 television show l–r Sneeky, Ethridge, Hillman, Clarke and GP playing piano

Frank Chino

Clarence White, Summer 1970

©1970 ED CARAEFF

Chris Hillman, 1980

The "Sweetheart Of The Rodeo" Byrds, l–r Chris Hillman, GP, Kevin Kelley, Roger McGuinn, 1968

Hot Burrito #1: Chris Hillman

Probably no musician worked closer with Gram Parsons than Chris Hillman. It was Hillman who wanted Gram in the Byrds and it was Hillman who joined forces with Gram a little later to form the Flying Burrito Brothers. For almost three years the two were musically inseparable and the union resulted in two albums considered among Gram Parsons' finest work, *Sweetheart of the Rodeo* by the Byrds and *The Gilded Palace of Sin* by the Flying Burrito Brothers. Chris Hillman wrote songs with Gram Parsons, sang harmonies with Gram Parsons and lived with Gram Parsons in the legendary Burrito Manor. This interview is his account of those songs and of his days working alongside Gram Parsons.

SG: *I'd like to start by asking you to clear up the facts about how you met Parsons. One story goes that you met him in a bank and one story says you met him through an accountant or lawyer he shared with you and McGuinn.*

CH: Gram had the same manager–accountant that Roger and I had, a manager–accountant who also handled Peter Fonda, Dennis Hopper and Brandon deWilde. I knew Gram but I ran into him in a bank in Beverly Hills and I asked him if he wanted to join the Byrds. And he tried out for it and passed the tryout and became a member.

SG: *What's the story that you told McGuinn he was a jazz pianist.*

CH: No, no, I never told him that. I don't know who told you that.

It was in a book on the Byrds.

CH: No, no, never did I say that. With Gram we needed a guitar player and a keyboard player because it was Roger and I and just a drummer. We were just a trio so we tried Gram out and he worked out well. He sang good, wrote good songs, and he played a little bit of keyboards but mostly guitar.

SG: *Who was the drummer at this time?*

CH: My cousin Kevin. Kevin Kelley.

SG: *When was the first time you heard Gram sing? Had you heard the ISB album?*

CH: I was familiar with the International Submarine Band before...and I liked that. He shared country stuff that I liked. I grew up from that and so had he.

SG: *One thing I was wondering was did you guys anticipate getting more country or did you just get him in the group and things began to happen that way.*

CH: Well, I started...people forget things ...with all due respect to Gram, who was a wonderful person God rest his soul, Gram and I started the Burrito Brothers together. It wasn't his idea alone. I was doing country things with the Byrds before we met Gram Parsons, on *Younger Than Yesterday*. Anybody that wants to can go back and listen to "Girl With No Name" or "Time Between", where I employed Clarence White on guitar, and that was the first jabs of country–rock right there. It was a year before we met Gram. All due respect to him. When Gram came into the group I had an ally in country music, somebody who understood it and who grew up with it. He helped it and sparked it some more and did help us into that direction of a full–out attempt at doing country. And from there the Burrito Brothers developed but I read Gram did this and Gram did that and...the Byrds recorded a country song on their second album in 1965, "Satisfied Mind", which is a Porter Wagoner hit I brought into the group and we recorded it. It's an old country song so we were really making those jabs. And I had come from a country background. Gram was the first person I had come

Burrito Heyday! The FBB's looking oh so country replete with de rigueur pickup truck and hay, l–r Ethridge, Hillman, Clarke, Sneeky and GP, 1969

across since leaving country music and entering rock and roll that understood what country music was, understood how it felt to play it, and by that I mean there is a certain way to play it, a certain lifestyle you have to feel and understand. It's an easy form of music if you are looking at it from a technical standpoint, it's 2/4...but I've had so many people sit in from rock bands when we were doing the Burritos that could not play it. That would screw us up when we were in such a simple three chord, I IV V combination of a standard country ballad cause you've got to feel that music and that's one thing I finally found in Gram Parsons. He understood what it was, he felt it. He knew what it was. He knew what it meant. That's how he wrote his songs, those kinds of songs and how to this day the most productive time I've ever had, including all the bands I was ever in, the most productive time was living with him in Reseda in 1968 when I was getting a divorce and so was he and we shared a house and we were putting the Burritos together then. We didn't have a drummer, we had Chris Ethridge and Sneeky Pete. We woke up in the morning and we would write every morning as opposed to the usual being up all night until 5 in the morning, which does happen. We were working in the morning, however. He woke up one morning and got the mail and found his draft notice. We wrote "My Uncle" because of that. "Sin City" was about our manager who had robbed us. He lived on the thirty–first floor and had a gold–plated door. And that was the most productive period I've had to this day, writing every day almost on a schedule but not announcing it was a schedule – spontaneously writing together. It was a great time. To this day I've never peaked like that working with other people. I've written a lot of songs, had a lot of fun and success but for writing that's the guy. We drifted apart after that.

SG: *When you say Gram really knew and felt country music are you talking about his feel for it musically or the sociological part of it, his being from the South?*

CH: Musically. Sociologically he grew up very wealthy. He grew up a Tennessee Williams character. They were new money in the South. It wasn't like the sharecropper's saving his money to buy a guitar. He didn't look at it like that. Gram could have been brought up in the North, attending prep schools and Harvard and all that. He just felt it musically and understood it. He was one of those people who really listened to it and understood it. Doesn't matter where you're from cause it's the workingman's song. It's the workingman's music. It's white man's music, as opposed to the black man's music.

SG: *White man's music?*

CH: White man's blues is right...you're darn right it is. That's the way we express it. I mean we are saying the same thing as a black man. "My old lady left me" or this happened or that happened because we have our way of expressing things and they have theirs.

SG: *On* Sweetheart of the Rodeo *there are two conflicting stories about why Gram's vocals were erased. Unless I'm wrong "The Christian Life", "You Don't Miss Your Water", "One Hundred Years From Now" and "Blue Canadian Rockies" would have had Gram's vocals on them, singing lead. But they are not...*

CH: No, I did "Blue Canadian Rockies".

SG: *That was your vocal?*

CH: That was my vocal. It was from the start. "Christian Life" should have been Gram's vocal but we had a contractual problem with Lee Hazelwood over Gram's vocals.

SG: *That's what I want to know about.*

CH: Okay, here's the story. Gram was signed to Lee Hazelwood and we had a problem letting him sing on a Columbia release. Lee Hazelwood International or whatever put out the Submarine album and we got Gram past on "One Hundred Years From Now" but we didn't get him past on "The Christian Life". I don't know why.

SG: *I thought "You Don't Miss Your Water"...*

CH: "You Don't Miss Your Water" should have been Gram. Those two. Those two are the only two that we didn't get by with and I don't know why. God knows

The Mach I Burritos, Jon Corneal at far left, 1968

why we didn't get those past it and Roger to this day is sort of embarrased with his vocal because we have this affected sort of accent. The original ones did have Parsons on them and they were real good.

SG: *There have been stories that you guys went back and pulled his vocals because of his leaving the group.*

CH: No, no. No way. His vocals were on and we really had to pull for them and that's the truth. We never would do that. Never would do that, never have done it. And I'll give you an example before I elaborate on that. On the *Notorious Byrd Brothers* David (Crosby) left in the middle of that and we did not pull his vocals off. We left them on and we gave him full credit even though he had really abandoned the project at that point. Roger and I did the whole album but we left them on. We did not delete David's part at all. Nor would I ever do that or allow that to happen. So Gram had the vocals on those two songs and Lee Hazelwood was suing so at the last minute Roger put his vocals on. We didn't want to Roger didn't want to sing over them. They were Gram's songs. Consequently that was the only problem. The album itself was a good step for us. It was a good album.

SG: *I heard that Gram was present at the* Notorious *sessions and said "Flying Burrito Brothers" over the studio mike and you guys wanted to use it then.*

CH: No, there was a group called the Flying Burrito Brothers playing at the Corral. Sort of a loose thing. We took that name. We stole it.

©1979 JIM McCRARY

McGuinn and Hillman, together again, 1979

SG: *From the J. Markham, Barry Tashian, Leon Russell thing?*
CH: I don't know who had it but I saw that name years ago and I said "Notorious Byrd Brothers". Parsons sort of adopted that name.

SG: *Ian Dunlop says he thought of it.*
CH: God knows who thought of it. It doesn't really matter at this point. I wouldn't even want to get into a discussion of how incensed I am that there is a Flying Burrito Brothers now. Let it lay, man. It is dead, let it go...

SG: *Did CBS ever record some Byrds' shows with you?*
CH: Not to my knowledge. The Opry... it would be interesting to look into that. Are those shows recorded? We did the Opry with Gram right after *Sweetheart* was recorded with my cousin, Roger, Gram and me. If they recorded those shows and have a file of the Grand Ole Opry Saturday night shows we are certainly on one of those shows. During that period in 1968. No TV shows and no live recordings. I don't even think we had a cassette recording from one of the gigs.

SG: *Somebody did.*
CH: Beats me.

SG: *Why are there so few photos of the Byrds that made* Sweetheart*?*
CH: I just don't know what happened there. *Sweetheart* was the last record I was involved in and the only one Parsons did with the Byrds. I have a photo of Doug Dillard, Roger, Gram, Kevin and me somewhere.

SG: *That might be my next question because there is a tape of the Byrds live with GP and there is a guy playing banjo on "Turn Turn Turn" and "Feel A Whole Lot Better" and on the country stuff.*
CH: That's Doug Dillard.

SG: *Who is in that lineup of bass, drums, 12–string, guitar and banjo?*
CH: Doug Dillard.

SG: *The Byrds with Gram toured the States once and then went to Europe?*
CH: Yeah, he wasn't in the band that long. Just a few months. Yeah, we did do the East Coast and then go to Europe. We did Europe and then South Africa. Parsons didn't go to South Africa, hence he left the band. We went to South Africa and we need not elaborate on that. We came back from South Africa and I left the band. Then Gram and I put together the Burritos. I was ready to murder him but then we did make up and became friends again. The South Africa tour was a stupid farce and he was right. We shouldn't have gone but he shouldn't have let us down by copping out at the end...though it really doesn't matter.

SG: *The few photographs I have seen of the* Sweetheart *era Byrds look like you guys really cleaned up with haircuts and coats and ties. I wonder if this is a reflection of Gram's desire to bring the country and rock audiences together?*
CH: No, actually it's because we were there from the beginning with long hair, the Stones look in 1964. The whole rag tag original Byrds look. Gene left and we weren't trying to conform or meet some audience halfway as much as it was us trying to look different for that time. Cut our hair short since everybody had long hair by then. By 1967 everybody had long hair and it wasn't being different to do so. And then that passed and we grew our hair long and now here we are again with short hair.

SG: Could you elaborate anymore about writing the songs on the first Burritos album where you collaborated with Gram? Are they true collaborations or are they Lennon–McCartney bits where one guy has one–third of a song and the other has two–thirds of a song and they match together?

CH: Those songs were written, as God is my witness, together and here's how we wrote them. I had an idea one morning. I said, "Gram, this whole town's full of sin, it will swallow you in." He finished that line with "take it home right away, you've got three years to pay." That's what I meant earlier. The most productive part of my life so far was with Parsons because it was a give and take thing. It was not "I have some music and you have some lyrics" or "sit down here's some music, put lyrics to them". We would sit down and do it with give and take on each line and that's what was neat. Roger and I work like that. It's being familiar with your partner, knowing and anticipating what Gram was thinking about because we were sharing a common thing then, both of us. We were sharing a divorce thing and we were also firing a manager who was crooked. "Sin City". There we were sitting in the middle of L.A. Our managers had stolen from us. Our old ladies had left us. That's what caused the creative working condition. That's what happened on those songs. "Hot Burrito #1" he wrote...I wasn't around. It was Gram working in the studio. And 'Hot Burrito #2" was written with Chris. I really don't know how they were written. You'll have to ask Chris Ethridge. But on the ones we wrote together that's how it worked.

SG: On The Gilded Palace of Sin *LP along with the much vaunted white soul influence, there is a black thing too on "Do Right Woman" and "Dark End of the Street". That's a fairly unique thing to cross Stax–Volt and C&W. It seemed to fade on* Burrito Deluxe. *Could you tell me about that?*

CH: You're absolutely right. We were more than aware of Percy Sledge and Robert Carr and things like that. Those kinds of singers and those kinds of songs like "Dark End of the Street". We were consciously welding the two. That was the merging of the black and white blues. The crying out... taking those R&B songs and putting a light country and western arrangement to them. We knew we couldn't...we were aware we couldn't try to be two black soul singers and try to do "Dark End of the Street". Not like Percy Sledge would do it anyway. So we did our own interpretation. On *Burrito Deluxe* we had a producer, Jim Dickson, who felt we should go more into the area. Maybe it was an attempt to reach more people or to be more commercial. I don't know. I don't like *Burrito Deluxe* all that much. There are a couple of songs that are funny, like "Older Guys". We also had Bernie (Leadon) then. I like the first album. It is my favorite record with Gram and the Burritos. Yes, on *Burrito Deluxe* we did stray from our roots and head more toward rock or rockabilly and less of the R&B thing. More uptempo things, not so much ballad, torch things.

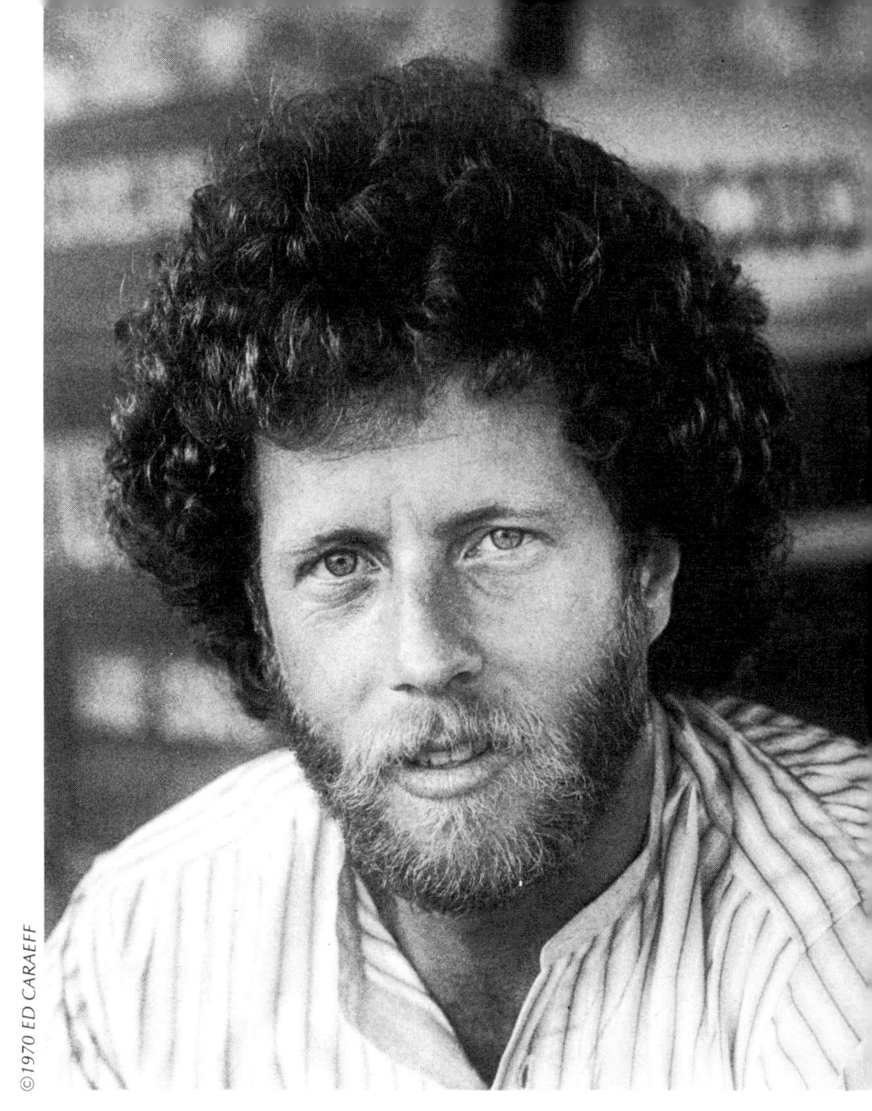

©1970 ED CARAEFF

Chris circa 1970

SG: A lot of the first Burritos LP is duets of you and Gram. How did you work those out? Were they spontaneous?

The Burritos in Nudie gear at unspecified television show, 1969 with GP doubling at guitar and piano

SG: Did you go back to the Everly Brothers or Louvin Brothers to get ideas, or what?
CH: They were Everly—type harmonies, firsts and thirds, and like "Devil in Disguise" Gram would sing the harmony to me and then I would switch on the chorus and sing the harmony and he would sing the lead. Basically, I love the first album although it is crudely recorded. We did those all live and we did them and sang them live and there was a lot of leakage. But the feeling is there. Yeah, mostly it's two—part. On "Do Right Woman" David Crosby sings the chorus with us. I don't think he receives credit on the record.

SG: Is that right? I thought it was a girl.
CH: No, it's David Crosby.
The real high "do"? That's amazing.

SG: CH: "Do Right Woman". Yeah. So he didn't get any credit but yes he was on there. He was walking around one day and I grabbed him and said help us out.

SG: Did the Burritos do any TV shows with Gram?
CH: We did do Dick Clark and American Bandstand. We did local TV shows across the country, meaning local rock shows. We did American Bandstand and we had Nudie on the show with us in his car... so it was quite an affair. But I do remember the very first Burrito Brothers tour; we would go to a place like Chicago or Minneapolis and do the local rock shows wearing our Nudie suits and stuff and lipsync "Devil in Disguise" or something.

SG: Some photos have surfaced of Gram and the Burritos on television and Gram is at the piano. What numbers would you guys be playing?
CH: "Hot Burrito #1" or "Hot Burrito #2".

SG: Promoting the "Hot Burrito/Train Song" single?
CH: No. Not the "Train Song". Either of the Burrito songs from the first album.

SG: So primarily Gram Parsons played guitar onstage?
CH: Yeah. We never took keyboards with us. If we were at a television station and there was a piano...we usually lipsynced these so we would all mug and ham and goof off and stuff. There is great footage of us from back East doing some weird TV show from someplace. It's real good and we are doing "Hot Burrito #1", the slow one,

1969 TV appearance

and Gram is playing the piano. It is real good. Chris Ethridge, Mike Clarke, Sneeky Pete, Gram and myself. The original group. I don't know what it is.

SG: Did the Burritos, when Gram was with them, record any shows? Like Gimme Shelter, *did they record all of that?*
CH: Yes.

SG: The whole performance is on tape?
CH: Oh, I dunno...I have no idea but I would imagine it was. It was edited out and put in there. If the cameras were going the whole time you could find some great footage, if you could find those people.

SG: I saw the Burritos on the David Frost Show. Would Gram have been on that show?
CH: The David Frost Show? You're kidding...

SG: Yeah, you did...you played bass and sang "Six Days on the Road".
CH: David Frost?

SG: Positive.
CH: Gram wasn't there then. It was later but I don't remember it.

SG: Gram would have been with the Burritos some eighteen months and he would have left in the middle of 1970.
CH: Yeah.

SG: What would have been his influences? I can't seem to get a grasp of the type of stuff he'd like to listen to.

HEATHER HARRIS

The Burritos at the Palm Springs Pop Festival Easter weekend, April 1, 1969.

FBB's at the Troubadour, 1969

CH: He listened to a lot of R&B. R&B meaning soul singers, ballads, Bobby Blue Bland, Percy Sledge, Robert Carr. And he listened to straight country like George Jones and Hank Williams. He was enamoured with the Stones at one time. They were the living end, could do no wrong.

SG:*What time was this?*

CH: We introduced him to Mick and Keith in 1968 when we went to Europe. Mick and Keith took us all out for the night. Gram started a relationship with them and that's why we parted company because it was becoming more important to hang out with the Rolling Stones and play rock star games than it was to do his own thing with the Burritos. It got to the point where we couldn't work with him. It just got to the point where Michael and I said "Out!" And that's when he left. But that's what he dug to do and listen to. That's what he dug, black music and lots of country. He didn't listen to any contemporary rock as far as I can remember.

SG:*Johnny Perez told me to ask about the Burrito Manor.*

CH: That was a house Parsons, Clarke and I rented off of Beverly Glen after the first album was done. During that time the Manson murders happened and other godawful things. I moved out. Mike moved out and finally Gram did too. Gram left the band and that was that. Things had progressed real fast.

SG:*Did you ever hear any of the things he recorded with Keith Richards?*

CH: No, I didn't.

SG:*Do you see a Burritos feel in "Faraway Eyes", "Country Honk" or "Dead Flowers"?*

CH: I can tell and do hear. When the Stones take a jab at country I can tell they have been influenced a lot by the Burritos. I'm sure Keith would agree with me. But their own songs...I think you might be reading a little of us into that.

SG:*As* Deluxe *goes, is there much of the Stones' influence coming back?*

CH: *Burrito Deluxe* has "Wild Horses" on it, doesn't it? Yeah, so that's their influence. They let us record that song. They had recorded it but it wasn't released yet. They let Gram do it and it

PHOTO COURTESY OF JOHN DELGATTO

The Burritos playing on a boat at Newport Beach, California, l-r Bernie Leadon, Sneeky Pete, GP and Chris Hillman, 1970

is sort of a Burritos type song. He was hanging out with them then and he was influencing what they would do on a song like that and consequently he ended up doing the vocal on it.

SG: *Gram always talked about bringing the country audience and the rock audience together. Looking back, do you think he achieved anything that he worked for in this area?*

CH: Gram was partly responsible and was an innovator in that area. Now if you will look at all the truck drivers; those guys have long hair. Country and western performers now have long hair. They are always five years behind everybody else, you know that. Country and western performers are doing rock and roll type songs with more emphasis on bass and drums and that's what Gram was talking about. We were doing that with the Burritos. The rock and roll stations said we were too country and the country stations said we were too rock and roll. You know why? Because we had more emphasis on bass and drums. That was the R&B influence. We took country songs and added more rhythm to them, more bass and drums. Now Dolly Parton and whoever are doing more rock arrangements. Dolly Parton cut one of the Temptations' songs.

SG: *She cut "Help" by the Beatles.*

CH: Yeah, so there it is. Sure there is a merger. He had an effect. So did the whole band.

Historic Country-Rock Summit Meeting: (l-r) Doug Dillard, Gene Clark, Gram Parsons, Michael Clarke, Richie Furay, Jon Corneal, Rusty Young, Chris Hillman, Sneeky Pete, Gene Parsons and Clarence White.

SG: So you are saying...

CH: Here's an example. We used to work the Palomino in 1969. And man we used to get yelled at from the audience. "Get off the stage, goddamn queers" and really, every cliche in the book. But we were playing Conway Twitty songs, Porter Wagoner songs and so we won people over. We actually won them over in the end. We were the rebel band. We were the original outlaw band. And I must say, in all honesty, the Eagles really developed out of that whole syndrome. And I'll never forget Glenn Frey and J.D. Souther opening for us as Longbranch Pennywhistle and they used to...Glenn Frey was just in awe of Gram. He learned from Gram.

SG: Like "Lyin' Eyes" is very Gram Parsons.

CH: He learned about stage presence and how to deliver a vocal and don't think Glenn Frey wasn't in that audience studying Gram. He was. I was there. And it is nothing bad, I have all due respect for Glenn and the Eagles. I think they are great. But they are really an extension of the Burrito Brothers outlaw thing, an extension itself of the Byrds– Buffalo Springfield family. It's a real heavy family tree. And someday it should be written down and shown on TV. The impact that came from the Byrds–Buffalo Springfield, those two groups and all of those guys influencing lifestyle, politics and whatever, is amazing. I got pissed...I mean you got all your New Wave bands and I was pissed off at the Records and this thing and this thing where they deny a Byrds' influence. Bullshit, man. Listen to their hit single and it sounds like the Byrds. And they say they don't like the Byrds and it isn't a 12–string...well, so what. They were probably ten years old in 1965 and they heard those Byrds and Buffalo Springfield records. It's a big circle that Gram is part of and it's neat, I like it. I like the New Wave bands. Tom Petty acknowledges Roger's influence and it's neat. Gram had a lot of impact on all that though country rock never caught on. Why, I don't know. But I've got a classic tape of Gram and Emmylou playing live in some club that will blow you away. They are so soulful. I don't know why it never caught on. It's like the New Riders of the Purple Sage are still out there working but they really don't have a market.

SG: Okay, so it's obvious in rock circles but do you think anyone past Willie Nelson knows about the Burritos in country music circles?

CH: Yes, I think so. I really do. I know Merle Haggard knows about Gram. Don Rich, Buck Owens' old guitar player, came to a lot of Burrito sessions. And a lot of the straight local country players from around town sure knew who we were. As far as the oldtimers, I couldn't say. Bill Monroe, one time I met him, he called Bernie and I "the Burrito Boys" like we were a bluegrass band. So he knew who we were but I wouldn't think that Hank Snow or Ernest Tubb or any of those guys would know who the Burritos were. But the younger guys like Waylon Jennings and Jimmy Rabbitt et al...Vern Gosden was a guy I used to work with in a bluegrass group called the Hillmen and he is having lots of country hits and he is doing real well. I used to work with him in '64, so, yeah, some straight country singers knew about Gram and us. Merle Haggard almost produced Gram's first solo album, did you know that?

SG: Yeah.

CH: But he didn't do it because Gram was drunk. He had started drinking again. So Merle quit. But that area has been exploited too much. Parsons was good. He was talented but he was...I don't know if he was a genius because that's a pretty heavy title to put on anybody. What he did he was real good at yet he was more into playing rock lifestyle. He was into playing out the role of Hank Williams. The reason we parted was this nature of his. He was a real good kid. He had a real good heart but he was unhappy and consequently he was...he was real talented. Songs like "Hickory Wind" are beautiful tunes. They are real soulful, and the vocal he did on "Hot Burrito #1"... well, you couldn't beat that. That vocal he does is incredible on "you may be..." and the "I'm your toy" parts. It is a killer vocal man. He *means* it. You get chills listening to it.

SG: In Gram's songs it is obvious he is very intelligent because there is a lot of humor and irony that doesn't appear at first yet comes through with subsequent listenings. Are these subtleties a conscious thing or is it simply the way things lyrically came from him?

CH: He was a very sensitive, bright kid. I mean the kid came from a prep school to Harvard and from a very wealthy family. He got the best of everything and as far as being a literate person, yes he was. He was very literate. Very well read and on the verge of being sort of an intellectual. He was more than aware of these subtleties, yes. It was no mystical gift coming through an illiterate person. He knew exactly what he was doing.

©1970 ED CARAEFF

©1970 JIM McCRARY

Burritos' publicity photo session shot at the A&M Records' Studio, l–r Clarke, GP, Hillman, Sneeky, Leadon, 1970

SG: *But they are your lyrics too, if we are talking about the Burritos.*

CH: Yes, well, I am basically a caustic person anyway.

SG: *But "Juanita" and "Christine's Tune" and "Wheels" have a lot of irony, humor and other things that you don't pick up the first time around.*

CH: It's basically back to collaboration, like on "Juanita". That's a great song. She was a girl I met at the Troubadour. So we wrote a song about her. All those things about pills on the shelf and suicidal tendencies weren't really there. Gram and I just added those for a touch of drama. It was just about some girl. "Wheels" is about motorcycles. We wrote the song..."we're not afraid to die" is about crashing our bikes. He could never ride his bike. He almost died. The first bike he bought was a little BSA and he could handle that, but when he got the Harley...I mean he was just a little guy and he couldn't...he wasn't strong enough to hold it all the time. I knew his accident would happen sooner or later. I knew he would eat it on that bike. Those songs were funny to us. We were actually sitting there going "what are people going to think". We were writing about our two bikes outside, the Triumph and the BSA. It was our weird sense of humor.

SG: *Who is Christine? I heard she was the hat check girl at Snoopy's.*

CH: No, Christine was this girl who has since died and it is real sad, actually. She was in a bad automobile accident and she was the type of girl who was making life miserable for us. Hence the name "Devil in Disguise". Just common day things, just like in a soap opera. We'd just jot it all down as it happened to us. Except that I felt awfully guilty and I know Gram did too after Christine died. So we changed the title for subsequent releases. I felt horrible about it.

SG: *In Gram Parsons' writing and singing, especially towards the end of his life, he gets more laconic and world weary. He sounds somewhat tired. He sounds like he has seen it all and done it all.*

CH: Sure, his experiences were affecting his whole life and that comes out in his music. Negative outside influences, shall we say, can hinder the whole process. I'm a team player, I like to work in groups. I like a clean team effort. The McGuinn, Clark, Hillman band was the way I liked it. Tight...good players and Roger on top of it. But it was definitely not working out that way in the Burritos.

SG: *Gram Parsons had a pretty rough go of it. His mom passed away right when he was getting out of high school and so forth. As you knew him, was he pretty much normal or did he seem mercurial, going way up and then way down?*

CH: Well, that's too bad. Tough. I may seem callous but we've all had family problems. It's tough out there. It's real tough, you know. I sympathize, yes. But of course it was tough for him, especially with money from the trust fund...but hey, people with no legs hold jobs and stuff today. He hid it real well. He was normal in the sense his ups and downs were not that often. He was a great charmer. He was good at it and he practiced it. When he saw something he wanted he turned the charm on and when he didn't need to deal with it he'd walk out of it. When the going got rough Gram would disappear. He wasn't one you could count on in a situation like that. I'm just giving you the truth.

SG: *Could you tell me about finding Emmylou Harris in Washington, D.C. and how you got her together with Gram?*

CH: Rick Roberts found Emmylou and he dragged me down there and we watched Emmylou and she was doing mostly Joni Mitchell and Joan Baez and some country songs.

SG: *With a three piece band?*

CH: Umm, I can't remember what it was. We talked and we got to know her and she sat in with the Burritos and I said you really should sing more country songs, they're great, they're really magical. They're what you should do a lot of. We parted company and I told her it would be great to do something with her someday. We parted company, Rick and I parted company...actually we ran into Gram as the Burritos were breaking up. Gram was back in the country from England and ready to do a solo record or do something. I said there is this girl in Washington you gotta meet. She's perfect for you. So I got her on the phone and I got her to talk to Gram on the phone. It took me an hour to talk him into driving there and meeting her. They met and the rest is all...there. They met and made records and worked together for awhile.

SG: *There is a story you guys asked Emmylou to join the Burritos.*

CH: No, no...never asked her to join the Burrito Brothers. Never. She sat in with us at the Cellar Door in Washington and that was it. She sang "It Wasn't God Who Made Honky Tonk Angels" but that was it. I quit the band a few months later because I had a nice offer from Stephen (Stills) and Al Perkins and I left. It wasn't making any progress and I'd stuck with it for three years. It worked out for everybody anyway. I had a good productive time in Manassas, Gram and Emmylou worked together and Rick Roberts went solo and then formed Firefall. Gram and Emmylou made some good albums. There it is; it's that simple. I wanted to do something with Emmylou but everytime I wanted to something would come up for me. Manassas was important to me and I didn't have time, but Gram did. I could see it. I could visualize the two of them onstage. They were the right height. They had the same hair, good looking and they both could sing. I was looking at it almost like a manager and still like an artist. I knew it could work and it worked great. Probably would have been a great success if Gram had not have fallen, if he'd stayed on the straight and narrow. One of the biggest myths in being an artist or a sculptor or musician is that you have to suffer to create. Bullshit. Gram didn't have to suffer to do all that. You can write and

This photo is purported to have been Gram's favorite of the "Gilded Palace" session because it featured the Joshua trees prominently, not to mention the models.

sing and create from your heart and soul without doing all that. We are all geniuses in hindsight, but if Gram had not fallen into...I mean him and Emmylou would have been huge. Like Willie Nelson. They had it, the looks and the style. And I think it affected Emmylou. I don't think it is the most important thing in her life to be a big star. She just wants to make albums and be happy and have a good time, which is nice.

SG: On Sleepless Nights *the liner notes call it the "Burritos attempt to make a pure, honest country album". Is this from after* Burrito Deluxe?

CH: I'll tell you what this is. This is all practice. We were using...these are outtakes recorded at a studio as we were waiting to do *Deluxe.* "Crazy Arms", "Sing Me Back Home", "Tonight the Bottle Let Me Down" and all that stuff were outtakes. The only good tracks on the album are with Emmy. The rest of this stuff is practice. A&M kept the tapes and put them out, since they owned them.

SG: Does anybody have the real Sweetheart of the Rodeo *with Gram Parsons' original vocals intact?*

CH: God knows...I wouldn't know who to tell you to ask. Who produced that one? Gary Usher? I don't even know where Gary Usher is. He owned Together Records also. But I have no idea...I don't know if record companies keep those tapes in their vaults or what.

SG: Who are the girls on the Gilded Palace of Sin *cover?*

CH: Two models we wanted to look like hookers. It was out in the middle of the desert. It was freezing and we were loaded...outlaw band, yeah.

SG: Sweetheart *is one of the poorest selling Byrds' albums. In fact, most of Gram's career didn't fare very well. Why?*

CH: I don't know. Why aren't a lot of people recognized? I think a lot of this business is luck. It's being in the right place at the right time and it is sometimes a disgusting business. The business part, I mean. The music part is wonderful. Playing music, doing all that is wonderful but I think of all the great musicians that never get a chance to make a record, that could outplay any of us, never get a chance, never leave the hometown, never get out of the club they are playing in. There's millions of 'em, and the odds are just so tough. Why those records didn't sell...and there is lots of music that didn't sell and all you can do is blame it on the people who are responsible for marketing and selling the record. That's all you can do.

SG: *I'm told that in August of 1973 there was going to be a reunion in Holland of all the Byrds from the varous stages for a concert in the country that appreciated the group and its offshoots the most. Then the death of Clarence White and the death of Gram Parsons stopped the idea. Is that true?*

CH: No, I never heard of it at all. You can discount that story. No one would have ever fallen for it anyway.

SG: *What do you consider Gram's best asset, his singing, his performance or writing?*

CH: He was a real good writer and a pretty good singer. Pretty good singer meaning he had a lot of soul in his vocal, a lot of feeling in his vocal. He didn't have the greatest voice in the world but what he had he used real well. He knew how to sing and make that commitment, make that lyric come out real well.

SG: *Do you listen to his stuff? Do you play the Burritos or have any favorite tracks of Gram's?*

CH: Once in a while I will put one on for oldtime's sake. I haven't lately...

SG: *Has all the material you recorded with Gram both as a Byrd and as a Burrito been released? Will we ever be pleasantly surprised to see a reissue or have some unreleased tracks surface?*

CH: God knows. There is a lot of stuff that the record companies have and you never know. I don't know, it just seems it takes something like a death to bring out all the things hidden away when the artist was unappreciated.

SG: *You best memory of Gram is the Burrito days?*

CH: Oh yeah.

Burritos, 1969 photo session in the desert for "Gilded Palace," 1969

BARRY FEINSTEIN

©1970 ED CARAEFF

Hillman, GP, 1970

The Flying Burrito Bros

Gram Parsons Interview: Burrito Deluxe

Gram Parsons, lean and lanky, given to mod–cowboy elegance, his gaunt face dominated by a fixed Georgia smile, and punctuated by a pugilist's scar across the eyebrow. Words float lazily from his mouth, carried by a gentle, expressive voice. A progressive family life and affluence on one side, the swamps on the other. Harvard hillbilly, once a Byrd of influence if not duration, now the #1 hot Burrito and another stranger in a strange land.

Gram brought Leon Russell's demolished gold high hat with him to New York. He also brought the still visible scrapes of a recent motorcycle wipeout. He greeted friends and strangers alike on this Saturday afternoon with credible warmth and natural ease. I was one of the strangers.

You're from South Georgia. Whereabouts?
GP: Swamps.
Around Waycross?
GP: Yeah.
I grew up in Atlanta. There's a strange kind of glean in the eyes of people who grew up down there. There are some bad things about it, but I think generally it was a pretty good place to grow up for me. Kept my head pretty clean.
GP: Uhm hm. Well, Southern people can talk to Jesus.
Can you?
GP: Yeah, yeah. I could be a preacher if I wanted to. Georgia peach.
Down in South Georgia, is the earth red and clay–based like it is around Atlanta?
GP: Yeah. Okefenokee, you know, means "land of the trembling earth". And everything down there is...mushy...and red, shifts and bogs, mud ducts.
Do you ever go back there?
GP: No, I'd like to go back on a tour, but I wouldn't like to just go down for a vacation. Nothing that I could hang out and do. I'd be at a loss. Probably don't know anybody down there any more and, uh, if I did, I don't know what kind of shape they'd be in.
Yeah, well, you're kind of the exception to the rule down there.
GP: Yeah, right.
They probably wouldn't know what to do with you either.
GP: No...they never did. I was a misfit from the start. But I never learned how to play games. It never really impressed me. I mean like I don't really have a Southern accent like most people from South Georgia do– –they have heavy, heavy Southern accents. You almost can't understand them when they talk. But I never developed an accent like that even though I spent thirteen years down there.
You were born there.
GP: Yeah, I was born in Winter Haven, Florida.
It's almost as if you were someplace else before that so that you'd have enough wherewithall to be able to look at it objectively.
GP: That's right.
It's kind of a karma thing.
GP: That's right, it is.
Which makes talking to Jesus a little more tricky.
GP: Well, uh, that's true, it does, but everybody knows it sorta makes sense– – everybody knows that some people can talk to Jesus. They know it; they just don't *know* they know it.

a 1969 publicity photo session, shot in the wild country of Laurel Canyon, Hollywood, l–r Clarke, Sneeky, GP, Leadon, Hillman

Life with Anita, Keith and Gram

It's an unusual thing that you happen to be who you are. And, uh, it doesn't add up in any logical, chronological way.

GP: No, maybe it adds up kerratically. That's what makes up for it. In that kerratically it balances out. Do you know what I mean?

Does that mean that time gets lumped together in places and stretches out in others?

GP: Right. It's a Greek word meaning "pregnant time"...(laughs) It's a heavy discussion.

Yeah, maybe we'd better start out easy. When your first album came out, I wasn't really into the Byrds' country thing, so I'd only heard Sweetheart of the Rodeo *a couple of times, and* Gilded Palace of Sin *really knocked me out. It was the first countrified thing and it wasn't just that it was country music; it probably has a lot to do with your personality as I understand it, because there's that thing about being very pure and moralistic and talking to Jesus on one hand, and then there's that tension through the whole thing.*

GP: I try to keep things simple as possible, and--we all do--and, uh, I think it's worked out for the best in all ways; inside my own head, I'm sure I'm not involved in any banalities of any sort, musically and otherwise. My foundations are pure ones. I remember when I was a kid playing music, I never gave the consideration to my audience that I do now; now that's the most important thing to me: touching those people who are watching me, you know. And you just can't expect to wash some people in pure, clean water all the time, you know, a lot of people like junk. And so you have to figure out another approach. Our approach is that we're a rock'n'roll band that sounds like a country band.

That's more apparent on your new album.

GP: Yeah. It will become more and more apparent.

McGuinn said that meeting the Stones had been an inspiration for you or something along those lines. He said, "I think Gram wants to be Mick Jagger now."

GP: No, Roger shouldn't say things like that.

But he always does. I can't print most of the things he says.

GP: I know... Mick Jagger (laughs); no.

After hearing him say that, I was waiting for your second album with baited breath because I really didn't know...

GP: (laughs) What is this kid gonna do now?
Yeah. But, if anything, I think you got more subtle rather than the other way around, and I never thought of the Stones as particularly subtle--good, but not subtle.
GP: You can only be yourself; you can't be Mick Jagger. You can be inspired, as you said, by the Rolling Stones, they're very inspiring people, great musicians, and I've taken their advice very often. Like: "Always make sure that you're yourself"--that's something they told me. When it starts to happen--so much has happened to them, and like a miracle happened to them in the middle, where they changed from a medium heavy English R'n'B band to actually a working team of creative genuises, you know. And they keep everything simple, down to where they can understand it, and lay back, you know, brilliant people. And not groovy to a lot of people, I guess, because they have to have their own privacy, it's very important that they do. Knowing them well, like I do, and since we are very close mutual friends, you know, they wanted to get further into what I was doing, and I wanted to get into what they were doing.
"Wild Horses" is very unlike most of their writing.
GP: Yeah, but a logical combination between our music and their music. It's something that Mick Jagger can accept and it's something that I can accept. And my way of doing it is not necessarily where it's at, but it's certainly the way I feel it, and not the way he feels it.
Have you done anything for them?
GP: No.
Roger says you sent some masters over.
GP: No, they sent a master over to me of "Wild Horses", but they didn't use it. I think they were dissatisfied with the basic track they did in Muscle Shoals, and they're going to re-record it--probably doing it right now. Jimmy Miller said at the end of this month. And they'll be re-recording it in England. I don't know if we'll be overdubbing it or what. The rock'n'roll I picked up from Keith Richards and Mick knows an awful lot about country music. I learned a lot about singing from Mick. And...it's all the same--that's what Keith said. "It's all the same." When the three of us sing together it sounds like Gaelic music. Like the Incredible String Band playing at the Palomino or something. We were doing Hank Williams songs and, uh: "I was ridin' number *nah-ne* in South Caro-*lah-na*." Mick's Southern accent and my English accent. What does it all tell you? It's the same.
Yeah, but it makes a lot of sense, though...
GP: It makes an awful lot of sense.
Because it's just pulling the roots back together. It all came from the same place.
GP: That's the kind of devils they like to conjure up. If the truth be known--not that anyone will ever believe it, 'cause they like to make up their own stories too much--and add an extra ingredient but they like to conjure up those kind of devils. While we sit at the piano and do that--and add an extra ingredient of Richard Penniman. With me and Jagger and Richards, we had Little Richard, (laughs) Jagger, Parsons and Richards. Two Georgia Peaches and two (laughs) English boys, stinky English kids. Fun.
You record any of that?
GP: Yeah, not that particular night--I wish I had--but I have a cassette of some of the stuff we did together.
It must be great.
GP: It's really far out. Drunk. *Drunk.*
Have the other guys in the Burritos been digging the Stones too?
GP: Oh, yeah. They all love the Stones. All listen to *Let It Bleed* a lot. I don't know if they were into *Beggar's Banquet* at the time I was, but I was closer to *Beggar's Banquet* at the time it was done. And I think the Stones have come further with *Let It Bleed*; it's a fantastic album. You know, everybody in the band has their own favorites off of it.
Yeah, that's one sign of a really good album, because there isn't one thing you can pick. I mean I have--I picked "Gimme Shelter".
GP: Right, that's Chris' favorite, and it is mine in a way--I can see why, you know. But I don't know if I have a favorite on the album or not. I like 'em all. I think, uh..."Honky Tonk Women" is a great song.
Yeah, "Country Honk". I was really digging that one initially.
GP: That's the way they originally wrote it.
Really. That would've really been something if they'd released that as a single.

DOMINIQUE

DOMINIQUE TARLE

The photographer of these pictures, Dominique Tarle, elaborates upon the ambiance of the Richards' estate and Gram, "When the Rolling Stones moved to the South of France, Keith and Anita invited me to stay for a while. Keith had a few LP's by George Jones in his collection but I could not get into the music. Then Gram came to the house. Gram taught Keith a lot of country songs. Those two people singing in harmony sometimes at the piano, sometimes at the acoustic guitar is definitely one of my best musical experiences. Music started at lunch. The summer was very hot and sometimes during the afternoon I would have a nap on the waterbed outside with Keith and Gram playing non-stop, exchanging guitars or going to the piano next door. In fact, they only stopped when the sun came up the next day. Nobody did any recording. I always thought Keith would record a solo album including the songs he did with Gram, but he never did."

DOMINIQUE TARLÉ

DOMINIQUE TARLÉ

GP: Right, and they recorded it and they didn't think it was a single. Collectively they didn't think it was a single; I think Keith did. Impish Keith the Gypsy. He sort of compromised and let them put the horns on it and put the screaming guitars on it and everything, to show them it was a really good song, that it could be number one. 'Cause they worry about that, like they hadn't had a number one song in six months. I think "Jumpin' Jack Flash" only got up to number three. And they were all freaked out about that, you know, they worried, sort of. And when "Honky Tonk Women" made number one, Jagger said, "Ah, phew, we can rest for six months."

But that single was really important; they were kind of down and out before that. And then by the time their tour came around--Jesus.

GP: They wrote that song in Peru, after they had left from doing the *Beggar's Banquet* trip and being with me as a result of running around to a bunch of honky tonks and going and seeing that, you know, they had never seen it before, really. I don't mean to say that Jagger didn't know about country music --he really does, and Keith does too, but he says that Jagger knows more, so I'll take his word for it. But Mick is a mystery unto himself--he doesn't really show too many signs of it until he's playing. Music and his personal life are so separate that it's hard to understand how he arrived at anything. Some sort of Rock Magician Menopause or something like that.

When you get to be a Rolling Stone, maybe a separation is good, or else you start believing the myths, you know.

GP: That's right, but a couple of screamers once in a while never hurt anybody. The people will never hurt you, but I guess in the Rolling Stones' case, you can make an exception and say, the people just might hurt you. People make up so much bullshit about them.

Well, maybe if there weren't a Beatles, there wouldn't be a need to counterbalance the Beatles with that black...

GP: Anti-Christ. Please give me some shelter, please (laughs).

Yeah. Lemme get to the Byrds for a minute.

GP: I thought you were gonna say that.

What?

GP: Go to the Byrds from there. 'Cause --are the Byrds rock stars? Are they really? Is David Crosby a rock star? Is David Crosby going to change the entire world?

What happened in Denver anyway?

GP: Bad day at black rock...Them ranchers, you know.

Do you still hang out with those guys? Are they still a part of that L.A. family?

GP: Well, they live up North. I don't have a ranch.

Do you want one?

GP: Prob'ly when I meet the fairy princess. Then she can design clothes and *eh*-v'rything. When I meet the right fairy princess.

Are you and Roger still buddies?

GP: Yes, we are, and I think Roger is a wonderful person, and a very good musician. And I dig his ol' lady. And I know he's been through a lot of heavy changes, and I know about the changes, and I know about the changes I don't know about. He forgets often when he's involved in whatever it is that he's doing that people really like him. 'Cause when he lets that warm part of him out, he's one of the greatest people in the world, and a joy to be with...

Did you always feel that way? Like around the South African thing?

GP: There was a lot of tension, and I think Roger was very, uh--he was less tense than almost everybody, 'cause he has a way of not showing emotion. And it was a little less important than I thought it should have been to Roger. He took it too lightly for me.

You mean the idea of going to South Africa?

GP: The idea that I wasn't gonna go. I mean he just sort of pocketed it and included it in his definition of rock music being a joke. And I walked off very disillusioned...

(At this point, John Nuese, an ex-cohort of Gram's in the International Submarine Band, entered the room to visit with his old friend. John was followed by two

maids, who had come to clean the room and wanted to know what was burning. Soon after, Sneeky Pete entered, fresh from a round–trip walk between W. 57th Street and the Battery. Just as quickly he was gone.)
GP: Hey, Pete...Anytime you want to talk to him, he just disappears...

(We then got into a discussion about the rock press.)
GP: I've got something against every one of them just about. That analytical bullshit, and reporting on what's happening, and where it's at, where they're at, where everybody else is at, and the exploitation of truth. Lack of real interest on their parts to tell the truth and not just make up something that sounds good. They don't have any real power, so they get on the weirdest fucking trips about everything.
I was over at Circus the other day and I noticed that you'd written them a complimentary letter. Is Circus an exception to the rule?
GP: It was the first time I ever wrote to a magazine.
I mean, you're not down on Circus?
GP: No, I was very impressed with them, because they had seen the Altamont Festival specifically, in a little bit different light than everybody else had. And I thought that was really a forward step on their part, being on the outside, not much more than a teen magazine, could accept the Free Press as sort of like their news service, you know, except they reported on it, but they didn't, see, they did their own research on it, and that in a crowd of 300,000 people, man, a lot of things were going on, a lot of things, and they took more into consideration than the brilliant staff of reporters that covered it for Rolling Stone, in a way. Those people were all boohooing in their sleeping bags...
I remember after the first album you were getting dumped on in your live performances. Was that warranted?
GP: No. We did a lot of things that people took the wrong way, I guess. At least we made our statement.
People either thought that album was silly or they thought it was great. But you've

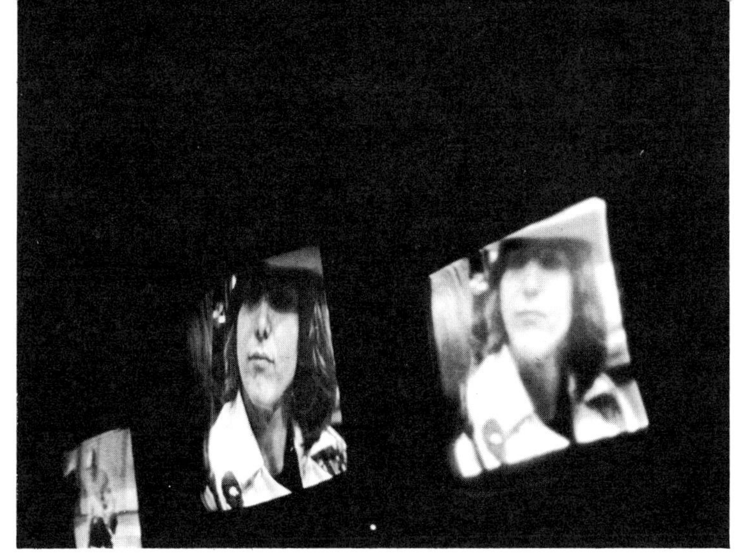

Gram in the media, 1969

never had problems with cohesiveness on–stage?
GP: Not the way they put it.

(Bernie Leadon comes into the room.)

BL: What are you doin'?
GP: Making a tape.
BL: Oh, yeah? I got some things to tell you motherfuckers, man.
GP: (laughing) Oh, no...no. New York's gotten worse.
BL: It has. I don't ever want to come back here. People are tryin', though. I was here last summer for a while. And I got into walking down the street and looking a lot of people in the eye, to see what they would do. Most of them look away, or just because you're looking at 'em, they get uptight, you know. But lately, man, there's just been more and more cats stridin' down the street, and you look at 'em, and they say, "Hello, man, how ya doin'?"
I was thinking on the way over, that instead of those dumb question and answer things, we could do a free association interview. I could say a word, and you say whatever comes into your mind. We'd probably get as much done. (Gram nods) You really want to do it?
GP: Okay.
Okay...Leon Russell.
GP: Beard.
Ah, c'mon.
GP: Leon's a magic musician. He has a great house full of very freaky friends. Lots of people living there. He supports a lot of people.

How about Poco? A lot of people have conveniently dashed the two groups together.
GP: I like Richie Furay's singing a lot, but I don't see that the two of us have anything in common more than a steel guitar. We started off playing country music where Poco was playing Buffalo Springfield music. That's about all I can say about that.
Uh...Buffalo Springfield.
GP: Sure...why not. Buffalo Springfield.
Sweetheart of the Rodeo.
GP: Any album, man, is a whole thing--it's a big thing, especially right after you do it. It was a big thing right after I did it, I didn't really appreciate...say their third album or their fourth album--I hadn't even listened to it. Since then, I have, and I can accept why *Sweetheart of the Rodeo* had to be--well, maybe you don't know about it, but the whole thing, the big thing about it for me was it was all changed.
How?
GP: A lot of things that were supposed to be on the basic track, when they released it weren't on it, and songs were taken out of the can that weren't supposed to be used. And all this was because Columbia Records was afraid that they were going to be sued by Lee Hazelwood.
'Cause he still held your, ah...
GP: Yeah, and so they just chopped up the album however they wanted to--I wasn't there when they chopped it. And it being before *Nashville Skyline*, I thought that it was very important that it should be kept track of, and this cat, the producer of the album, decided it should go Hollywood freaky, you know. And it wasn't the time for that; I thought it was the time for a *Nashville Skyline* or something like like the album was as I remember it, I'm not sure. It was a great album that might as well have never been recorded. So there's another *Sweetheart of the Rodeo*. And, ah...I dig it.
What did you do between the time that the album was completed and the time you formed the Burritos. It seems to me it wasn't too long after.
GP: I started forming the Burrito Brothers right after I left the Byrds. I got in touch with Chris Ethridge and we decided to get a band together. Then we started playing with Chris Hillman as well, because he came back from Europe and whereas Roger sort of disappeared--apathy, you know--Chris at the time was very upset about it and came back and said, "I was wrong, man, I'm not mad anymore." That was really nice of him, you know. And the three of us started playing together and decided we needed a steel player, and it was just like that, one thing after another.
You couldn't find a drummer, though, could you?
GP: No one who particularly fitted what we wanted to do.
Did you think of Mike Clarke at that point?
GP: Apparently Chris was; I didn't know Michael that well because he had left the Byrds before I came...It seems strange now that Chris Ethridge, who was the first person I talked to was the first to leave. But there was no way of knowing then that the band was gonna be doing what it is now.
In other words, you were thinking more of a straight country band then than a rock'n'roll band.
GP: We were thinking in terms of the music that we'd played together before, which was--not totally country music, we just jammed. We didn't know that we could do what we're doing now. I've heard other people say that before, and it's true in our case.
Did Chris leave because of the change in direction?
GP: He wanted to do something for himself...
How did you come up with the name Flying Burrito Brothers?
GP: Ian Dunlop came up with it.
John Nuese: He was the one who named the International Submarine Band. He was the bass player.
GP: Besides that, I was with Ian while they were recording *The Notorious Byrd Brothers*, before they had a title for the album. And, uh, I just happened to go to a Byrds' session. And I said "Flying Burrito Brothers", while they were still doing their real Byrd tunes, you know, Crosby was wearing his velvet hat. And they said, "What are you playing with

Chris and Gram, Laurel Canyon photo session, 1969

now", and I said, "Flying Burrito Brothers", over the microphone, 'cause that's what we were calling the International Submarine Band, or some such nonsense. And they all freaked out, and wanted to use the name for the album, and if they had, we wouldn't've had a name. (Laughs) I told them they couldn't do it...
Do you have any intentions of playing on the same bill with the Byrds again, 'cause Roger said you didn't want to anymore.
BL: When did he tell you that?
Back in January.
BL: Well, we've been talking about it since then...
Are you oriented toward music of social comment?
GP: Only if it's positive. I don't like the "I ain't marchin' anymore" attitude. Only if it's positive and not deeply philosophical any more than I can avoid.

-Bud Scoppa, 1970

Vintage Nudie-suited Burritos, 1969. What do the individuals above have to do with the provocateur below?

Kim Fowley more recently

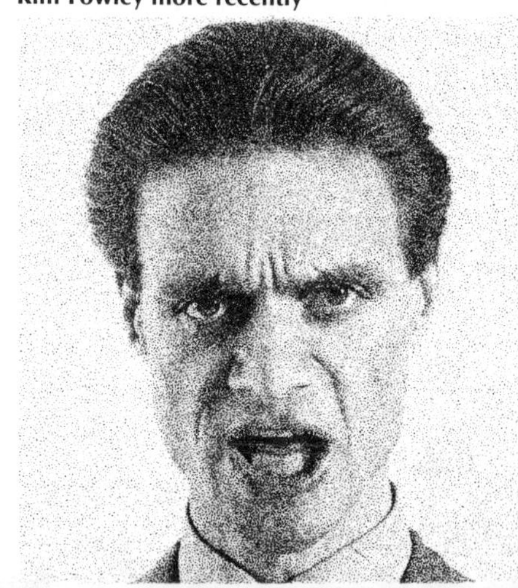

Northern Quebec Medley: Kim Fowley

Fowley: When I first met Gram he and I were dating the same girl and he had just started out with the Flying Burrito Bros. The Burritos got off to a good start because they were ex-Byrds and because these personalities were known as Byrds and therefore people were willing to give a listen to anything they had to say musically. Not like today when Sex Pistols' fans don't follow a John Lydon into PIL.

Gram was doing the Palomino and other clubs like that, doing George Jones songs, a pure country thing, on some nights moonlighting from the Palomino. He and some other Byrds and country rockers used to all go to the Sundance Saloon in Calabasas once a week and jam.

He reminded me most of another bad boy in rock, P.J. Proby, who at that time was a star in England doing Johnny Cash songs and things like that. They even looked a lot alike. Proby was constantly having personal problems too, like a John Barrymore meets Johnny Cash thing. Both basically were country musicians with a rock n'roll attitude as opposed to Poco doing rock with a country attitude. That's the subtle difference. And people couldn't believe this was going on in the middle of the Syndicate of Sound era.

Q: What was happening at the Chateau Marmont?

Fowley: Rick Grech, myself, Gram and a lot of other people were living there. At the time it was a cross of the Fitzgerald and New York's Chelsea. Lauren Hutton and Faye Dunaway lived there alone at the time. It was a prestigious place to stay in its own way. Gram met Rick Grech at the pool there.

I got the impression Gram did not sit around listening to records and reading *Rolling Stone*. I don't think he cared I was working with his old band, the Byrds. He seemed to be a guy who listened to

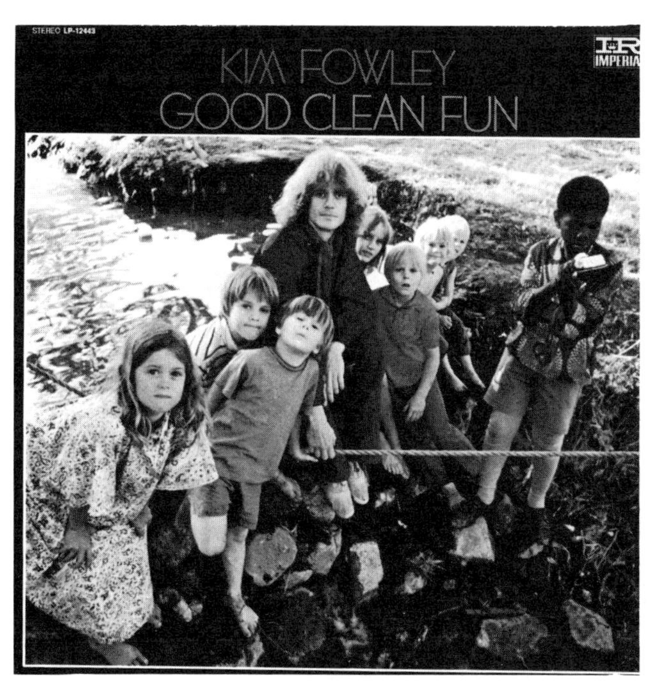

Kim Fowley album from the early Burritos era. It contained songs by a then unknown Warren Zevon as well as Fowley originals

The Modern Lovers 

The Modern Lovers official publicity pic. In addition to the involvement with Gram mentioned by Kim Fowley, the Modern Lovers performed at a "benefit" to cover Phil Kaufman and Michael Martin's alleged grave-robbing fines.

himself and music from his past, the stuff he dug before he came to Hollywood. Very polite guy. "How's your room? Drafty? Ours is a bit."

Q: What about Gram's involvement with Jonathan Richman and the Modern Lovers?

Fowley: The original Modern Lovers were a great band. Jonathan Richman on vocals and occasional guitar, Ernie Brooks on bass, David Robinson of the Cars and Jerry Harrison, now with the Talking Heads, on keyboards. They were Lou Reed's Byrds. I met them in 1972 when I was an artist, and I use the word loosely, on Capitol. We went to Dinky Dawson's sound retreat to cut the first record. He was the sound man with the original Byrds.

Eddie Tickner was managing them and he managed Gram too. Gram showed up with Phil Kaufman one day and he gave the band a real Knute Rockne, told the band to have a great session. We cut them in the dark and let Jonathan get the right feel.

We decided a test gig was a good idea so we set up one for the Modern Lovers at the Swing Auditorium in San Bernadino with the Tower of Power. It was a primarily Chicano audience and they were being hard on the Modern Lovers, throwing things like rocks and bottles.

Backstage there was a lot of "hey, Man" macho Chicano aggression against the very white skinned New Englanders in the Modern Lovers. All of a sudden the back door opens and it's Gram with his wife and someone else and he says "what's the problem here?" He took a very fatherly attitude toward these guys, and he had a real intimidating presence to these people who didn't know who he was but immediately respected him. He was dressed in full Nudie regalia and he looked great. He had an Elvis Presley sense of right then, "I beg your pardon, these are my friends, sir." I mean he took the time to go all the way out to San Bernadino to see them play on a weekend and he also stuck up for them when they were being harassed by a number of tough looking people.

Q: What about your credit on the Grievous Angel *LP?*(Fowley appears on the *Medley live from Northern Quebec*)

Fowley: Gram had gotten together with Hugh Davies, the engineer for Merle Haggard, in order to try and get that kind of sound. so there was this song, *Cash on the Barrelhead*, where me, Larry Larer (who was called John Doe on the LP), Rick Grech and Tickner and Kaufman were supposed to make noise and clap, to be this crowd in the background. That's us clapping away.

There's also the sound of glasses breaking. I'll tell you how that happened. Gram set out these strategically placed buckets and put them on the floor of the Capitol studio. Gram threw bottles at the buckets near our feet to get us to scream and yell while glass is breaking, like in the cowboy movies where the toughs make the stranger dance by shooting at his feet. Needless to say we did it in one take. That was the last time I saw Gram Parsons and he had gained a lot of weight.

©1970 ED CARAEFF

An official A&M publicity still from the Laurel Canyon session

I know Gram influenced a lot of people. Like John Phillips on his first solo album. Now where else would he get the idea of using those players but from Gram because they are C&W players. They had that terrible motorcycle accident together.

Terry Melcher made two very, very good solo albums. Now where did a kid from Beverly Hills get the idea to do *Rolling In My Sweet Baby's Arms* and a Stephen Foster tune? I think Foster's whole life is like Gram's anyway.

Gram was born into the right place at the wrong time. If he'd have been born ten years later he could have been a singing cowboy because the Urban Cowboy thing had no single band or act to carry it over completely. He was a guy who was a visionary and an innovator at a time when no one needed one. The roots of American garage rock were being laid then and Gram went relatively unheard. There is something about the South which is diametrically opposed to California anyway. I wish he'd have gone to Nashville and been an Outlaw..

GINNY WINN

Gram, June, 1973

My Memories o

Miss Mercy, formerly of the GTO's

Miss Mercy was a member of the GTOs, an all-girl group from the late sixties/early seventies. At a Long Ryders gig she came up to me and pressed a rambling yet moving account of her memories of Gram Parsons into my hand. After reading it I decided her recollections were a strong example of the various influences and powers of that period in Los Angeles rock 'n' roll. I hope it gives a glimpse into many of the facets symptomatic of the time.

The first glimpse I got of Gram was at the premiere of *Yellow Submarine*, a gala event, and then I went comatose as I was captured and captured and spellbound from here to eternity because he was so real he was unreal. I was with my group the GTOs and precious Miss Pamela had grabbed my arm and pointed my eyes to the left aisle, the lights dimmed, and a tall lean cat in a sparkling Nudie suit drifted by. He was true glitter, true glamour rock. The rhinestone suit sparkled like diamonds: it had submarines all over it outlined in rhinestones and the color was scarlet red. It sparkled so bright it made Gram sparkle through the movie show, contrasting with the phoniness of the screen and the Beatles. His Nudie belt hung on his hips like a gunslinger and that was his ammunition, his exaggerated entrance into my life.

Pamela always raved on about Gram too and I'm the only GTO who listened. She always was in contact with the special earth angels on this planet, so during a recording session for *Permanent Damage* she called Gram and we got an invitation to visit him and we took advantage of it. The other girls couldn't have cared less about Southerners but I was looking for one since the British Invasion had made me bloody sick. I could recall screaming in the midst of it all "if I could just hear a Southern accent," and I believed in

Gram Parsons: Miss Mercy

Pamela so off we went to the outskirts of town into the San Fernando Valley. We drove to a modern cowboy ranch with wagon wheels paving the driveway. At this point in his life Gram had swiped Chris Hillman and Mike Clarke from the Byrds after cutting *Sweetheart of the Rodeo*. We entered the house and shy Chris Hillman and the cat in this Nudie suit greeted us with a grocery bag full of grass and He was downhome dazzling with sensuous Southern hospitality which just slayed me. But the first words I recall him speaking to me were as he leaned over his pile of records and put on an old George Jones album (whom I had never heard of) right by my face and as a tear fell from his eye he said "This is George Jones, the King of Broken Hearts." Imagine crying over a hillbilly with a crewcut. Gram put George on and I've been indebted ever since.

Gram was on the battlefield to cross county music over to rock 'n' roll and vice versa. Unfortunately the Okies from Muskogee ruled the Palomino jukebox and although Gram was wealthy through his inheritance he never bought his attempts at success. My God, he could have bought the Palomino. He even tried the Pal's talent contest but lost to a woman yodeller. He would sing in the most remarkable Nudie suit but this was his weapon against him. The suit was the standard cowboy cut in white but he replaced the usual roses and cactus and other acceptable cliches with nude girls on the lapels, marijuana plants growing up the side of his pants, pills on the shoulders and, although he was a devout Christian, the cross which sparkled on the back was believed by the conservative cowboys to be sacriligious so they persecuted Gram for it. Gram had hair so long the audience would attend his Pal dates to call him a faggot and ridicule him for it. I don't believe they ever listened to his "Hickory Wind". The beginning of his downfall..He believed in flying saucers and even had a flying saucer Nudie suit, which is why he was enchanted by Joshua Tree and attended the various flying saucer conventions.

One wonderful night Gram called Pamela and me all excited about his black T-Bird he had purchased with his actor friend Brandon deWilde. They picked us up at the Landmark Hotel and drove us to Venice for dinner at the Lafayette restaurant on the eerie beach. It still haunts me every time I pass it. Another time the GTOs played the Shrine Auditorium and Gram came and took Pamela and me for a high ride, later dropping us off. Miss Christine was enraged, grabbed me by my neck on the balcony and said "If you mess up I'll kill you". After the show, which went perfectly anyway, I looked for Gram but he had vanished. I felt empty.

The Burrito recording sessions were always my favorites, and I even sang on "Hippie Boy". They were always a celebration and Gram came to ours. Unfortunately Lowell George would not let him play even a tambourine. I can remember the tarot card readings I did for him. One night I read for Mick, Keith and him before Altamont and that was in the cards. Gram used to bring back Holy Roller tent revival meetings on tape and play them for me at the Chateau Marmont and I brought him some Percy Sledge because the Burritos sang "At the Dark End of the Street", and he lived it.

by Mercy of the GTOs

Did You See: Rick Roberts

Rick Roberts

In 1970 Gram Parsons left the Flying Burrito Brothers to begin a solo career which amounted to nothing for two years or more. The Burritos faired little better without him. For four months in the early summer of 1970 the band continued without replacing him, gigging around the West Coast as a four piece. In late summer a newcomer to the L.A. scene was asked to join and while none of the Burritos said so outright, Rick Roberts was the man chosen to fill Gram's role.

While Roberts proved to be a fine singer and surprising songwriter he was unlike Gram Parsons in many ways. His temperment was different, probably due to the usual differences between two individuals and also because of his lack of experience with a music business which had already frustrated the talents and temperment of Gram several times before. Roberts was new to this lifestyle and he was just then learning what Paul Surratt calls the "rock n'roll rules."

Rick Roberts talks easily about the old days in the Burritos and his memories are fond ones for the most part. He was a tireless worker and a fine performer whose tendency is to recall the good times and give little thought to the bad. His job following Gram was not easy and he talks with candor about his efforts to do so and the relationship he had with GP.

SG: When I was at the University of South Carolina your name came up several times. Lots of people remembered you and how you said you would go to Los Angeles and make it.

Rick Roberts: That's basically true. I originally went to L.A. thinking I had a deal together. This guy came in one day to the place I was playing in Washington, D.C. and it was Paul Rothchild. I thought "that's easy, the Doors, Janis Joplin, Rick Roberts, of course that's my style... that's my league." He said he was committed for the next several months but if I would make my way to Los Angeles he would put me on a retainer.

I should have known from making my way out there but I was nineteen years old. So I hitch-hiked cross country and finally reached L.A. with six dollars in my pocket and I got to his office and it wasn't the same man at all. He just didn't look alike. I thought "uh-oh, trouble now" and I was right. I spent a year from then knocking on doors trying to get it together. It was about a year later when I joined the Burritos.

That happened thanks to Chris Hillman and Eddie Tickner through several time consuming steps. Through every step I would get discouraged again and think about going back to Colorado. I left South Carolina in July 1969 and was living in Colorado for awhile. I arrived in Los Angeles on my mothers' birthday, September 14. I was telling her and everyone else I was going to L.A. to become famous. I wasn't aware of anyone remembering me.

SG: Yeah, they did remember you. You were a big hit at Budget Tapes and Records on Main Street in Columbia. It's right by the Capitol. All those guys used to talk about you.

RR: That's great, I consider it a real compliment. I always check out the local bars and if they are playing my songs I'm sincerely flattered by those kinds of things.

SG: What music did you listen to growing up in Clearwater, Florida? Specifically I've always heard you dug the Byrds and then were given the rare opportunity to play with guys who you had admired for some time.

RR: I was, specifically, a very big fan of the Byrds. They did everything but change my life. I came from a classical music background and I did not like country

Four Burritos

music at all as a kid. I had very big adenoids and sang and people always told me "you'd make a great country and western singer." I'd hear myself on tape and I'd freak out, I hated the way I sounded.

And then the Byrds came along, with the Beatles and the Beach Boys whom you mentioned, and they showed me something I had never seen before. They harmonized. And Little Anthony and some of those bands but the Beatles and the Byrds had something that really blew me away. They were self-contained bands, they didn't just sing. Before that bands had one singer or were doing instrumentals. And they had meaningful lyrics. So I bought myself a 12-string, and granny glasses and went for it.

SG: The Byrds had gone through "real" country music with Gram Parsons right before you came out West. How did this change strike you.

RR: The Byrds had weaned me to country music by this point. When it got down to *Sweetheart* and the first Burrito album... I was not a big fan of the first Burrito album at the start. Now I love it dearly. My hard sensibilities against country music had been softened by that time. Now I love those two albums.

SG: What was it like meeting these guys whom you admired and were then playing with? Were they friendly toward you?

RR: I was awed. I considered myself to be one of the most lucky musicians around. They weren't condescending... you are only subordinated when you put yourself in a subordinate position. Here I was getting to play with two guys, Chris Hillman and Mike Clarke, whose records I'd admired. The last album I listened to before I left South Carolina was *Gilded Palace of Sin*. I thought, "boy, they sure are getting a fill of country music, that's real country music." It is weird because a lot of the people I grew up listening to I got to play with eventually. It was an ongoing education. I still have the greatest respect for Gram and all these people.

SG: You replaced Gram in the Flying Burrito Bros., essentially. Could you tell me how this came about?

RR: Yes. It was an offshoot of my supposedly budding solo career. Paul Rappaport had taken me around and this one A&R guy said "you're really good but you need a band." Which I'd heard a million times. This guy called Eddie Tickner phoned and I went and played my songs for Eddie Tickner and he introduced me to Chris Hillman. I went and played for Chris at home. Chris said I should come rehearse. Now they weren't looking for a singer and I wasn't looking to join, they were just helping me out. My first gig with them was the Whisky.

SG: After Gram had left the Burritos?

RR: Gram had been gone for about four months.

SG: They had played without him?

RR: Yes, for an entire summer. They were a four piece; Bernie Leadon, Chris Hillman, Michael Clarke and Sneeky Pete. Bernie particularly resisted me because he had become the harmony singer and my joining would be another major change in the band after they had just finished a major change.

I had not met Gram at that point, he was persona non grata with Hillman then but I had heard a million stories about him. I didn't meet him until we were in Washington, D.C. when we found Emmylou Harris. We were going to play Davidson College and I was told Gram was coming. He met us at the airport with a van and we drove to the college some 60 or 70 miles in the van.

Gram didn't look anything like I had expected him to because he was real beefy at the time. He was not the thin country rocker and he was healthier than before. We told him about Emmylou at that point and the next gig was in Baltimore so he decided to join us for that one too.

I didn't see a lot of Gram during the trip but I know Gram and Chris were sitting a lot and talking about Emmylou. Chris thought she was wonderful and so did Gram so he grabbed her for his own work.

SG: Tell me about finding Emmylou.

RR: I had lived in Washington, played those same clubs. I had been told there was a hot new lady singin' in this place so I wanted to go over and see her. By coincidence Chris and I had been talkin' about the feasibility of asking Linda Ronstadt about joining or getting some woman singer. Bernie had left by then to form the Eagles and we had Byron Berline and Roger Bush with them doing the Country Gazette on their own.

We were thinking about how we could class up the act and what we came up with was adding a woman singer. So I went to hear this singer in the club. Kenny Wertz and I went to see her sing. We walk in and she was phenomenal! She was singing a few Joni Mitchell tunes, some older country stuff and a few of her own tunes. The older country stuff impressed us the most. Nonetheless I called up Hillman and Chris has never been much for going out. "What are you talking about," Chris said, "I'm already undressed and I don't wanna go out," "Chris," I told him, "get down here."

He came under protest. He let it be known it had better be good or he was gonna kick a little sense into me. He comes in the door looking all around and by the time he got to our table he wasn't even looking at us he was looking over his shoulder at Emmylou, smiling away. And we were going "told you so." We asked Emmylou to sit in with us and she came and sat in the next couple of nights. We proceeded to tell Gram about her and hype her to him. Hype may not be the right word because we gave her a buildup which was deserved. Gram went and saw her and soon after asked her to work with him. It worked out somehow.

Five Burritos

DOUG HANNERS

Gram and Emmylou, 1973

SG: Did Gram ever rejoin the Burritos for a few gigs?

RR: Gene Clark did a little of that. Gram played at Davidson and at Baltimore, sitting in with us. In 1972 it could have been... well, the Burritos were short-lived after this time.

SG: What do you think of Sneeky Pete's revival Burritos? Chris Hillman was quite upset by it.

RR: I usually don't have much bad to say about someone's artistic endeavors but I think it's cheap, real tacky. It couldn't be more of a fraud. They changed the name to Sierra at one point but that didn't make inroads to people's pocketbooks so they changed it back. It was never a legitimate regrouping attempt. Everytime I'd see Chris Ethridge he'd apologize about it. Apologize to Hillman too.

They should have let the band rest in peace.

SG: Did Gram sing any on the third Burrito album?

RR: No, he didn't. He was still persona non grata at that point. Gene Clark did and we used one of his songs. It was Chris Hillman's idea and I thought it was damn nice of him. He's a goodhearted man.

SG: Didn't you take over Gram's vocals onstage? Didn't you become the guy singing "Wild Horses", "Devil in Disguise"....

RR: Yeah, what happened was I took over the dual leads with Chris from Bernie who had been doing "Sin City" and so forth. And I sang "Wild Horses."

SG: Did you ever sing "Hot Burrito #1" onstage?

RR: I love that song. (sings) "You may be sweet and nice..." No, we dropped it. Of course Gram sang it and "Wild Horses" real, real well.

SG: Was Gram receptive to what you were doing as a Burrito?

RR: Yes, he was. I was the new kid, he wasn't real cold or real warm particularly. We sat backstage and played some country songs, Gram knew so many melodies and lyrics to old country songs, songs I couldn't remember. We had grown up in the same state and I couldn't remember a lot of the things he did.

I remember one night at the Chateau Marmont. Gram and Michael Clarke were visiting, their suites next to each other. Chris Hillman had given me a buckknife for my birthday. Chris hated me then, couldn't figure out why I wouldn't take my guitar home and practice to become the lead guitarist. I never will be a lead guitarist. He never told me what was wrong. Gave me a buckknife and told me to use it on my throat. Well, those were his sentiments anyway.

At the Chateau Marmont Gram and Michael were visiting and pretty drunk that night. We were in Michael's suite. Michael had a buckknife too and Gram was playing with it. He took Michael's knife and was fooling around with it. Suddenly, with one quick gesture he throws it at the door.

Buckknives are not throwing knives and the knife hit at a funny way and two inches of the blade snapped off. Michael was really pissed. Just decimated. "Damn," he said. Gram said he was sorry but too bad. Both went from friendship to hostility in a second. So Michael said to me "lemme see your buckknife" and Gram goes "yeah, let him have it."

Michael says "I'll get you Gram, I'll get you." And Gram says "c'mon then. Just try it man," says Gram. They are now both trying to get me to give my knife to Michael so they can have a knife fight. And I was going "not a chance, man, I'm not gonna let you have my knife." "Gram," I told him, "your knife doesn't even have an end on it, it doesn't have a point." "I'll slice him," drawled Gram. "Go ahead, Rick, he won't hurt me."

I told Michael it was not that I worried about him getting hurt. "Well, don't worry about me," said Gram real quick, "I won't get hurt." Okay, I said, I told them I was worried about me getting hurt. They then both agreed not to hurt me. "I won't hurt him if you won't," mumbled Gram. "I won't hurt him either then," said Mike.

I said, "ah, c'mon, what is this?" I said "not a chance" and split; they probably passed out a little later. But you shoulda seen it, Gram with a knife without a point is trying to get Michael who wants my knife so they can have a fight. God, what a wonderful story.

But going back to the original question I don't know how easy it is for anyone to objectively accept what happens to a band after you leave. You want your friends to do well but you want to be missed also. Everyone wants to be needed. Robert Hilburn sure missed Gram in the band.

SG: Did you ever see Gram perform at one of his own shows?

RR: Yes, at Max's Kansas City. That's where I met Jock Bartley. I thought Gram was good and I thought Gram and Emmylou together was wonderful. Gram was fairly loose that night.

SG: Firefall has you, Gram's replacement in the Burritos, Jock Bartley, Fallen Angels' lead guitarist and Michael Clarke who drummed for Gram in the Burritos. How much of a Gram Parsons influence does this give Firefall?

RR: I don't know... I don't hear that much similarity although I do have one song that's real country which I keep getting told is a hit. It's hard to pick out Gram in our sound, I mean, how much did he influence Chris Hillman? How much did he influence Chris Hillman that in turn had Chris Hillman influence me? And what about Jock Bartley and Gram? It's really hard to answer that question.

SG: The Stones had a real Gram edge for awhile.

RR: I would say Gram Parsons gave more of himself to the Stones than us. Or Emmylou. Gram and the Rolling Stones were real tight friends, that's how "Wild Horses" came about. The Stones have that closet country urge. Jagger using that lazy kind of voice....

SG: Yeah, I figure the Burritos were Hillman and Parsons' C&W answer to the Stones' attitude and stance. Bad Boys.

Chris and Gram on the 1969 Burritos' "Train Tour"

RR: Absolutely. Gram was a country-rock Mick Jagger. He was flashy and naughty. Chris told me Gram studied Jagger's moves, not his physical moves but his conceptual ones. It made up a great portion of his panache, no one had applied this attitude to country.

If you ask me they were the original Outlaws. Waylon and Willie came along a lot later. They were getting a lot of play off the top and then people saw they were long-haired boys. And in those days there was no crossover. The image could have worked against them. In the country market.

So many people who are artists or innovators are not appreciated in their lifetime. Gram was a tremendous influence on a tremendous amount of people but most never realized it when he was alive. He was an innovator, he opened a lot of doors. A crazed genius.

Gram Parsons Interview: Big Mouth Blues

The following interview was taped and conducted by Chuck Cassel at A&M Records on March 3, 1972 in order to get some background information for the upcoming live album by Gram Pasons' old group the Flying Burrito Bros. The LP, which was to be their last release of the original band (meaning with Chris Hillman), also featured interviews with other Burritos and even a family tree. At the time of the interview Gram had not really started his solo career but was formulating more than a few ideas which we now know came to fruition in the *GP* album. If the Greivous Angel seems a bit hard to pin down here it should be remembered a certain evasiveness was necessary, his answers only adding to his legend and his plans not being completely formed.

G.P.:...didn't even know what an international submarine band was.
Interviewer: No, from a cartoon—film?
G.P.: Oh, from where the name came from, yeah. A cartoon called OUR GANG—the old OUR GANG... there was Spanky I remember.... They had a band one night—they were going to win a radio show—a talent contest for kids and so they got a band together full of incredible equipment and stuff—hoses with things attached to them—and stuff and put them all in their dog cart and got them roller skates and a whole bunch of them invaded this radio station—this pretty little blond girl was singing her 1920 kind of song with her mother looking at her girl like that—and this bunch of kids with hats on and little black kids and all, and ah... the guys—were the International Silver String Submarine Band. (laughter)
Interviewer: Do you ever listen to the album now?
G.P.: Yeah, once in a while when I get a chance to.
Interviewer: What do you think of it now looking back on it?
G.P.: It's all right for the time.
Interviewer: It was very early for this brand of music, I think.
G.P.: Yeah...
Interviewer: When was it... '67?
G.P.: Well that would be... yeah, I guess so, '67.
Interviewer: It was ah—between Everly Brothers and...
G.P.: No, it was early '67 or late '66.
Interviewer: Late '66 or early.
G.P.: It might have been—well, the Submarine Band was together in '65 when we recorded it in '65, yeah. No, in early '66, and a couple of times for Columbia and for Ascot, this really crazy label—I don't even remember who they are. And we had to do a couple of things on the 'A' side that were like—one was a thing for film and another thing was a thing for ah... things for like the Beatles in a way—but on the other sides of both records were like—one was a Jerry Lee Lewis tune—the other was a song called "Truck Driving Man." That was the first one that we really got to do... hard rock or rhythm and blues and country music at the same time. Nobody understood it. And we were so nuts anyway. A lot of people were real nuts back then. It wasn't bad, being produced by a bunch of kids. Everybody took advantage of us.
Interviewer: It was... I mean this combination of either hard rock or straight country-western... Commander Cody does it now more or less, it's different from what you did at the time. Did you hear his first two albums and how did you like them?
G.P.: I only really heard the second one and I heard the first one is better than the second one but I don't know, I like the second one too. They're pretty good.

ram and assorted totems from the Laurel Canyon session, 1969

Interviewer: They also succeed before a straight country-western audience, this is of course something we get at that time, you know, with the Supremes and the Everly Brothers which was unthinkable. What sort of audience did you play then?
G.P.: One or the other.
Interviewer: Yeah?
G.P.: We would play to rock audiences but we would play country-western music and they just didn't like it. Some of them did, some of them didn't and some of them—like in New York man, Young Rascals were the thing then and we played a couple of bills with them. It was really insane, you know... chewing gum, looking up at the stage, they were still into their natty New York pop period thing that happened.
Interviewer: What time was that?
G.P.: That was early '66, late '65. I don't know, I was there in '63 and '64 doing the same sort of thing only by myself in small coffee shops and things and it was easier there because you could control the audience. You could talk to them, somehow get something across. We started playing big things and we didn't have any equipment and road managers were a luxury that we ran into every once in a while. They didn't know us or what to do with us, our crazy mismatched equipment. It was really funny trying to get that feeling across. It was easier when I came to California. That's why I got an album together but it took breaking the group up.
Interviewer: Was it an inevitable consequence which you could foresee?
G.P.: Yeah, well it seemed like the only thing to do because everybody wasn't into country music. They were sort of into small rock clubs and stuff like that, and I just kept going. I was one of the only guys who had a car and I would keep going to all these clubs way down Lankershim Boulevard. (laughter) If you had a car you could get all over the place like that. Got to a lot of country clubs, was at first gigging it, got to know some of the people and then started sitting in. It worked into a country music session every once in a while. At the same time I did the International Submarine Band, which isn't the International Submarine Band at all except a bit of the guitar player and crazy things like that. I can't even go into it.
Interviewer: Apart from the album there were some singles also in there you managed to do. Was it a Jerry Lee Lewis number on one of them?
G.P.: Oh yeah, well it wasn't a Jerry Lee Lewis number it was a Jerry Lee Lewis number that I wrote that Jerry Lee Lewis never got a chance to do. It was the same sort of feeling. It was trying to do what nobody was into trying, straight from 1953, and a lot of people had a good time in music, da-da-da-da-da-da.

When you look back on it it's silly, trying to do country music. There are a lot of people in New York who understand country music and a lot of people in Europe.
Interviewer: I was at a concert at the Academy of Music last week, people were stamping and so now it's catching on. When you joined the group, how did this come about? Was McGuinn actually looking for a replacement?
G.P.: He was looking for a replacement and...
Interviewer: You joined after David Crosby I think.
G.P.: Well, it seemed like the last one to go before I joined was I guess Michael Clarke. But I'm not real sure. (laughter) It probably was Michael. David left early. And I wasn't a replacement, they needed another musician, they were working as a trio at that time and they figured they needed a keyboard man. Peter Fonda had recorded this song I wrote and somehow it got connected we had the same business manager, and so they said well why don't you come down, try playing some of our stuff—they they liked it and Chris and I immediately got together as far as country music because he had been just wanting to do something like that.
Interviewer: That was the first album which was released with you, also the only one. It was definitely the most country album which they made. Obviously your influence, but it was also because of Chris Hillman.
G.P.: Definitely. Chris had been waiting to do that kind of thing for a long time. Maybe even longer than me because he was playing a real authentic bluegrass band a long time ago where I was playing rock and roll a long time ago and we sort of forgot about country music. We would do it but we would do the kind that... we

did electric country once in a while in a rock and roll set, get away with some country ballad or something and that's all anyone knew. Tired of playing 12 bar blues, people weren't going for it anymore. (laughter) We did a country song and see how that'd sound. Chris and I, even though the album didn't come out like we wanted it to, were both pretty happy to have a chance to learn a bit more, get to do a bit more.

Interviewer: You said there were some things you were not happy with. It's surprising how ahead of the times it was. The ritual of country music was pretty ingenious, the arrangements, etc. What were the things you were not happy with on that album?

G.P.: Well, I don't know, about that time you got Nashville Skyline.

Interviewer: It was earlier.

G.P.: You did get a little forelook. For some reason they, being Columbia, for some reason were going to get sued because my release with LHI was kind of shakey. And so a few songs they overdubbed completely and that shouldn't have been overdubbed and my voice was used way in the background, a guide to go by, it didn't work. It gave too much of that old Byrds sound which we were fighting against at that time. Not because it wasn't any good but because there was all this other stuff to work with and it didn't need to look back as Bob Dylan once sort of said. And we had a chance. Things really came out well until this thing about the suit and I don't know, everybody remembers it that way and The Byrds and I certainly do and I think Chris does too. They had to pull a few things out of the can that we weren't going to use, "Life in Prison" and "You Are Still on My Mind". Those are great songs but we just did them as warm-up numbers or something. We did a lot better. They were just about to scratch "Hickory Wind" when somebody ran in with a piece of paper, that's the last one they had saved.

Interviewer: Your voice on most of the tracks, at least on the first side, is your voice solo. It's very much in front.

G.P.: On the first cut only. We didn't keep going that long, yeah, that's fine, we had something else we wanted to do. They're great songs.

Burritos, 1970

Interviewer: I think the group split up pretty soon after that album. You toured with them?

G.P.: I toured with The Byrds a good while.

Interviewer: You went to Rome as well?

G.P.: Yeah. We went to Rome. I think maybe right after we recorded it and it wasn't out yet. I'm really not sure of the times, things get so lost.

Interviewer: Soon after that Chris left The Byrds. Made one more album with them I think.

G.P.: No, I don't think he made any more albums with them after that.

Interviewer: Which group let's say was the best to play in front of an audience.

G.P.: The Byrds, because you had more of an audience. They were already set to dig what you were going to do and it's nice to have that sort of advantage on your side because then you can introduce new things without people going to sleep. They might say, "What?" At least you got their attention.

Interviewer: I once heard the whole first album was cut in one slice in the studio, it's almost incredible. Is that true?

G.P: The first Burrito Brother album?

Interviewer: Yeah.

G.P.: At once? Live?

Interviewer: Yeah.

G.P.: It's most certainly not true. I'd like to say it was, but it's not. They wrote a lot of things that were cut live. Things that people sort of like. But these things took a long time to do.

FBB's onstage at the Troubadour, 1970

Interviewer: Many outtakes.

G.P.: Well yeah. Sneeky Pete, at that time we overdubbed all those things. But Sneeky you see, I think he could always play all those things at once if he wanted to. I've heard him do it before. I've looked around and seen him do things that would take people three or four overdubs, and look at Pete, he did them all at once. (laughter) But it wasn't done live. A lot of it I think, what I like about it, one of the reasonsyou brought it up, and I like it better than the second album is that some of it was actually done live and just kept the way it was and there might be some bass notes or guitar overdub.

It was basically, maybe Chris and I sitting and singing while the whole band was playing, I don't know, maybe that didn't make the mix so great—it taught me a lot about what I'm doing now, which is getting a live feeling and then maybe overdubbing the vocal, but trying not to.... The guys I've been working with lately, Burton, and Tutt, and Harvey, Emmylou Harris, this chick I've been singing with and this great singer Barry Tashian, he used to be around the original Flying Burrito Brothers and was then called the East coast Flying Burrito Brothers, when Flying Burrito Brothers actually came to the East Coast on a tour and they came there and there was already a group there called that. (laughter) Ah... it made it possible to get a live sound in the studio. A lot of what's on my albums is done live.

Because there's such a great engineer, I got Merle Haggard's engineer, Hugh Davies and those people and, they didn't have to tear up the studio to get really crisp sounds out of their instruments, and I had a rock.

Interviewer: There's also the heavy soul influence in the first Burrito album. There are two straight soul things. Which sort of music were you yourself involved in before you ever, ah... joined a group? Which music did you listen to when you were twelve years?

G.P.: Twelve years ago?

Interviewer: No, when you were twelve years old, I mean, this period...

G.P.: When I was twelve.

Interviewer: Yes. Twelve or fifteen. What sort of music did you listen to?

G.P.: I always used to listen to rock and roll, and black gospel music.

Interviewer: That was in Georgia, the music that everybody listened to at the time?

G.P.: Yeah. Really.

Interviewer: And black gospel music, after that...

G.P.: Well no, when I was twelve...

Interviewer: Later on.

G.P.: On our local station, which I would get either music—I would get country music mixed with some rockabilly and I would listen for the rockabilly and I liked some of the country music, some of the early Ira Louvin and Charlie Louvin stuff and Louvin Brothers stuff, early Everly Brothers, the stuff which was considered country at first, turned me on, and so I listened to this combination of rockabilly, where I first found out about Presley, who was a hit in a little area in Florida and Georgia before he was a hit anywhere else.

His early Sun records weren't really big in New York or Detroit or Chicago or Minneapolis or anything like that. A lot of people down there picked up on him. I saw him when I was like... I must have been seven or eight. And I went with a couple of twins who wore bobby socks, my mom let me take them because I wanted to go. He was billed second to Little Jimmy Dickens on The Grand Ole Opry Show, and Little Jimmy Dickens, he had some ridiculous hit at that time, and I actually just walked up to the front row and the aisle seat was empty, it was a basketball gym that held about 700 people, and I just sat down and nobody ever came and said you can't sit there or anything like that. After a while I got to wonder where he was and what he was going to do and I started looking for him and finally after all this craziness, Mug and Jug or Minnie Pearl all came on then finally he came on, and the whole place just went bonkers and the chicks were all moving down and stuff like that. It was just... well... like it's still the same now, then none of the rest of the country was hip to it. Just then it just fell out.

And I said, gee-whiz, in my mind. It all penetrated my mind, and I just walked through Little Jimmy Dickens' dressing room back into Elvis' and said, "hello there you're Elvis Presley and I'm the little kid who buys his records and I think you're all right." And he said, "Yeah," and shook my hand, put me on.. gave me an autograph, sent me... made sure I was with the twins. It's funny, it's ironic that I should be playing with his band now.

Interviewer: Would he remember it?

G.P.: Of course not. Or course not. I doubt if he'd even remember Waycross, Georgia. We didn't get into Louisiana. It's sort of a little circle around New Orleans where things don't get in as much, unless you go looking for them. You have to find them, but in that area you're likely to come upon a juke box and it'll have James Brown, Otis Redding, Merle Haggard, Jerry Lee Lewis, some old Kitty Wells song, a couple of black gospel songs, Reverend James Cleveland. You still see that.

Interviewer: Things were in a very pure form and played then, because in most parts of the country it was either the one or the other, straight country or the soul. The soul for the big cities, etc.

G.P.: I think that was true with Presley in so far as your radio stations. all over the Southland there were various pockets of... where things like that were happening, places in Texas and Oklahoma, probably even Baltimore.

Interviewer: You played on two of the Burritos' albums, didn't you. You weren't as satisfied with the second album as with the first? Was it one of the reasons you left or was it for other reasons?

G.P.: It was so much a reason as a result. I was just getting bored. And it was the result of my getting bored. Um... shouldn't say bored though, I was unhappy... (laughter)... at the time.

Interviewer: Your group had a really big following here, records sold but you were always billed under, let's say, Jefferson Airplane.

G.P.: Right, of course, but we had a pretty big following, as compared to a lot of people at that time. Because I don't know about your country, in this country it seems to be that kind of charisma or Whisky A Go Go charisma let's say is sort of beginning to die out a little bit and people are either returning to something they really like, that they don't have to shake their feathers or there are a lot of young kids who like all sorts of weird things and they like to hear psychedelic music on Saturday morning at ten o'clock. (laughter) They get out and have their Cheerios and then watch a crazy bunch of people playing or cartoon shows with psychedelic sound tracks—but there was a very hot period. I know over in Rome and places like that and the Burritos were surviving pretty well. During our first album and stuff things went pretty well. And it was exciting but in a way you're right, we never really had a definite audience we could play to all the time. We were big at, say, the Whisky and a couple of clubs like that and sometimes big in concerts but it just took the right sort of combination.

Interviewer: No, I say it because at that time it was one of the biggest groups in our country together with The Byrds, although a lot of people had never seen them, compared to let's say the big psychedelic groups, you were more popular than you were here. This is because of the reasons you mention. How long has it been since the second Burrito album was released? Three years.

G.P.: Three years.

Interviewer: Yeah. (sigh) You haven't made any records yourself after that. You played with Delaney and Bonnie, were there specific reasons why you didn't play solo? Was it from your disappointment from the second Burrito album?

G.P.: No, it wasn't that. I was trying to find out more about everything I wanted to do and the kind of way I wanted to do it. And sometimes it's not as easy as popping a pill and sitting down and having a big light bulb shining about your head, sometimes you really have to get down into it. Clean out all the old ideas. Takes a while sometimes. Shouldn't expect miracles. It's come together, I'm glad it has, maybe it could have a year or so ago but that doesn't matter now. All that matters is that I keep playing music. That's what I want to do.

Interviewer: Yeah. You did play in the meantime....

G.P.: Yeah, I played a lot of sessions, but I played mostly with friends. It's a hard thing to do, making a living, but I had some good friends and they all wanted to play music and that kept it going. I got over to Europe and I got together with Keith Richards, but it was hard for us to find any really contemporary country music records. I would bring as many as I could with me but they would get worn out and smashed and sat on. (laughs) Somebody would pour their champagne on them.... After a while we got down to a pretty narrow collection, you know. I'd try to find things, but it was pretty hard. In England they seemed to be ready for country music in a big way and I met a lot of people who were into it but for the main part all they ever get to hear is Jim Reeves and old Patsy Cline singles and things, and I think that's terrible. (laughs)

Interviewer: Pretty strange, yeah. You've just recorded your new album, is it a recording with a definite group which you're also going to tour with?

G.P.: I'd like to tour with that group, but I think a definite group will probably be a long time coming because I just ain't into the whole group thing too much anymore. I like working as a solo artist. There are a couple of people I like to sing with and if they want to stick around, fine. I think a lot of musicians these days feel that they don't want to be tied into an organization inside a record company. It's like being in a penitentiary. They'd rather work just as solo, freelance people, get connected and get an identification with a couple of people, sure, if that happens fine. But people should understand you can't stick together as Billy, Buzzy and Boffy for very long without losing part of your mind. (laughs)

Interviewer: When you are going to perform it will be you solo with a backup band?
G.P.: Yeah, other solo artists and other solo bands. I think The Country Gazette is a very fine band. We shouldn't even really call them bluegrass, they do some other things as well. I guess the people in Amsterdam got a chance to see that. You know, where a lot of people didn't. I hear they were over there last time with the exception of Rick Roberts...
Interviewer: Yeah!
G.P.: ...who once in a while stepped in and did balance or something.
Interviewer: Yeah, Byron Berline and Al Perkins I think was in there and...
G.P.: Byron, Al, wasn't there Kenny Wertz along?
Interviewer: Yeah.
G.P.: And Alan the banjo player? Wasn't the banjo player there?
Interviewer: Kenny Wertz was?
G.P.: Yeah. Kenny and the... the other guys, Roger, Roger Bush.
Interviewer: Bush, yeah Bush. Uh huh.
G.P.: He plays bass. Didn't he do a bluegrass section?
Interviewer: Yeah.
G.P.: That's turned into a group now.
Interviewer: And that's the Country Gazette?
G.P.: Yeah. I'll get you the album cover and show it to you, it's really dynamite.

—BREAK—

G.P.: Amtrak is a super moving service, the train people all got together and they also got together like a love-three thing. Travel in the bedroom, from coast to coast, once again without getting in a fist fight with some guy in Kansas City—"my girl friend's pregnant na na na"—but that died out with that wasn't even possible anymore and they got Amtrak together. Amtrak was sailing across the country and they had a couple of setbacks, the government subsidised them and said, that's okay, that's good, that's a good idea and all the railroad guys were happy men, all the old porters had a job again, and then the fucking thing went through Kansas. One too many times. They been going through there and going through there, either they didn't notice it or just waited for the right moment to bust it. As soon as it hit Kansas City, all of the sheriffs in Kansas practically came on the train and busted everybody in the club car who was... and the train people and took them all to jail. (laughter) While they were having their tequila sour or something and since then Amtrak has been a lot of trouble because people... they just don't like that eight hour wait. Something else might have

Scenes from the 1969 Burritos' "Train Tour"

happened by now, I'm not up on it as much as I should be, but I'm up on it more than most people.

Interviewer: Can you tell me, ah... ah...

G.P.: Get away from Kansas. (laughter)

Interviewer: Yeah. Can you tell me something about the album which you just completed. Anything you want to tell about it, as far as material, style, etc. Are they mostly your songs?

G.P.: Yeah. They're mostly my songs but the album is full of surprises. It's still... a lot of people did a lot of things on it and I'm glad they did, I wouldn't have it any other way. There's a few things with saxophones.

Interviewer: Is Joe Blow on sax?

G.P.: No, no, just Harold Batiste, he used to play with Fats Domino. And he's great. There's some great steel work and some great singing.

Interviewer: Who's the steel player?

G.P.: Buddy Emmons and Al Perkins. and Emmylou Harris is an incredibly good singer. And Barry Tashian, a great singer and sort of mood generator. All the studio musicians I mentioned before. Engineers. Our executive nanny made sure everybody was safe inside the recording studio and didn't have to wander out and he got things done in time, instead of spending 42 hours on something when you can get it done in three hours. What in the world do people want to spend 42 hours on a record for? Then you're just taking a chance on being able to punch in and come up with something that sounds decent when everybody knows that the real thing to do is to get it down the way you want it, so you don't have to punch in. Hell, there's enough to mixing that... eight different kinds of leads to use. There's no telling what can go on in the studio. You're in there, you're up for a day or two, you don't know what somebody's going to forget to do or....

Interviewer: Did you sign for more years for more albums with Warner Bros.? Have you been independent? How do you decide with each different album?

G.P.: No, I'm doing another album right after this one. Two in a row.

Interviewer: You must have had a lot of material... since you haven't made an album for so long a time?

G.P.: I had a lot of ideas and a lot of material. Books and books full of them. But when you're recording you have to be selective. That's the thing about this album, it's full of a lot of different surprises. More people will be able to dig it than just certain spots of people.

I like to see that. I don't know if I'm playing with fire or if I'm doing the right thing even. I think I am. When I say that long hairs, short hairs, people with overalls, people with their velvet gear on, can all be at the same place at the same time for the same reason, that turns me on.

Interviewer: You're already working on the second album or thinking of making those arrangements?

G.P.: Arrangements have been made for it. Thinking of the logistics of it. Material is pretty much settled for it, of course anything can happen when you actually get down to doing it. You might change your mind about one thing or another. But then again, it's just as well not to have 36 versions of 12 songs on your hands. But maybe just one version of 36 songs is a lot better. (laughter)

Interviewer: Are you going to do singles or not? Picking them from your album, issuing them as a specific single, you want to hit that market?

G.P.: Hit that singles market? Yes, I want to hit the singles market, with a country single and a pop single at the same time.

Interviewer: From the album or...

G.P.: From the album.

Interviewer: Yeah? Do you know the titles already?

G.P.: Yeah. The pop single is going to be a song I wrote with Chris Ethridge called "She". And the country single is going to be a song that's going to be billed as a classic country duet called, "That's All It Took," with the B side on it a piece that I just wrote called "Kiss the Children." It's really a piece from 1953. Deja Vu.

Interviewer: Have you ever recorded a number called, "She Thinks I Still Care"?

G.P.: "She Thinks I Still Care."

Interviewer: It's suited for you, I think.

G.P.: I recorded it and sang it lots of times, but I've never released it. I was going to but I never, I just... George Jones is a pretty hard man to compete with when it comes to doing his stuff but "That's All It Took" is a song that he did.

Interviewer: Really.

G.P.: Of all people, he did it with Gene Pitney.
Interviewer: Oh yeah, they were embarking on a music career, yeah.
G.P.: They did a couple of albums together and this is a duet with a girl and she does a really great job. Best coverage of a George Jones song I ever did.
Interviewer: George Jones and Merle Haggard your country-western heroes?
G.P.: Oh definitely. Oh yeah, yeah. Merle Haggard is a great artist and a great person, a great human being. Great everything.

—BREAK—

Interviewer: ...do you prefer the earlier things or the latest, ah...
G.P.: I prefer Merle's earlier stuff, and some of his latest stuff I did.
Interviewer: I like the album called, ah... I think it's one before the last, I didn't like Let Me Tell You About This Song too much.
G.P.: You like *Hag.*
Interviewer: Yeah, Hag. *And the one after* Hag, *it was um... "California Cotton Fields" was on it, did you know that, and "To Larry Dust," "California Cotton Fields." he...*
G.P.: "To Larry Dust," well. "Someday We'll Look Back."
Interviewer: Yeah, "Someday We'll Look Back."
G.P.: Yeah, yeah, I like a couple of things on that album quite a lot. The difference between where Buck Owens went and where Merle Haggard has gone, are two completely different things. When I say that I liked much earlier stuff... yeah sure I liked it, I don't know if I could compare the two. I wouldn't compare the two, but Merle Haggard seems to keep on going in a lot of other ways. Did you ever see that television special that he did?
Interviewer: No, no we didn't have it in our country.
G.P.: He's supposed to do another one. Great things... him singing in concert and on trains and things like that and the next one they're going to try to do some recording on a train which is something I've thought of a lot of times but if you've sung in a club car for a bunch of Marines you notice even when they shut up it's so loud, the sound of the train is so loud you can't really get anything really together acoustically, but Merle told me they were going to fix that somehow.
Interviewer: There are a lot of people who were into country music at that time in our country who were a little shocked by "Okie From Muskogee". They didn't expect it from someone like him.
G.P.: Yeah. It's a shame he got famous for a throw away line.
Interviewer: Is it the song which he does in concert or not?
G.P.: He does it in concert cause people want to hear it, but he doesn't do it as much... it's one of the songs that Merle Haggard doesn't like too much that he's done. I don't mind it, I like it—but Merle, he sees it differently. People are always asking him, how serious are you about that? He's not, he's no more serious about it than he is about whether he catches fish that day or not. He's more serious about singing songs to people. That's how he made his living, was like going through places like, well, to Larry or before he got polished, just going to bar rooms and stuff like that. And like a painter, paint what was going on and then, ah... all my social friends would be on their noses. That kind of stuff. Painting, that actual seeing, that actual feeling. Like one day, now he's on two busses, one for the band, one for him and his wife, and they passed through Muskogee. And he likes to drive the bus a lot, too and stuff. He's a real hunk-a-man. (laughter) Really rugged individual. He just saw Muskogee and painted that picture.

He's not overly fond of hippies, by hippies, I mean the whole race is dead already anyway, maybe Merle doesn't know that, maybe. I think he does but he just doesn't have another word for them because there are a couple of hang-ons here and there. He'll get a fiddle album, somebody'll lay on him a picture of this guy with hair down to his knees swinging this... the guy is playing the fiddle like that and he'll put on the record player until he busts out laughing (laughter) someone takes it off, that ain't the one. It's nothing about hair or all the connotations that people would think there are in "Okie From Muskogee," beads... and sandals and dope, and L.S.D. and shaggy long hair, and...
Interviewer: Burning draft cards.

Michael Clarke and GP on the train

G.P.: Right, burning draft cards at the courthouse, you know. Fuck man, maybe what he was really thinking about was burning down the courthouse, along with Old Glory and everything else. There are a few people who talk that way.
Interviewer: I was in ah...
G.P.: Know where they're all going to live and burn it all down.
Interviewer: Yeah. I was in Oklahoma during a rodeo...

—BREAK—

G.P.: I've only met him a few times, we never got a good chance to talk, I don't know him really well.
Interviewer: You ever played with him?
G.P.: Never got to play with him. We were talking about the concept of him doing an album with me. He never really let on that he knew what it was but he wanted to do it, which is saying something. And then—we both figured that we didn't have enough time. If we were going to do it together it would be sort of difficult. Because he's got his own way of doing things, and I've got my own way. And for the two to blend it would take longer than I have the record budget for, frankly. And I just don't want to stay up that much. (laughter) I need my sleep.
Interviewer: What are you doing apart from playing most of the time now? Are you reading?
G.P.: Playing with different guys I know.

—NEXT TAPE—

G.P.: Sneeky was going to be the steel player for Echo Crane. And a guy from Nashville was going to be the steel player. I'm trying to think of his name, Chris is going to play guitar, the bass player who sang tenor, God, it's so long ago. It was what you would think it would be, a hot country group that we could provide material for that would become famous. Ideas for classic songs that everyone would record, that kind of thing.
Interviewer: You were really a small group. There was only the four of you. Well, according to the cover there were the four of you, but there was a drummer who...

G.P.: There was Eddie Hoh. Eddie just wanted to get the advance money and then he scored and left town or something. (laughter) And he was smart to do that I guess. Sneeky wasn't going to play steel. I can't for the life of me remember that guy's name. But he was some friend of Jonny Corneal, who played drums on the first album and was from Nashville. But like all people, he had tie-ups with his old lady and ten children or something. Steel players... and then we found out he was going to split and we were going to get Morse Hart to play drums, who played with Jerry Lee Lewis. I always thought that the Burritos had a drummer problem. Don't put that on it. God knows I love old Michael Clarke. He's not a country drummer. It just didn't work out. There's Herb Alpert, look at him.

Interviewer: That's kind of a specialty item.

G.P.: Oh, I guess it is. I never thought about it. (laughter)

A WOMAN: Is he still as cute as he used to be?

G.P.: He's cuter, in fact.

Interviewer: The fact that this is the end of the Burrito Brothers, you know after four years, things over, and I said you know in my words it was kind of 'now that it's all over let's go back to the beginning. There's nothing more you would provide a historical perspective to...

G.P.: Yeah, that's what I'm trying to do. You know, I start over from the beginning.

Interviewer: Yeah. I know it's kind of hard to relate back four years to everything that went down but just kind of a brief chronology, you know, the days you were together, what happened...

G.P.: You provide the sodium penethol and I'll.... (laughter) Trying to think of just the good things. Gosh, that guy Al Perkins sure played nice steel guitar. Then I've always dug Chris Hillman and the way he likes to... the music he likes to listen to, influences.

Interviewer: Maybe there's a point, maybe there's another point, going back to The Byrds.

G.P.: There you go.

Interviewer: Take it from Sweetheart *and what happened with that. And from there how the Burritos came about because of that because that's really the formative stage.*

G.P.: I suppose I convinced The Byrds that they should be doing country music instead of trying to write their own Bob Dylan material. I guess Chris had been trying to say something like that all along but he wasn't sure it would wreck his whole life, that he would be out of money and The Byrds would be out of a job. After a while he saw that he could make money with country music and The Byrds started to become a millstone around his neck more than anything else. And we fell out, we were bitter enemies at the time that I split, cause of the South African tour. Cause Chris was really humiliated to go and just play bass with McGuinn singing and Kevin Kelly playing drums and nobody else doing anything. Wasn't Mike Clarke on the *Notorious Byrd Brothers*? I guess it was just Chris, McGuinn, and the horse. Yeah, I think it was, Michael was the Byrds drummer, he wasn't the Burritos drummer. Oh God, these things inside my mouth are killing me.

Interviewer: From there it went to, you broke away and then Chris...

G.P.: Then Chris followed. We sat up in Topanga Canyon and smoked a lot of dope and sang a lot of country songs—"gee that sounds good," you know. And then Mo Ostin from Warner Brothers called me and said, yeah I sure like some of the stuff you've been writing and Joan Baez had just recorded "Hickory Wind", and wouldn't you like to do something for us. It was his dream about doing stuff in England, starting a country band in England. England is so unjaded that way, they're so open-minded about it. Really, they're so open-minded they're ignorant, they don't know. Maybe it's just a dream but it seems like the perfect place to start a country music scene. Only the musicians can't support it. You had to take over American musicians, it's a whole lot of bread, right? You need a lot of front money, we needed a good contract. Jerry and Herb came in really fast and said, oh well gee, you can start right away here and we'll give you the equipment and stuff.

Interviewer: How did they find out?

G.P.: I guess they heard it through the grapevine. You know, these guys talk to each other.

Interviewer: Yeah right.

Fashion courtesy of Nudie

G.P.: So we got it all together very fast, I think Larry Marks did a real good job getting us enough reins on the first album to get a group started, but because of hassles, and not getting the right personnel in front because there still wasn't time... you can go all the way back to the International Submarine Band or Chris' Scotsville Squirrel Barkers, which is really a long time ago. We all had trouble getting people to believe that it could be done, cause your connotations of Oakie this and Oakie that, they like the Christian aspects of it, the gospel feeling of joy that people... sort of hootenanny 1970 or something.

Interviewer: It probably had most to do with the image of longhairs doing country music.

G.P.: Yeah. And longhairs can't quite cope with it. Since it's the only music I know how to play I don't worry about it so much. Some good things are happening though, really good things are happening. The other month, a couple of months ago I went over there with the Burritos and played with them, Baltimore and Charlotte, North Carolina. It was really fun. Byron Berline and Al Perkins added something that had been missing from the Burritos the whole time. And that was just a quick musicianship, spontaneity and super good at their notes and stuff like that. And Michael's... I hope you erase everything I say about Michael.

Interviewer: Yeah.

G.P.: It was... another thing I couldn't believe it that is, Chris came up with the tape that we did at the Palomino Club right when we were recording the first album and it's five sets of madness, a 45-50 minute break and a lot of tequila and Clarence White sitting in and this really good singer Jimmy Morse sitting in and all this playing the best we could and some of it sounded great, but the singing sounded great, and guitar sounded great, some of Sneeky's stuff sounded great. I couldn't believe, I knew Michael wasn't at his best, I couldn't believe the way Chris sounded, I didn't realize it, he wasn't a country bass player. It should have been obvious to me because he's such a great fucking studio musican but he's not a country bass player. He didn't know it, he realized it before anyone and said, oh man I'm sorry. What we needed was someone who could play country shuffle, du-du-du-du-du, and it wasn't happening and I never heard that, I don't know why. I looked at old Chris Ethridge playing the bass and I said, wow, he's got to be great. (laughter) And he wasn't. But you know, Chris, he understood that. So he split. I suppose about the time he split I got sort of disillusioned.

Interviewer: Why?

G.P.: He'd become part of the group. He was part of the group. He was the person who convinced me to come back from England when I had already split with the Byrds, he told me, oh man we got to get something together. And I liked writing with him a whole lot. And it just blew my mind that he wasn't the right bass player.

Interviewer: Yeah.

G.P.: So when he was missing it seemed... the idea had been wrong, you know, we had picked the wrong people. I didn't know quite how to say it to Chris Hillman without getting in a fist fight. So I tried to stake it out and make it work.

Interviewer: Right after you left, the second album...

G.P.: The second album was a mistake. It was a mistake to get Jim Dickson involved. It was all done. We should have been more careful than that.

Interviewer: Yeah, it's really funny you know, from an untrained ear, an untrained

ear in knowing all the facts behind what happened with the Burritos, yet you can listen to the albums and know that this was a period of everybody being really not together.
G.P.: Uptight. Yeah, really uptight.
Interviewer: Just like a completely different album from the first and the third is polished in a different direction, it's really got its Crosby, Stills and Nash slickness.
G.P.: It's commercial.
Interviewer: Yeah, really commercial. But good in a way.
G.P.: That's what Jim Dickson was aiming at, he was trying to make it commercial, and when he finally got rid of me he got it that way. You know he had his brother Leonard and Rick Roberts. Kept Sneeky from playing too much. And he dictated to Chris Hillman for some reason. Chris is always listening to what Jim says. I think it's because of the Mr. Tambourine Man album.

You can make mistakes like that. I didn't listen to Jim Dickson, I listened to Terry Melcher about three months later. And I made the same mistake. Because I was floored by the Mr. Tambourine Man album and I thought Terry has that charisma, he says, man that's great, wow...
Interviewer: And Jim, too. Jim's got the same kind of... whatever he says is coming from some place, he's been to a lot of different places.
G.P.: Sure.
Interviewer: He says, that's great man, that's great, this is the way to go. And you say sure, whatever you think. I know that you've been there and I haven't.
G.P.: Yeah well, he's a good producer in that sense. He knows how to—this is a Leon Russell quote—put everything into a little box. He can draw a little series of boxes and put everything into a little box, I don't remember how it goes. For a producer that's great, unless he does something like some producers get really screwed up somewhere or another, we won't mention how. I don't even know if anyone knows how. And they forget their little boxes about half way through the song. (laughter) That can mess you up. Sometimes I guess it's not good to have a producer, who does a little box trip. But probably guys like Bob Johnson, that's what they do. I've never worked with him, but I guess that's what he does, and guys like that are good producers. Denny Cordell does it. and Denny does good work. That's it, either Jim himself didn't fit

GP

the method or the method didn't fit. But whatever it was it didn't fit. I can't even claim to have really participated in that. I did what was asked of me and that was it. It's a pretty lousy thing to have to admit.
Interviewer: After you started...
G.P.: Yeah, and especially when you're going to have to leave everybody else holding the bag.
Interviewer: Had you drowned by that time?
G.P.: Yeah, pretty much. (laughter) No, I left...
Interviewer: ...had been...
G.P.: ...I waited to see if the album was going to be a freak, and then split. I was starting to duck out of my own gigs about that time, I just can't handle it, I don't want to go to Seattle for $800.00, no thank you. Chris and I though... he hit my guitar once. We always understood what the other one was going through. So that was nice. The old country flavor, it was always there, somewhere, and so we drove from New Jersey to South Carolina to hear the Burritos. He could get off one way or another, he wouldn't be disappointed. He heard us getting drunk in the dressing room, singing songs or more than we did on stage, there was always some reason for it. And then finally when it became too much, I split. You could probably, from what I said, get an idea of what happened.

Interviewer: From that point how did you look at the Burritos—when the album came out, how did you react?
G.P.: My first reaction was when a mother looses one of her young. My eggs were broken—jealousy, kind of disappointment that Chris could prostitute himself in such a way. They got here a little late. That sounds real nice. I wish Al Perkins would have been on that album, I think he would have added that steel guitar spirit to it which the Burritos always needed, and Sneeky provided magically on the first album. I think Larry Marks had a lot to do with providing that, because he let Sneaky go with some of the weirdest ideas that I... there were times during the first album when I wanted to quit (laughter), when I couldn't understand this guy doing eight steel overdubs but I liked it. You know, Jerry Moss said, you're a second album group and just don't expect your first album is going to be the greatest thing in the world. He was probably thinking things like Chris Ethridge isn't a country bass player, I can't tell these guys this. But he knew we were a country group and knew what would make a country group—it's just that we didn't really have it together on the first album, he was hoping we would on the second. I don't know why A&M didn't stick with us to make sure.

I know why. Maybe they just didn't have the time or something. To find them Al Perkins, to find them Morse Hart, to make sure the drumming was tight and you can't really say that's our responsibility because that kind of thing takes bread more than anything. I can sit here and name steel players all day long. And good drummers. But when it comes to telling somebody they have to... on the one hand they have to go and somewhere on the other hand they have to put up with three months of not eating until we somehow get it together.

It's hard. You can't do it. It's much easier to say, let's go into the studio and collect studio musicians and say let's do the album and see how it turns out. Then you've already dug yourself in so deep and they've got to pull you out from there.
Interviewer: Do you think the first album was premature?
G.P.: Yeah, I think all those albums...
Interviewer: ...Bob Dylan didn't get any sanction to do country music. I mean not indirectly, he came out and just yelled it.
G.P.: Think of how I felt after the initial Submarine album. And I knew Dylan was going to get into it sooner or later. Cause I mean, well, nobody loves Dylan more than I do.
Interviewer: Me.
G.P.: No, you don't more than me. Maybe as much, but I love his sense of humor. The guy is such a fucking great writer and I wish that he could do the country thing better but he can't.
Interviewer: He's got his own...
G.P.: He's got his own style, right.
Interviewer: He even said that.
G.P.: I wish he'd make me laugh a little bit more, like he used to.
Interviewer: He might have been, you know...
G.P.: Catching dinosaurs. Making love to Elizabeth Taylor.
Interviewer: Yeah. That'll happen again. I know that'll happen again.
G.P.: Yeah. Yeah.
Interviewer: It has to. It has to.
G.P.: Yeah.
Interviewer: I mean if he's around to do it, he'll do it, because it has to come back here. It all happens like that. It all comes back.
G.P.: It's all come back to the guys who I'm talking to right now, the first managers of the first International Submarine Band which was conceived of in Massachusetts as a rhythm and blues country and western group.
Interviewer: Who started that group?
G.P.: I did. The only way it got recorded was by... I had to split and let all these guys down because it wasn't that... Two guys, a hard kicking rhythm and blues drummer and a rhythm and blues bass player who played horn and this country guitar picker who played upside down and hit the ceiling and he sings like James Brown, trying to harmonize with me and we wrote some dynamite stuff that never got recorded. We had this real enthusiastic manager, this guy named Jack Lewis, from Monte Kay, who handled Flip Wilson and stuff like that and they loved us man, they thought this has got to be a good idea. Jack is crazy though and the time wasn't right and we got disappointed and we were broke and hungry. So we said, shine it and I came out here to California and had to hustle a street album, had to go to Lee Hazelwood, and say, okay just let me record an album, I won't take any money

for it, that's pretty much what I was saying, unless it's a top album (laughter), and just give me money to go into the studio and he said, okay but my old lady has to produce it. I said, yeah great, anything. Glen Campbell sang harmony on it, J.D. Maness played steel, Earl Ball played piano, Jonny Corneal played drums and I was thinking about it the other night, it's probably the best country album I've done because it had a lot of really quick shuffle, brilliant sounding country.

Interviewer: What was it called?

G.P.: Safe at Home. Once in a while with the Burritos I would run into some freak who had nine copies of it or something. Nobody else ever heard of it. And a lovely black and white album cover, and like it had four songs that I had written, good.

Interviewer: Whose label?

G.P.: L.H.I.

Interviewer: Oh, it's L.H.I.

G.P.: I mean, it's really young. I got real carried away with some Arthur Big Boy Crudup, things like "That's All Right Mama," and the other one which sounds like that. I wrote a song called "Luxury Liner." Did "That's Alright Mama," "Miller's Cave," and "Folsom Prison Blues." But it was all recorded in a week. Mixed in one day. (laughter).

Interviewer: The first one, it was done supposedly, recorded, mixed and pressed and packaged in two weeks.

G.P.: Yeah, well. Then again, that's the thing about having a studio in your house. It's different. This was like four three hour sessions at Western Studio and I didn't know any of the musicians or anything. I love those old records. I love all those guys. I might as well throw something in about them in the middle of this because they played a part, them all playing together, when you consider the inputs of Billy Bogeman, Junior Markham, Jimmy Carstein, and Leon, and Mark Benno, even the road managers, Shade Tree, Gary Sanders and all those people. Boy. They had an electricity going. And it blew up. I've heard some of the weirdest things from some of those guys now, stuck back in Tulsa. Crazy, there you go, they are always lending things to each other. Billy Bogeman and Jimmy Carstein, Junior Markham. Where else could they lend their influence except to that kind of thing, I don't know. And now Leon is the ringmaster but I really dug what was the

JOHN LOMAX III

Backstage, 1973

sort of country feeling, kind of hostile feeling that I don't even feel so much in Leon's music anymore. I think Leon's gone beyond it, what has to be his own style, but that was really a nice scene. Beautiful scene. If you have everything at your disposal, your own recording studio or even a houseful of sound equipment and you're in the right town and things aren't driving you crazy or if you can put up with it long enough, get an album out and make the rent then you got it made. We wanted the big money so bad, needed it.

Interviewer: Yeah. Sneeky, something about him having a lot of material not a lot but maybe his own material started coming out about the time he started up with the group.
G.P.: True.
Interviewer: He didn't have an outlet for it because Chris was kind of...
G.P.: That's true.
Interviewer: What?
G.P.: What was true all along was that Sneeky, it sounds like I'm repeating myself, wasn't the right steel player for the group. Chris sort of has two opinions about this. In a way he digs Sneeky more than I do because he likes that dit-dit-dit-dit, which Sneeky could sometimes pull off—but probably more steel players can better that Randy, what's his name, Rusty Young and people like that. I wanted Tom Brumway deep inside and when it came down to it I just settled for anybody who can play flying guitar with pedals on it, but I wanted a brilliant sounding pedal steel player, and Sneeky was cutting it on the first album. In rehearsals he would come up with some really tender pretty things, and not too whiny. I think a lot of critics started to think that Sneeky was the whiniest steel player in the world. It's probably because the guy was down, man, he felt horny. Sneeky had a lot of material, it wasn't suited for... I tried to get into it with him, and so he probably thought Chris was against him, because I tried to.... But it wasn't right, it was probably good material. I heard that he's producing Spencer Davis?
Interviewer: Yeah.
G.P.: Sneeky?
Interviewer: I asked him last week or whenever, he said now he's producing Spencer Davis and I said that's a long way from getting your own material through, you know.
G.P.: That's Sneeky.
Interviewer: Yeah, that is.
G.P.: He had a sort of Paul McCartney type material, not Paul McCartney so much as... what's that guy's name? Randy Newman. A real polished kind of stuff, a thirty-four year old guy might write. (laughter) Looking back on life I see anything through the antique store window and he never got a chance to do it, that's true.
Interviewer: I told him I bought the first Spencer Davis album at a swap meet three weeks ago for a quarter and he went right over, he didn't even hear me, you know. I said, "Gimme Some Loving" album...
G.P.: Swap-meets are such a part of his life. (laughter).
Interviewer: Yeah, right.
G.P.: By the way, I have a copy of...
Interviewer: Crimson Yellow.
G.P.: Yes sir, I went to see my Chinese dentist the other day. (laughter).
Interviewer: ...found Dr. West.
G.P.: Did he? A Dr. West? Who...
Interviewer: Chicago.
G.P.: He planted...
Interviewer: Your Chinese dentist reminds me of "The Egg Plant that Ate Chicago." Dr. West Medicine Show and Junk Band.
G.P.: Oh yeah. Dr. West Medicine Show and Junk Band, who did that? Was there a Dr. West?
Interview: It was Norman Greenbaum's first group.
G.P.: Oh... Norman Greenbaum.
Interviewer: Getting back, the name of the album is "The Last of the Red Hot Burritos."
G.P.: They did do Red Hot Burr... see now, I tell them things and it comes out just the next day. They came to me...

Robert Franks came to me last week and said we're going to call it The Hot Burrito Review. Because it's something Leon said one night, it should always be called the Fantastic Flying Burrito Brothers, you shouldn't just say the Flying Burrito Brothers. They flipped Jim Dickson out doing something, making our Mexican road manager do radio spots (laughter), Fantastic Flying Burritos or something, like he was introducing his parents at a wedding. And The Last of the Red Hot Burritos. That's good, I like the album cover. The Hot Burrito, the Red Hot Burrito album cover. I thought that was great, I thought it should have happened a long time ago.
Interviewer: Yeah. This one is much different. This one is like... it's not really reminiscent of Burrito, you know it's really...
G.P.: It should be something else, exactly.
Interviewer: Beautiful, it's really beautiful. It's airbrushed. Plastic 30's design.
G.P.: Boy we sure got cut out on the short end of the album covers. I got to tell you.

Interviewer: The second album, is that yours?
G.P.: Nothing was mine but the name man.
Interviewer: Oh.
G.P.: When they said we're going to do a sitting in the garage back here in the A&M lot for the back cover, I said, okay, great. (laughter) I broke out in white suits. (laughter).
Interviewer: Right, where was that thing...
G.P.: Yeah, a guy that I was sharing an apartment with at the Chateau Marmont was quite a loony character and had these white suits, these sort of cocaine tester suits. (laughter) German lab suits, it was the perfect opportunity, (laughter)—take all these dumb pictures, either in Topanga Canyon near some paint splattered wall back there and I was just so bugged because... well first of all I was disappointed. I think Barry Feinstein as a photographer and the first album cover picture was such a bring down man, it's just killed me. The suits were alright, they could have been photographed well but the picture itself, like there were other pictures in that session that were good, actually. There was one on a poster where we were standing in front of a Joshua tree, it is a lot better than that one is. Everybody that's ever seen that picture has commented on it, it seems... why did you use that one? The way I feel about the first album is that it could have made more noise than it did. When we went on the tour A&M set up across the country, God bless A&M for that, wonderful, people really dug us, man they were really excited about us and they had no reason to be, nobody had ever heard of The Flying Burrito Brothers. I mean, A&M bought some record spots on underground radio stations and shit like this spends the money but nobody had ever heard anything we'd ever done, our album wasn't out yet. We were playing with groups like Savoy Brown, people that had big teeny bopper followings and like people loved us. I was used to people being very cold to country music and from the moment, the very moment we started it got really exciting, you know. I was really having a ball, I guess so was Michael Fosse. A lot of other people... it didn't get handled but Jerry was probably right, we were a second album group, if the first album would have been right. Anyway I thought it was a pretty good album... we were capable of doing good stuff back then. Times like when we would be playing...
Interviewer: Why was that? The reception you got at the time was not precedent.
G.P.: I don't know. I'm sure you have a lot of different opinions on that.
Interviewer: What was the other music at the time that was close to your music?
G.P.: There wasn't any.
Interviewer: There really wasn't any?
G.P.: Jim Kweskin, maybe. Or, no no. We were still trying to do my deluxe number, a dream of soul-country-cosmic, what I called in my earlier college days, Cosmic American Music. I would do numbers, buy a bottle of tequila, five turbans, and I always insisted on having an organ around so I could do Jerry Lee Lewis numbers and try to get a big sound and then get a real little sound. I guess people like Crosby, Stills and Nash made a ton of bread doing big sound with Dallas Taylor and Greg and then switching to acoustic guitar, but that kind of shit always impresses me as just a side show number, doesn't get me off, it doesn't have enough spirit that involves everybody. It puts me to sleep is what it does. And I need excitement. I like going to hear somebody and getting surprised and thinking the music is good. Even if I don't think it's so polished either. I guess Leon did that, Leon really did it hauling everybody he knew onto the bus and depending on them to sail all over the stage and get kind of a feeling going. And we were never that kind of group, though. I mean even if we would have had the money to do that it wouldn't have been quite right once we were really big and famous. It had to be something we provided and the material we had just wasn't there in the group. The musicians were there, like we had one of the best bass players around, but he wasn't a country bass player. If he had been both it would have been all right, but he...Chris is a country person, but like so many people from the country they turn the other way, turned his back on it. He didn't want to hear anything but Bobby Blue Bland when he was a kid, you know, I'm sure he cried when Hank Williams died, like you said, but he never really studied that kind of music, didn't want to play it. There wasn't much money in the South anyway, ten bucks a night.

©1973, Kim Gottlieb

Relaxing during rehearsal at the home of Phil Kauffman

END OF SIDE 1 SECOND TAPE

G.P.: ...and ah... I dug them so much and Snoopy's Opera House and to sit there all night... we were the only people in the fucking place. And Chris was still with the Byrds. Michael had just been fired and I can't go into people like... but I would say, "you got to go hear this band," and Ethridge would too and nobody wanted to hear it. "Oh bull, the Valley"—and finally Chris started going and that's when we really started to get tight. It was me and Chris and Chris. We'd sit and listen to Bonnie and Delaney, and Mike Clarke—found out it was a good opportunity for a drummer and he loved it.
Interviewer: Where was it?
G.P.: It was at Snoopy's Opera House and The Prelude on Monday nights and Snoopy's Tuesday through Sunday. And Snoopy's is past Sherman Way, past the Palomino, I think.
Interviewer: That was the whole...
G.P.: It's not past the Palomino? Well... it's near Sherman Way. They were the closest thing to what we were doing really but then I think they changed an awful lot before they did any sort of recording—and this is... I'm talking about Bonnie and Delaney, Bobby Keyes, various bass players, J.J. Cale, Jimmy Carstein, Junior Markham. That was their horn section, Junior Markham and Bobby Keyes. And Greg and Lennie, complete freak, got two chicks to drive out of the parking lot of Snoopy's... this is when they were starting to get more well known. I had told Alan Pearser and Sid Kaiser and they went down there. One night right around that time two broads in a cocoa brown '68 Cadillac, brand new Cadillac, pulled out of the parking lot of Snoopy's and went down the street and made a U-turn and pulled right back in the parking lot and drove right through the wall. (laughter) And this car, with steam coming out from the hood was like half way into the club, all these swingers were in it... it was the Prelude, it wasn't Snoopy's, it was the Prelude, and before they got out of the car they lit a cigarette. (laughter) Red velvet curtain hanging across the top of the car with steam coming out and this faggot in tight light blue jeans, jumps up on the stage and yells, "business as usual tomorrow night". That was the rhythm section without Bonnie and Delaney. That's what I think kept it going so much was like... they'd have a different personality every night sort of like, um... Leon would come and sit in if he was bored, or Jesse Davis would come and sit in and everybody would split and go over to the Plantation and get drunk and that's where it all happened. That's where ideas for big time country music started hitting me cause I started hanging out with these freaks and I realized that it could be done again and the Hazelwood thing was a shuck. These guys would make it, and I could do it too. People were not so hung up on sick music as I thought. There was a little room for funk and stuff. I got that crazy idea...
Interviewer: What did you classify then as...
G.P.: Oh... bubble gum music.

Interviewer: You mean as real music as opposed to some other fantasy?
G.P.: As opposed to the sort of folk vocal kind of music going on at that time. I have really nothing to say about things like Bobby Vinton. I don't think about that too much but there was a lot of imagery type of mind garden stuff going on then, it was really boring and I started getting into the thing and we were really close, Bonnie and Delaney. They first did their tour or they hadn't done a tour yet and when they finished doing their album and we just came back from our tour, they gave me this plaque. I guess it was the first plaque they gave out, somebody told me they probably gave out a lot of plaques in those days but Delaney's brother was a trophy maker and he gave me this and it was signed Bonnie and Delaney instead of Delaney and Bonnie and Friends. That was nice, we were close not only sort of musically but in our heads we were close They were always you know, pulling us aside and saying how much country music meant. It was important that somebody did it and almost sort of like swearing on momma's old Bible that we mean this, we're not just drunk and saying it and listen pal, you got to keep doing this, so we kept doing it. Things like that mean a lot, you know, it's the next best thing to money. It's better than money, but you can't eat it.
Interviewer: What's your involvement now with country music?
G.P.: It's really crazy.
Interviewer: Is it going back to it or is it...
G.P.: Oh yeah. People like the Rolling Stones, that nobody's going to forget about it—people like even Crosby, Stills and Nash, but everybody who has anything to do with it is doing something good, almost like Delaney said, you know it can't be all bad trying to do something for country music. It's a beautiful, beautiful idiom that's been overlooked so much and so many people have the wrong idea of it, God, I just can't believe it. When you say country music to people, what some people think, you know, how little they know, what they haven't listened to, what they missed... it just takes somebody like Merle Haggard. You say, Merle Haggard and he's probably not the most important thing to come along since Lefty Frizell by a long shot but he's good, you know, he's real good and a lot of people don't know it, much less than when Lefty was around.

Doug Hanners

Live at Liberty Hall, Houston TX, Feb. 1973

Interviewer: He had the longest title of any record... what was that song he wrote?
G.P.: I don't know, "If You've Got The Money, I've Got The Time"?
Interviewer: Yeah, "If You've Got The Money, I've Got The Time."
G.P.: What a song, man. But he did some good shit, like "Mom And Dad's Waltz", and stuff like that. When I think of him I also think of "Rock 'N Roll Notion" that Hank Snow did and people when they think of these guys they can't think of anything but bad stuff, they think of Hank Snow or Tennessee, they think of Tennessee Ernie Ford and one day they think of country music they think of a WASP white cab driver (laughter) and listening to three chord music and I don't know. If they accept Appalachian folk music on the one hand and really super ethnic stuff, I can't think of the particular example but if they can listen to mountain gospel, B. Mitchell Reed can play that to them, they sure ought to be able to kick some shit. Because that's where it comes from, where the whole feeling comes from.

Doug Hanners

Both photos from The Fallen Angels' gig at Liberty Hall, Houston, Feb. 1973. Kyle Tullis at far right.

Doug Hanners

Just because somebody studied it and wrote a book on it doesn't mean it's got to be done in a hostile atmosphere. No one can get contaminated by it. Or the dulcimer... Ah... well you know what I'm saying. People call me a purist.
WOMAN: People call you what?

G.P.: A purist. For sticking so close to (laughter) oh... I really don't stick very close to the rules. I don't know.
Interviewer: Are you going to go back in?
G.P.: I'm about ready to go back in, but I don't know what it's going to turn out as.
Interviewer: ...someone?
G.P.: I don't know if I'll wind up recording for Rolling Stones Records or some small company. I'm thinking about recording with a smaller company where I can be more of a big fish. I just can't get it out of my mind so I might as well, like I found a chick singer who's real good who I want to sing with. I like that idea. I've always had problems with guys who can't sing high enough. (laughter) I have to kick Chris Hillman in the ass.
Interviewer: You should sing with Brian Wilson.
G.P.: Yeah, or Terry Melcher. No, I mean someone with that kind of a voice, you take Don Rich, right, he's perfect. He plays lead guitar and has that perfect... like a steam whistle, his voice. It's real high and penetrating. His phrasing is perfect, the way he pronounces words is perfect and he knows an awful lot about recording, and he smokes grass (laughter). He's probably one of the only, big straight guys who does, you know. I wonder if Merle does yet or not. It's not really very important, is it? But I just threw it in there. So anyway, women always seem to work it out at least half good and if you get a really good woman it works better than anything, because you can look at each other with love in your eyes, right. (laughter) She's a gas. Her name's Emmylou Harris.

G.P.: I won't say where she lives. She lives in Virginia.

I don't want one of these mustache Petes from around here to steal her away.
Interviewer: What ah... well Gram...
G.P.: Yes. I'll tell you anything I can.
Interviewer: I just feel like Walter Winchell or something.
G.P.: Yeah. I know what you mean.
Interviewer: You know. Go ahead, do whatever you want.
G.P.: I don't have any...
Interviewer: What do you think of the world situation, Gram? I just want to wrap up.
G.P.: I talk a lot.
Interviewer: Good.
G.P.: Did a lot of tapes.
Interviewer: That's why I'm here. You didn't talk a lot though.
G.P.: I hope you don't play them back.

Interviewer: No, I said you didn't talk a lot. Maybe we should do some more tomorrow.

G.P.: I have gotten a real nice feeling lately, Rick Grech and I, we've been living in England, working on a farm with the guy who was the bass player in the International Submarine Band, same fellow who thought of the name, the Flying Burrito Brothers. Do you know how that was thought up?
Interviewer: I heard... there's so many decorated stories...
G.P.: It proves what I've been saying, it's the most obvious thing, but the Flying Burrito Brothers was... The International Submarine Band had gotten a name, we could sort of work for five hundred bucks around L.A. I started cutting these guys out and working with strictly country hicks. So Ian and John and Mickey to make money got together with this guy Barry Tashian of the Remains and Leon and people like Junior Markham and even Bobby Keyes and J.J. Cale. Whoever was around would play, and that was called the Flying Burrito Brothers and I would sit in. It was at the Prelude where they would play and all those clubs up and down Lankershim, like the Hobo and the Red Velour and...
Interviewer: Who's name was it originally?
G.P.: Ian Dunlop's. And I stole it from him. (laughter) He split to England to... he was

Spring, 1971, Tregidden Mill, Cornwall, England. Gram visits Ian and Valerie Dunlop (below.)

an art student, a very far out guy, Ian Dunlop. He was born in Cornwall, England. And his father is a psychiatrist. There was the old country doctor, who moved to the United States and had a lot to do with inventing librium of the psychotropics — had a real interesting (laughter) medicine cabinet. And Ian decided he had had enough of it all and he went back to Cornwall and has a little organic farm down there, he's married, he's like really living tough, shoveling cow shit for 95 cents an hour and stuff like that, big arms. I got very good feelings about music down there, not only the old Celtic and the.. flipping you out now, aren't I?... Judaic vibes and I saw the monoliths and megolithic art and pre-bronze ancient vibes. Ian's very much into a free Cornwall, the Cornish Nationalists, that's where the world's at today, man. As far as I'm concerned, there's like people who want to get back to where it's at. You talk about getting back to where it's at, that's the end of the circle and Ian's trying to find out. I mean he just had to go there and start farming and noticed this going on, he wasn't on a pilgrimage or anything, and he has become interested in this and he reads papers about it. He has this old water mill that he is restoring. He loves old machinery, buys it and works on it. Everybody he knows is like 80 years old, old farmers and stuff. Terribly honest people. Wonderful people. And he still keeps playing bass, his last band was Harvey and the Sequins. It was him and an 85 year old accordian player. Jesus, I said, who are the Sequins? He said, "Well we were always looking for another guy" and his last group was the Cornish Red Hots and they're pretty silly. But I get wonderful feelings about country music from Ian, always have, and I was getting into writing some things with Ian and then just sort of trading ideas back and forth about what should be going on and he's very sentimental, soft-hearted sort of bloke, he really digs the dust-on-mother's-Bible syndrome. He has no designs about "let's all hock our tractors and buy a bus and go and try to make the big time", he just has the other way, he can't fathom it.

G.P.: ...terrible trumpet player that Ian... Funky Potatoes.
WOMAN: Real big gig.

G.P.: No that's the name... they're a weekly gig. Ian talked to some art student who had to make up a poster and the guy said, tell me something about your job, and he said what goes on there and he said something about I don't know, about blues, pine salad, beer. And that's what the guy called it.
WOMAN: Ian is so crazy.
G.P.: Every name is...somewhere...
WOMAN: He's more nip than he would want you to think.
G.P.: There are people that will never know about Ian.
WOMAN: Probably never, till it's too late.
G.P.: He's really a very good musician. He's a tremendous artist. But he's going back to the woods.
Interviewer: You know, talking about going back to the woods... if you could just give me the time, cause you have been gone two months. When Rick came in...
G.P.: I thought it was longer than that.
Interviewer: How long was it?
G.P.: I thought it was more like six months. When he said he'd been in the group a year and a half I thought it was really shocking. I thought he had been in the group less than a year. Because it seems like they would have done more than one album.
Interviewer: I think it's '70. Or '71, I don't know.
G.P.: Maybe he thinks he's been in it longer than I have. I think he's... (laughter).
Interviewer: In the Byrds since '65.
G.P.: I knew that, I knew because he reminds me an awful lot of one of the Byrds... I didn't say that.
WOMAN: You did so.
G.P.: I don't ever remember saying that. I think Chris said that.
Interviewer: After you left it was all Rick Roberts, talk of getting him and then actually getting him.
G.P.: I guess he had to get his name around. It seemed to me Chris was really the front man. I was really impressed at how much Chris had come out. If only Chris had been like this a long time ago it would have been a lot better or our chances would have been a lot better. Because his voice was... wow... not having to depend on me to sort of do the high points in the show. Having to depend on himself, which he never did in the Byrds. In the Byrds he was always turning his back on the audience, they had their personal problems too but then in the Burritos he felt funky and out there but he felt like more of a quiet power behind me, he used to say things like, I'm going to manage you some day, kid. I always wished he would come out but it seemed to me he just wasn't a solo singer, it wasn't in the cards and I was knocked flat when I went to Charlotte, because Chris not only sounded good on stage but when I listened to my little Sony cassette he actually was projecting a feeling, a really good singer to the audience. Steve Stills got himself a bargain. Especially with Al Perkins too. Those are two heavy guys to depend on. They're very consistent, solid guys.
Interviewer: Yeah. Maybe it was the fact he was the bad guy...
G.P.: Well...
Interviewer: I mean, it's that simple I think.
G.P.: Yeah. I never heard much about Rick Roberts before...
Interviewer: He thought it was your show.
G.P.: Yeah, I guess he did.
Interviewer: So he didn't want to steal it from you. That was cool.
G.P.: You see, it was tough on me. I tried to push Chris and then when I thought he couldn't do it I guess I started to agree with him a little too much. Didn't keep pushing. But it's all right now, who likes to be up against the wall all the time? I encouraged Pete, but it wouldn't work, at least I couldn't see it anyway. I suppose a group shouldn't be something like that, it should happen...
Interviewer: Yeah, I think it was Sneeky, I asked him the last time the group was together, you weren't doing gigs or recording and it was just like you and Chris were together but everybody else was studio people, everybody met at the studio or wherever or met when you had to meet, it just wasn't a spontaneous...
G.P.: That's true. You can think of all sort of reasons for it but the basic fact is it was that way.
Interviewer: When you think back to the beginning of the Beatles, I mean Hard Day's Night *probably was what happened.*

JOHN LOMAX III

Backstage

G.P.: When you work for eight years, you weed out the good and bad points, don't you?
Interviewer: You got to go through...
G.P.: No matter how much it hurt, if you've got to get rid of somebody, you've gotten rid of them by then, and without bringing any names into it. It should have happened before it was too late and it probably wasn't too late until after the second album. That just seemed to seal it for me, I mean, after the first album I wasn't really upset or down or anything or hadn't given it up, and even though Chris Ethridge leaving the group was a disappointment it was the right thing, but the second album was a death blow to The Burritos. When you split from something like that you have to go on to something else, so I just started doing better things, think better thoughts, do better things. Chase dinosaurs.
G.P.: There's a weight off me, really. It's a great relief. It's hard to even think I could be accurate at this point because, um... it was right on the tip of my tongue. I am so far away from it now, none of it really seems too important to me anymore. I'd like to be able to come up with something that would be a wonderful obituary for the Burritos but the idea'll keep on going, it's not like it's dead or anything. Whether I do it or anybody else does it, it's got to keep going and if it can exist in Cornwall then it can exist anywhere.
Interiewer: That's kind of a nice way to end it, the idea will keep on going and there are how many Burrito Brothers albums?
G.P.: A lot, more than I ever thought.
Interviewer: Yeah. Right. What, five, four? It must be the fifth.
G.P.: Yeah.
Interviewer: You know, so they'll keep on going. When it's the end, you still have it.
G.P.: That is the purpose of a recording, that's the only way you can do a recording, that sure is, you're right.
Interviewer: Yeah, like when I think of Dylan, I think of never wanting to be able to end my Dylan collection, you know?
G.P.: Yeah.
Interviewer: It's like I've got some stuff that nobody has ever heard, I don't think, probably some people in Cornwall have, but...
G.P.: No. I doubt anyone in Cornwall ever has. Dylan might have copied it off of them. (laughter) I always had trouble with understanding the necessary business requirements and then wanting to ignore them. On the other hand, not wanting to hear about the big time. But knowing

certain things were necessary to get anything happening. If you don't do it that way then you have to just face something I can't really face, which is not having the best equipment or musicians you can get your hands on to do what you're doing. Like I couldn't do Ian's thing, unless I change as I get older, playing with Barney and the Muscletones or anybody. What really matters is my form and my peace and being happy about music, that way, going and finding a piano in an old cow barn and cleaning the shit off of it, making it work, being happy about it. To me that seems sad in a way. Although I know it's fun for other people, it's not fun for me. I like the bright lights. That's part of country music. Cause that's kind of tragedic. A country kid in the big city, doesn't know where to go. And I hate the city man, I hate it, but I always got to come back to it to hustle something or make something, some kind of deal, I know. London isn't much better than Los Angeles, but it's a start.

Interviewer: This is John Cameron...

G.P.: Signing off.

Interviewer: Yeah that's inevitable. That's the problem with the city. And knowing all the facilities and everything you need is going to be there and you don't have to deal with the other half.

G.P.: Right and you keep avoiding it and you keep waiting for... everybody hopes that someone with the big hand is going to reach down and somebody is going to discover you, make your whole life a dream and easy but it never really happens that way.

Interviewer: Yeah. Sometimes it does, you know.

G.P.: It hasn't for me. (laughter) I don't care about that so much. I can face making the phone calls myself and going around and doing that. It doesn't flip me out. I don't get schizted. Business meetings and stuff. There have been times when I was close to pulling my hair out and killing a few people, or just calling them

GINNY WINN

GP in his own promotional T-shirt, 1973

Philistine mother fuckers and telling them exactly what they've done to my life and my integrity. But I chicken out at the last minute. I go meditate. Clean my head out. Such thoughts, I don't like be violent.

LIBERTY HALL
★ 1610 CHENEVERT - 225-6250 ★
FEBRUARY 22-23-24 and 25
ADVANCE $2.50 AT DOOR $3.00
Shows Thurs. & Sun. 8 p.m. ★ Friday and Saturday 8 p.m. & 11 p.m.
COUNTRY
ROCK
SHOW
★ In Person ★
GRAM
PARSONS
and BAND

Down In the Churchyard: Emmylou Harris

Tracking Emmylou Harris down was no problem. Getting to speak with her was another. As a Grammy award winner, country music superstar and spiritual as well as musical heir of Gram Parsons' legacy she is an extremely busy performer whose time is quite valuable to her. A friend of hers gave me her manager's phone number and I called Ed Tickner (manager of the Byrds during their heyday and at one time Burritos' as well) the next day.

Our negotiations started from there. I called the whole thing Salt III. First I had to present my case sincerely because so much trash had been written about Gram that both Tickner and Ms. Harris were none too sure I wouldn't add to the damage already done. Secondly I had to prove I knew what I was talking about and that I would ask intelligent questions on music and music only. Even a prestigious national publication such as *Playboy* called Parsons "Graham Parker" in their April issue's interview with Linda Ronstadt. And third I had to have the patience of a saint since it took me five months of trying before I actually got to see Emmylou Harris, the interview being called off several times.

Along the way I heard some interesting stories. In October of 1979 I met with Ed Tickner in Santa Monica where we discussed the questions I wanted to ask. He cleared up a lot of misconceptions I had and I thanked him for it. As Gram's manager at the time of GP's passing he was aware of a lot of things I was not.

"Emmy doesn't plan to have one GP song per album," he told me that day, "that's just the way it usually worked out.".

Tickner said there were no outtakes from the GP sessions, unlike the three *Grievous Angel* cuts which later surfaced.

I asked him why Gram didn't do the Fallen Angels tour with Glen D. Hardin, James Burton and the rest of the Elvis Presley players who later formed the first

A Warner Bros.' publicity shot of Emmylou Harris

An official Emmylou Harris publicity shot

Hot Band behind Emmylou Harris. "Warner Bros. felt Gram should go out with his own personal band so the individual players behind him would not take some of the spotlight away from him."

My session with Emmylou was conducted at Ed Tickner's home in the San Fernando Valley. Several things are noteworthy here. One is that I immediately felt right at home calling Ms. Harris by her first name (something I do not usually do until a formal introduction is made) and another is her astonishing resemblance to a cousin of mine back in Kentucky. We spoke soon after she had gotten her Grammy and I think our conversation reflects some of that excitement.

I'd like to thank both Emmylou Harris and Ed Tickner for being so kind and remind myself once more of something she said after we were done. "You know Gram's a lot bigger in Europe than he is over here. He was the most popular male vocalist in some of those countries," she remarked. I said I'd heard he was a big deal over there but I had no idea how much of one. "Before I recorded my first Warner Bros. album I was voted the eleventh most popular female vocalist in Holland. All due to my association with Gram Parsons." She looked wonderingly at Tickner. "And I hadn't even shown them what I could do yet."

SG: *To test this machine I want to ask you something.*

E.H.: Okay.

SG: *I'm from Louisville, Kentucky and in the Summer of 1978 I had some friends out here and I took them to the Roxy to see you. They were absolutely thrilled you had a fiddle player in your band with a University of Kentucky basketball jersey on.*

E.H.: Yes, Ricky Skaggs. He's from Lexington. He's a big University of Kentucky basketball fan and he follows all their games and stuff. In fact I'm surprised they didn't know who he was. I guess they must not have been into bluegrass music.

SG: *One of them went to UK and he knew who Skaggs was. The other guy didn't know and frankly I didn't recognize him either. I'm a little embarrassed I don't know more about bluegrass.*

E.H.: If you are into bluegrass you are into it all the way. Ricky is like the Paul McCartney of bluegrass, I mean he is the young genius who has worked with Ralph Stanley, and he's been singing things since he was five and he's a real prodigy. So if you're into bluegrass at all you know him. Usually the people I meet are either into bluegrass and know everything about it or they know nothing.

SG: *Right. Did Ed tell you about our book and everything?*

We're real excited for this is sort of like the last thing. I figured if we are gonna do it once let's do it once and do it right. The first thing I want to say is all I have is second hand information about you were in Washington playing some club and Chris Hillman....

E.H.: It's a neat story.

SG: *I talked to him and he corrected everything I said. Not being belligerent or anything just...so could you please tell me about your first meeting with Gram?*

E.H.: I hope I tell it correctly, as I remember it. They were playing at a club called the Cellar Door which is sort of the club in Washington for the out of town groups and I was playing down the street at a bar called Clyde's which was sort of a single's hangout place but they had this room where they couldn't get anybody to go in so someone got the idea to hire musicians to play. We won't give them a salary but we'll let them have 30% of the gross of the room. That way the club wasn't taking that big of a chance.

So I was playing there. Actually Rick Roberts came in with Kenny Wertz who was playing with them then. The first night they came in they heard me. I got up and I sang, "It Wasn't God Who Made Honky Tonk Angels" or something like that. I'm sure that's the number. And the next night Rick brought Chris Hillman so Chris came the second night. Chris was the one who asked me to come sit in with them.

I was working all that week and I would finish up my shows and they were playing later than I was so I would go and sit in with them. There was real strong talk about me joining the Burritos.

SG: *Yes, I was going to ask you that. You were going to join but they broke up.*

E.H.: Yeah, that's true. I mean there was talk about me starting to work with them.

SG: *I've interrupted you.*

E.H.: What did Chris say? Because I don't remember exactly but it seemed like it was moving in that direction.

SG: *I feel like I'm a detective because I know a lot of stuff and I don't want to start a fight but I asked him that and he said no, that it was ridiculous. He said "how could you have a girl be a Burrito Brother?"*

E.H.: I do think they wanted me to do some work with them, just for a change of pace. It just never...it was just like a fleeting moment and then all of a sudden the Burritos had broken up. And that was that.

But what came out of that was when the next gig was in Baltimore for the Burritos and Gram was there. He had mentioned to Chris he was going to do an album and he wanted a girl singer. Really this is all secondhand too because Chris....

SG: *How could it be?*

E.H.: In other words I wasn't there during the conversation between Gram and Chris. I got a phone call from Gram because there was this girl hanging out at the concert who had done some babysitting for my little girl and who gave him my phone number. This is all very strange...so I got a phone call from him and he said "I'm in Baltimore, could you come pick me up?" And I said no, that's fifty miles away! And he said "oh, is it that far? " I said yes, why didn't he then take the train down because it's a really pleasant trip and I will pick you up at the train station. So that's what I did.

SG: *Had you heard of him before? Were you familiar with any of his material?*

E.H.: He was a vague name in my mind. I was not really up on what was happening in the music world because as I was getting involved in music I also became pregnant and was completely out of the scene for a long time. I was struggling to make a living and waiting tables and stuff so I wasn't that familiar with the Burrito Brothers and I wasn't all that familiar with Gram. I came to know his music as I got to know him and as I got to work with him.

SG: *So you didn't see it as "now's the chance, my big break"?*

E.H.: With Gram?

SG: *Yeah.*

E.H.: No. I was pretty jaded at that point, I didn't expect anything to ever happen to me. I was very cautious and extremely reserved about the whole thing. I mean that was my reaction to "will you come and pick me up?" It was kind of like "hell, no, I've got to work tonight" cause it was pouring down rain and I had to work for the ten people that were gonna come in the club tonight! I was gonna make maybe five dollars that night. It was that kind of thing.

I was simply very reserved about the whole thing because a lot of people had said to me over the years they were going to do this for me and they were going to do that for me and I realize it wasn't anyone not meaning well but I understood the reality of the business. And I realized I didn't have any of those hopes anymore, that I'd had a child and I'd just gotten back into playing music because I didn't think I was ever going to do it. So I was in a strange place as far as music is concerned.

SG: *When you did meet Gram the first time were you impressed with him musically?*

E.H.: No, it's more I wasn't impressed and I wasn't unimpressed. Gram had not sung for a long time at that point and I didn't think that his voice...you've got to understand it was not just Gram either, it

The chemistry between Gram and Emmylou's duets is readily apparent in these two shots taken at a rehearsal at Phil Kauffman's house in Topanga, CA.

was me. Gram was the person who brought me to life musically. I never heard things in music, the things I can hear now until I worked with him, my collaboration with him. And so even though I had done some Country and Western I wasn't aware of what he had inside of him as an artist, what he possessed. Yet the first time we sang together our voices seemed to blend together pretty well even though I hadn't done a lot of that, dueting singing.

We ended up singing together. He ended up singing at Clyde's at my gig. It was a rainy Monday night and there were three people in the audience and I remember a waiter there who must have been a really big fan of Gram's because he took a piece of cardboard and wrote "Appearing Tonight, Gram Parsons" and stuck it in the window. Nobody saw it but I remember that.

SG: *Are you saying you were not aware of some of the country things as you are now?*

E.H.: No, not at all. I liked country music but not on a very deep level, I wasn't into it that much. It was like day and night, the time before and after I'd spent with Gram.'

SG: *When you did sing with him did you both work out the harmonies? Did Gram say do this, do this and do this? Was it spontaneous?*

E.H.: It was totally spontaneous. Sometimes he might suggest "why don't you go low on this line" but other than that...that was purely for the fine points. As far as sitting down he would sit down at the piano or with a guitar and start singing and I would sing with him and we would never polish it up formally. It became more polished just by singing. I mean there are things that we do on *GP* that we just rehearsed it a bit but basically we just did the things live and then went in and never worried about it. Something like, for example, "That's All It Took," he said at the very end "why don't you do low at the end line instead of going high. Let's go low," he said, "instead of doing like everybody else."

© 1973 KIM GOTTLIEB

N.D. Smart II in Mickey Mouse shirt and Kyle Tullis in background. GP and Emmylou rehearsing

It was things like that where he would suggest bits but for the most part we never worked anything out.

SG: *If you never worked anything out but you sang them through two or three times were they then sung the same way from that point on?*

E.H.: Yeah, we worked it out by just looking at each other and singing. Phrasing would come from honing down the things we did naturally.

SG: *That kind of tosses the next question out the window. I was going to ask if Gram based the duet singing, the George and Tammy stuff, on modern or Appalachian harmonies or what.*

E.H.: It was spontaneous you see but while it was in that style and in the spirit of that style I was not aware of it. I think perhaps what Gram did was turn my head around in subtle ways like he gave me this cassette one time. He said it was the original version of "We'll Sweep Out the Ashes in the Morning," We had already recorded the song so it wasn't like he was saying "I want you to have this ready," he said "why don't you listen to it".

On the cassette was Charlie and Ira Louvin. He knew I would listen to it and he knew I would be knocked out by Charlie and Ira Louvin but I had never heard of them before. Once I had heard them I became a great fan and I had to have everything they recorded.

SG: *Did you perceive it then as modern country harmonizing like the Jordanaires or the Appalachian type where one guy is almost nasal like bluegrass?*

E.H.: I don't think we had any perceptions of that at all. I think we wanted to sing together like George and Tammy sang together and it wasn't a thing like anything else. We simply wanted to sing together and we wanted the harmony, the level of harmony that I have now, that...I mean everything I do now is built around harmonies and I sing them and I don't think of them as this harmony requires you to do this and so forth. I think of them as melodies. It's

The Fallen Angels' class portrait: (l-r) Kyle Tullis, Emmylou Harris, Jon Corneal, N.D. Smart II , Gram Parsons and Phil Kaufman with dog

basically the song is not complete unless the harmony is there and if I leave the harmony out it's intimated in my mind.

SG: Right. You mean you hear it and it comes back?

E.H.: Even if you decide to leave it off it still...when I sing along and listen to it it's there. Sometimes it is just more effective if its a ghost.

SG: When you rehearsed with Gram for the GP tour was that a productive time for you musically speaking?

E.H.: Not really, it was pretty hectic. I think we worked on all his stuff but Gram knew so many songs we never finished anything. We realized after the very first show we didn't have beginnings or endings to end the songs. As far as arrangements go.

We must have gone over fifty songs but we didn't work out a single one. Everyone sat around and played and there was no structure and after that we decided we had better really rehearse so we went back to the hall and picked out about 12 songs and we decided on beginnings and endings and breaks. The next time we played completely blew the roof off the top of the Armadillo World Headquarters in Austin, Texas. In fact we had to go back and re-do a song for an encore because we had been called back so many times we didn't have anything left. So we started doing the show over again.

SG: There is a song called "If You Don't Love Him" you sang in that set and I don't know who did it.

E.H.: Oh, the Paul Siebel song. "If you don't love him" (Emmylou sings)

SG: That's the one.

E.H.: Paul Siebel.

SG: 'Cause I heard a tape of you guys doing it.

E.H.: It's amazing, I'd completely forgotten about doing that.

SG: Some guy sent me a whole tape of this show in the mail and either you or Gram introduce it. Did you or Gram ever get stage fright?

E.H: No.

SG: Really? You were that seasoned a pair of pertormers?

E.H.: I don't know about him. I wasn't in the sense that I had never worked with a band before. I had been performing for quite a few years as a solo artist and Gram was in groups of course. I don't know where Gram would have been coming from because all I know is we did a show and I'd come out and play guitar and sing harmony with him. But you see I had no stage fright because the show wasn't on my shoulders. All I had to do was sing harmony and play, I didn't have to say a word. It was incredibly wonderful, too, I had no idea, it just brought me to life, since I had never done anything like that before. I must say too how I thoroughly enjoyed being up there as a harmony singer.

SG: When you did record were the vocals and instrumental tracks usually first takes?

E.H.: On the albums? The music tracks?

SG: Both.

E.H.: On *GP*, I really don't know how many tracks there were of every song. Some songs went fast and others took a lot of time, like I had to spend a lot of time with "Brass Buttons." We also spent a lot of time on "She" and then songs like "That's All it Took" I remember we ran out of time and Ronnie Tutt kept saying "oh c'mon, one more take." We got it and we were like three minutes over or something. But it was a fast take.

And we sang along but usually Gram and I went back and live, did the vocals.

SG: You mean once the track was done?

E.H.: Once the track was done we sang along with the track.

SG: Erasing the original?

E.H.: No, we sang along as it was being recorded and then in some cases we went back and overdubbed but we still did the vocals live. As far as the two of us singing together at the same time is concerned. Then on some things on *GP* I was having to sing harmony with Gram, like on "A Song for You", and of course I couldn't follow him too well at that point as his voice did all these little things. I had the lyrics written out and I had these little lines written out over them moving up or down so I'd understand when to go high or low a little better. Somehow I understood what I was supposed to do as far as phrasing went. It's hard to explain. So I did some harmonies like that. Some of the things like "We'll Sweep Out the Ashes" and "That's All It Took" were not hard to me.

The official Fallen Angels touring bus, left to right, Neil Flanz, Kyle Tullis, N.D. Smart II , Gram Parsons, Emmylou Harris and Gerry Mule.

Then on *Grievous Angel* sometimes we would overdub the vocals but always together. Most of those songs were written on the bus and sung in the back of the bus and we had sung them so many times we knew exactly what we were doing. And some of these are the live vocals.

*SG: Are you familiar with say, "Apple Tree", the Gram Parsons song Johnny Rivers recorded on his **Slim Slo Slider** lp in 1971?*

E.H.: No, I'm not familiar with it. I'll have to hear it. I'll have to find it.

SG: Did you ever have serious musical differences of opinion with Gram?

E.H.: No, he was always in charge. I don't think we had any disagreements at all about anything He was...the only thing we had disagreements about was I was upset when we did "The Angels Rejoiced in Heaven Last Night." That was all live. I was assuming and hoping it was going on *Grievous Angel* and one of the last conversations I had with Gram was when he called me and said he wasn't going to put it on the album, that it would go on his next album.

And I said "oh no, that's my favorite", or something like that, I can't remember exactly. And he said "it'll go on the next one, there are enough songs about angels on this one." It was just little things like that. I don't know, our musical partnership was a good one. Perhaps if we had stayed together longer we'd have had our problems but I pretty much trusted his taste and his knowledge about what he was doing. Also I was the novice in the sense he was the one who brought me into this and turned me onto a whole different world of music and he

JIM McGUIRE

Emmylou Harris

brought out whatever music was in me. He was the one who drew it out. So even though it was an equal partnership and I never felt I was an underling or something...because what I think I did for Gram is he was inspired by singing with me. He enjoyed it and he loved singing with me. We were a natural duet.

I think he got a great deal of joy from that and I, in turn, got a great deal of joy from knowing that and feeling responsible for it in some way.

SG: *You are credited as the co-author of "In My Hour of Darkness"?*

E.H.: You know Gram and I would sit down and when he would have difficulty with his song I think he had difficulty with his songs only in the sense that he needed somebody for the input so he could finish them. And I feel that the only thing I really contributed to the song is when I would sit down and sing it with him with the melody. He was the one who said after the song was finished "I'm giving you half the credit on this song." I never said anything and I always felt a little small scale myself. I realize how much effort it takes to write a song and I felt my contribution was not great enough to merit a songwriting credit on it. But he was very adamant about it.

I mean I would just do things like on "Las Vegas" where he had a line about "spend all day in this funky old hotel" and I said "why don't you say 'spend all day in this Holiday Inn' because that's the reality of the situation. If it was it would be all right but unfortunately it's a Holiday Inn." Things like that were about as big a contribution as I would make to a song in all honesty.

SG: *GP is credited to Gram Parsons but on Grevious Angel you moved up in the world as it is credited to Gram Parsons with Emmylou Harris.*

E.H.: That was also him, he was very insistent that it be on there. I think he felt the album was a culmination of the months we'd spent together.

SG: *Were any of the Fallen Angels shows recorded?*

E.H.: Yeah. We did a show for a radio station that was a live show with an audience, a live show with an audience in a recording studio wasn't it?

Ed Tickner: Yeah.

E.H.: It was WLIR in Long Island. There's talk it will be put out as an album but

©1973, Kim Gottlieb

Topanga rehearsal, 1973

the only way I'll let it be put out is if N.D. Smart's name is as big as mine on the credits. It should be a Gram Parsons album, not a Emmylou Harris with Gram Parsons album.

SG: *When I hear "Faraway Eyes" by the Rolling Stones I hear a lot of "Hippie Boy" by the Flying Burrito Brothers, not in the sense it is a rip-off but thematically they are quite similar. It is an obvious Gram Parsons type number. Are there any other artists on the scene today who you see some of the Gram Parsons influence in?*

E.H.: No. That's one of the obvious examples. I agree with you, that song sounds to me like Gram wrote it. I'm hardly saying he did write it but the style is so much there it is a real Gram feel to it.

I have a real general feel about all this, that Gram started it all and that all of us out here doing country material or

DOUG HANNERS

ne Fallen Angels at full tilt, live at Liberty Hall, Houston TX, Feb. 1973, left to right Jock Bartley, Gram, N.D. Smart, Emmylou and Kyle Tullis

country-oriented material are a direct result of some kind of association with Gram or some indirect influence of his music.

SG:*Of all the work he did, not just the work you did with him, which songs are your favorites?*

E.H.: I don't think of it that way. I really don't know how to answer that because I can't.

SG:*Did you ever hear the story of "Radio Sweetheart" by Elvis Costello?*

E.H.: "Radio Sweetheart". No...I listen to KLAC, I'm sorry! (laughter)

SG:*Well, so do I. But to tell you about it in case you get curious, Costello put it out on a little EP with his first English album. Just on the first several thousand copies. The significant thing is it is like "Stranger in the House" or the Eagles' "Lyin' Eyes" in that it is a real GP type number. I mean his influence extends to the English New Wave!*

E.H.: No but I'd love to hear it. If you've got it can you get it to me?

SG:*Yeah but it will be a cassette with hiss on it.*

E.H.: That's okay.

SG:*I mentioned it because of what you said about "all of us out here playing country music" since Elvis Costello is hardly "one of us".*

E.H.: I meant in the cosmos (laughter).

SG:*Oh! I see. I thought you meant the country-rock snowball.*

E.H.: No, no, no, no. I meant the left-field of county music as far as those of us go who didn't come out of Nashville. Actually his influence is really strong in England. In Europe he is much, much bigger than he is over here. You know how big Gram is over here, people throw his name around but they don't know his music, but over in Europe...the whole reason I got so popular in Europe is because I sang with him.

SG:*Really?*

E.H.: Yes, I started out as the 11th most popular female vocalist in Holland before I had ever cut a record. Before I had ever cut a record, a solo record. That's how big he is in Holland.

SG:*Why does the music of people like you and Gram Parsons seem more traditionally country, whether it really is or not, than the stuff coming out of Nashville at the same time?*

E.H.: I don't know how to answer that. I guess I don't have an overview of country music and what's going on in it. Perhaps Nashville music became a little self-conscious of what it was and tried to change into something else. It's real hard to say.

Listen to a country music station today and when I try to find it when I go into a new town it is not real obvious to me, I have to wait for a few songs before I know whether I have the country music station or not. Unless in Santa Cruz and I'm listening to KFAT, which is one of the best stations and one of the key stations that plays Gram.

SG:*How were you affected by all this? What made Gram Parsons so special to you? Where was his magic?*

E.H.: As an artist?

SG:*Yes.*

E.H.: First of all, for me, there is his voice. There is a quality in his voice that was just so, so special and if he had just been a singer I think he would have been special to certain people but now some people hear Gram singing and they are affected in such a way that...well, that feeling they get is really what singing is all about. After all if you are touched by someone, and I know that happened to me....

I had been singing with Gram for awhile and one night we were listening back to a tape of the show and for the first time I was really able to step back and listen to Gram's voice and I was amazed that I had spent all this time with him and never really heard him. Never *really* heard him. From then on his voice had a truly deep affect on me. I also think he had a way of incorporating culture into his songs. Country has always been a traditional, cut-and-dried form and he was always injecting incredible poetic images that were so down to earth. It's like taking Hank Williams' stuff forward. I mean Hank Williams is wonderful but at the same time things progress. We have consciousness of new things. Some things are the same, some things are always basically

DOUG HANNERS

Liberty Hall gig, 1973

true and Gram was able to keep both parts in his songs. So I can only really describe why he affected me from a personal point of view. I don't know why he affected other people so. On one hand I don't understand why people respond like they do and on the other I don't know how they can't respond and why he remains unknown in the musical community except to me and other artists that knew Gram. but basically the public is not aware of his music.

SG: *Did the traditional country artists like Johnny Cash and George Jones know of Gram Parsons?*

E.H.: They probably know.

SG: *But did they recognize him when you were all Fallen Angels?*

E.H.: Probably not but that's understandable. If Gram had lived I think this fusion would have eventually taken place.

Marley Brant, above and John Delgatto, below right

HEATHER HARRIS

California Cottonfields: John Delgatto and Marley Brant

John Delgatto and Marley Brant were the main forces behind the release of the *Gram Parsons and the Fallen Angels — Live* 1973 album which came out in 1982 to great applause of Gram Parsons followers everywhere. Both knew the Grievous Angel and both logged in some pretty long hours to make certain Gram's final musical contribution would be one of his finest. They should be congratulated on a job well done. "Love Hurts," a track from the LP won a Grammy nomination for Gram and Emmylou Harris as "Best Country Vocal By A Duo/Group."
Though the interview covered many subjects including the trials and tribulations of getting the record out, I have limited the comments here to Gram and his music. Naturally when three GP fans get together there are all sorts of digressions from the norm so here is the most imporant part of Gram discussed that evening in West Los Angeles: his music.

GP with Phil Kaufman and Eddie Tickner at a record company picnic, June, 1973

SG: John, my first question is to you. We've talked about Gram's live LP doing well so can you tell us if there is going to be any more GP stuff coming out anytime soon?
JD: There may, but unfortunately it is either poor quality cassettes or it is poor performances like any group gives sometimes. I mean either the tapes aren't good enough sound or the playing isn't quite there. The only thing that could probably be of any interest is perhaps some live Burritos material but there you are talking about some problems because A&M would have the rights to it and trying to get the okay from the other members of the Flying Burrito Bros. would be difficult. But again we are talking about songs they recorded on record done live and I'm talking about a show done in San Francisco at the Avalon Ballroom which isn't a great quality tape.
SG: Yeah, that's not such a great show, they sound kind of blase.

John Lomax III

GP backstage

JD: Since there isn't that much Gram Parsons material that's kind of unfortunate.
SG: Nuese and Peter Fonda both said there were International Submarine Band shows recorded.
JD: John Nuese was interviewed by us for two hours and he said there were tapes done at Gold Star and those tapes were in the possession of Gram and Brandon deWilde. When Brandon died his girlfriend took the tapes and she was living with some guy and he split on her and took the tapes and they're gone. They could be destroyed or they could be anywhere.
SG: What about the tapes Gram cut with Terry Melcher in 1971? Paul Surratt was there at the sessions.
JD: They did about four or five songs and either Melcher kept them or Gram did. What I've heard from people involved with that is they weren't that good, they were more or less demos to see how things sounded. And then there's the alleged tapes with Keith Richards which have never been verified and I've got the feeling they are just party tapes. You know, "let's get together and sing a couple of songs and turn the machine on."
MB: There's a lot of stuff in a lot of places. Who's to know, really, what will ever surface? You really can't say as to what might surface.
JD: I'm trying to find video, visuals, film, anything and that's even harder. There is the thirty seconds of Gram in *The Trip* and the brief clip from Gimme Shelter and we talked to the Maysles about their film.
SG: What'd they say?
JD: They said "What you see in the film is all we had. We didn't shoot that much. Just that little bit you see is all we did." They also said the strangest thing was they talked to Gram about doing a film on him right after that. They said they were really into Gram and his music.

I talked to them on the phone and Paul Surratt went and visited them in person. The Maysles said they used everything in the film, there were no outtakes, they said they just weren't thinking that day or something. One of the brothers said he wished they did have it. But all they have is what you see in the film. They said, "hey, wish we did have something on him, it'd be great to have something on the Burritos but we simply do not".

Yeah, they were going to do a short music film on Gram but they said they got involved inother stuff and never did much about it.

It would be great to put together a video thing on Gram but the legal hassles are enormous. Everyone on the set, whether on camera or not, they would all have to be repaid. You're talking big bucks and all that. But who knows, perhaps one day. I have this vision of putting together the *real* heroes of rock n'roll, people who may not have been known mass media-wise but who influenced so many others like the Everly Brothers, the Kentucky Colonels, Gram and the Burritos, groups who had influences which went on and on.
SG: I suppose the great fear is someone putting out an inferior performance because the artist has a big name.
JD: I always worry about that one. I certainly have heard a lot of Burritos things but the quality is just not there one way or another.

MB: You know this live album is a Gram Parsons record, it had his involvement and really always did.
SG: You'd better explain that one.
MB: Gram called me one night after it was recorded and said this would make one hell of a live album and how he would like to put something like it out. Years later this inspired me to get in touch with John when I heard he had a copy of the tape and was going to do something with it. I had two copies of the tape, a bootleg and one that I think was Gram's.
JD: Someone told me the boot was aired in Holland on the radio, Gram being a huge star over there.
MB: Gram was excited by it. He felt so positive about it. He felt his records were fine but they were *studio* recordings. He wanted something out which showed how he related to his audience,that his studio albums were stilted in some way. Gram was really excited about the fact he could possibly put a live album out. One that would really show how he felt about relating to a live audience.
JD: Compared to the other Fallen Angels tapes this is another world, real tight and playing like they truly meant it. Another good point about the album. I've often thought *Grievous Angel's* two live tracks were a reflection of Gram's enjoyment of the tour and the WLIR show in particular.
MB: But to put the WLIR tape out after GP when it was almost the same thing...So Gram merely held onto it for the future, possibly some type of retrospective album.
JD: I consantly get letters from people saying "well, Gram did those two live tracks on *Grievous Angel* so there's got to be more," I always try to explain it was live in the studio but you know how it is. They did a good job getting an artificial live show though, you have to give them credit.
MB: I think the live album is as much Gram's as if he was here working on it all along.

That's another thing, he had a lot on his mind about what he wanted to do, where he wanted to go with his music and I think these ideas would have surprised alot of people. It's all been kind of glossed over, in light of people wanting to repeat all these stories you hear about his personal life.

JOHN LOMAX III

Backstage with Rocky Hill

JD: Yeah, I'd personally like to hear more about his relationship with Clarence (White) and some of their musical ideas and some of the things they were going to do. Some of the concepts they wanted to do musically were unbelievable.
MB: They would have been! They had that goal set out for them...you read these things about *Grievous Angel*, about how the sessions were so tough. You read about how the guy had floated away for two years and was now getting back to work. But, he had so many things going for him then. He wanted to do a straight gospel album, not country but straight gospel with a Louvin Bros. kind of feel, Carter family stuff. He wanted to do an album of Everly Bros. songs 'cause he loved them so much. He wanted to do an LP with John Phillips and bring in some of the people who were instrumental when he was forming his ideas.
JD: Like you have all these people thinking the Shilos were Kingston Trio influenced and in reality it was much, much more a Journeyman influence. Which is John Phillips, Scott MacKenzie and Dick Weissman. They were very good friends with Paul Surratt and Gram.

Steve Weitzman

Clarence White at the Philadelphia Country Rock Festival with Gene Parsons and Gram (not in pic) mentioned in text at right, June, 1973

MB: We should talk about Clarence some more because those two were working together and forming some ideas which kind of died with them. That's rather myopic of me I guess but their ideas of these two country rednecks playing this rock n'roll music was sort of... they both realized they wanted to go in so many directions. Combining country with rock, and rock with gospel and getting this potpourri of music to lay out on the public.
JD: Yes, they seemed to have this urgency to get all this done. Do it all at one time, playing with all these different people, trying to get it all in like they had so much to do. Clarence even told some people he knew he wasn't going to make thirty. You'd always have to say "stop talking like that, Clarence, that's silly."

Yet he wanted to get involved with all these different projects. Okay, he was not a songwriter per se but he knew Gram was so he figured he could learn that side of music by working around Gram Parsons. They were seeing things eye-to-eye, no rubbish about Mr. Mystique or the great guitar player hanging out together. They'd gone through their turmoil on that.

It happened at a concert in Philadelphia, the very last time they played together, that anyone saw them live. It was this country-rock festival, two shows the first weekend in June of 1973. One in Annapolis, Maryland, and the other in Philadelphia. It was Gram, Emmylou, the Country Gazette and Clarence White. The Country Gazette would come on and do bluegrass and then they'd go off and on would come Gram Parsons and then Clarence White would do his thing.

One set was Clarence, Gram, Gene Parsons on drums, Sneeky Pete on pedal steel, Chris Ethridge on bass and Emmylou singing harmonies. This is probably the band that would tour in the fall. Gene told me the story that Gram was doing his Mick Jagger stance with Clarence on stage, kinda showing off and Clarence is merely standing there being the studio professional onstage at a gig picking away. After they came backstage Clarence picked Gram up by the collar and read him the riot act, telling him never to do that upstaging stuff again. Telling Gram "we're all onstage together," that type of thing. People expected a fight but no. Clarence was probably the first person to really talk to Gram no nonsense in a long time and Gram just looked at him and was completely brought back to earth. He needed that, to see someone actually cared about something around him. And this was the birth of a great rapport between the two of them.

Weeks later Clarence was sitting in a rocking chair on a porch somewhere and, to finish the story, apparently Gram came up from behind him and tipped him over onto the lawn. But they were laughing about that too.
SC: What's the dedication about on the live LP, John?
JD: Lots of people ask me this and I've told the story a lot but here goes. At Clarence's funeral it just seemed a whole bunch of us died too, we knew the rush of music from January of 1973 to his death was now over and it was such an incredibly sad thing to lose this man, just the bluest. It was a Catholic ceremony and the priest did not know the White family very well and it was the most staid

DOUG HANNERS

Liberty Hall, Houston TX 1973

situation you can imagine. Everybody's there, Kristofferson, Rita Coolidge, The Byrds, all these music people. Clarence had the knack of being a brother to everybody.

So here's the ceremony, a hot day, lots of flowers, so forth. And all his plans are out the window. Everybody's standing there and the ceremony ends. Now what do we do? Do you say "nice seeing you" and split? Because we all still felt terribly empty after the official ceremony was ended. Gram starts singing "Farther Along". No one else would have the guts to do that but him. Starts singing "Farther Along" acappella. Bernie Leadon is standing next to him and he starts singing too. I'm standing in the back with the Country Gazette. Remember Clarence recorded the song with the Byrds and Gram cut it with the Burritos. We all knew the song.

We all started singing it and within the one verse everyone there was singing "Farther Along". I can't tell you what it was like. It lifted this incredible despair we were all in, relieved the tension to a certain extent. You wanted to scream or something. And that day I said to myself if there was ever anything I could do for Gram I would. Which is the story of the dedication on the album jacket. The record's a small way of me paying Gram Parsons back for his feeling that day.

There was definitely another side to Gram and he showed it that day. It took something like the funeral for me to realize the feeling the guy had. Nobody else would ever have done that either, the singing.

SG: What did you think of the "Return of the Grievous Angel" single re-release by Warner Bros.?

JD: It really got to me. No remix at all as was the word. A totally different, and I might add here inferior take where Emmylou is singing offkey.

SG: Yeah, the fiddle/guitar solo is a lousy splice, it broke meter!

MB: To go back to Gram's definition of Cosmic American Music; nothing ended with Gram's death, musically speaking. Cosmic American Music wasn't merely what Gram recorded up to that point, it's everything he and people like Clarence did and influenced right up to the present day. All these musics interbreeding. Some people will like this aspect of it and some folks will like this part of it but the general idea of what was evolved is certainly not unlike what Gram had hoped for.

To me, an important part of remembering Gram is knowing he is alive in music since his music and his influence lives on. He was a wonderful, gifted person.

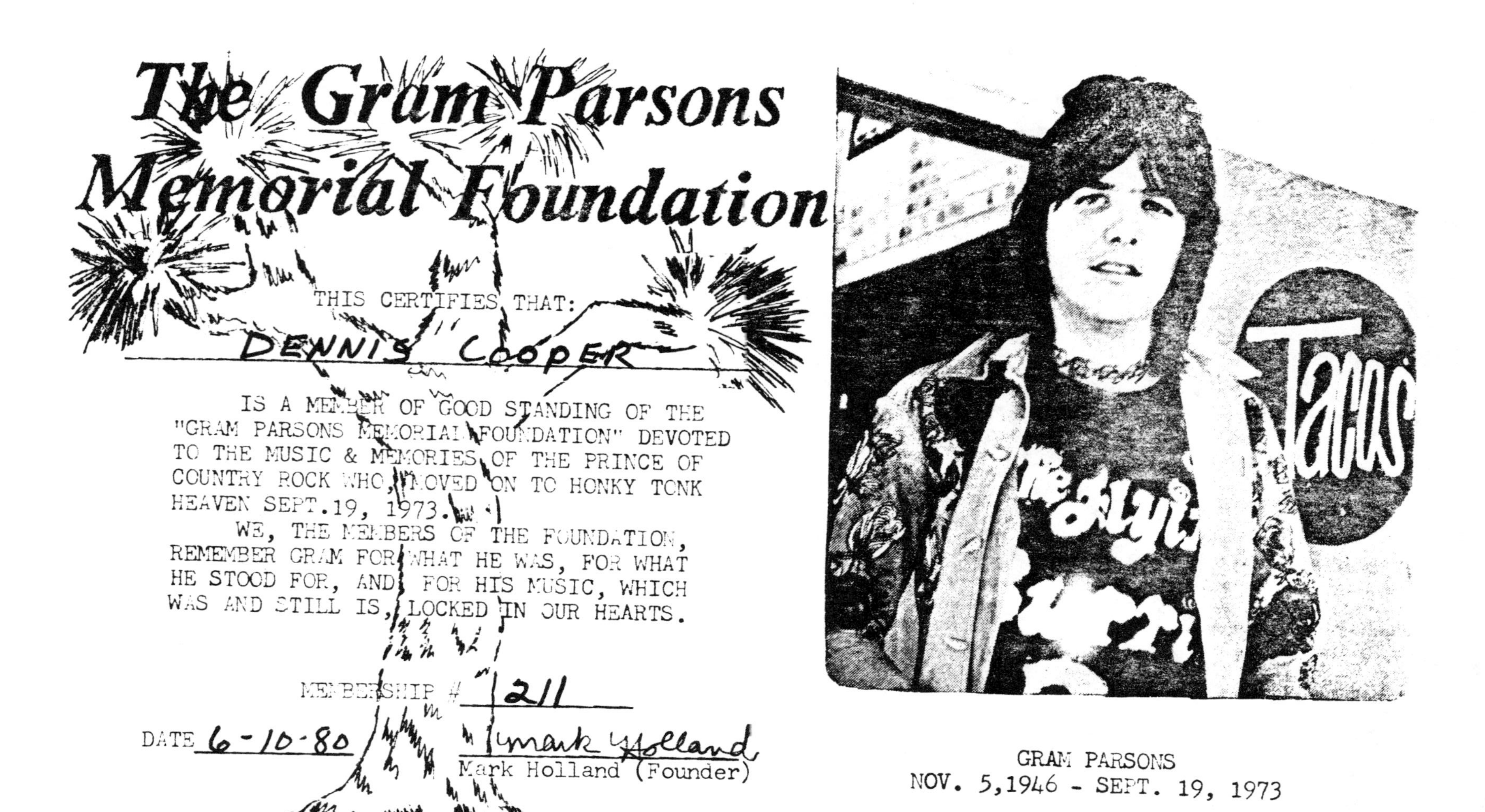

The Gram Parsons
Memorial Foundation

THIS CERTIFIES THAT:

DENNIS COOPER

IS A MEMBER OF GOOD STANDING OF THE "GRAM PARSONS MEMORIAL FOUNDATION" DEVOTED TO THE MUSIC & MEMORIES OF THE PRINCE OF COUNTRY ROCK WHO MOVED ON TO HONKY TONK HEAVEN SEPT.19, 1973.

WE, THE MEMBERS OF THE FOUNDATION, REMEMBER GRAM FOR WHAT HE WAS, FOR WHAT HE STOOD FOR, AND FOR HIS MUSIC, WHICH WAS AND STILL IS, LOCKED IN OUR HEARTS.

MEMBERSHIP # 211

DATE 6-10-80

Mark Holland
Mark Holland (Founder)

GRAM PARSONS
NOV. 5,1946 - SEPT. 19, 1973

Honorary Member

A Yankee Looks At Gram Parsons: Dennis Cooper

Unlike my fellow editor, nothing in my upbringing or place of residence or early musical education would naturally have caused me to love Gram Parsons' art. I was born, raised and remain within Los Angeles County limits. When *Sweetheart of the Rodeo* came out in the late Sixties I considered it the downfall of the Byrds. I blamed this mysterious Gram Parsons character I was reading so much about for the switch to Country, a music which, to my ears, should have stayed down South and on the one or two sorespots across my AM radio dial. I had been intrigued by the Byrds' turn toward electronics and textural experimentation. I hadn't noticed the C&W influence lurking beneath. At the time I wanted music which seemed profound, spacey, chancey, lengthy, played by bands I now wouldn't own up to having worshipped. The Country element Parsons was infecting the Rock World with sounded like one big step backwards.

I paid more attention when the hip artists and intellectuals began to, but my headphones were still plugged into Pink Floyd, King Crimson, Yes and other units my cronies and I figured were leading Rock up the primrose path to modern Beethovenism. I liked the Burritos' "Wild Horses" when it came out as a single, before I knew it was written by the Rolling Stones, a band which remained hip no matter the twist or turn. I liked it enough to stay after–hours at my high school to see the Flying Burrito Brothers play in a special assembly. I wasn't exactly knocked over, but I did begin to realize they had *something*. My chief impression of the band was of Gram Parsons, the guy up front dressed in black and transcendentally cool, no matter the lyric. The students around me went crazy; I nodded along. So began my interest in the music of Gram Parsons.

It wasn't hip in my circles to admit to a liking of "shit-kicking" music and, to tell the truth, it was mere admiration I felt for Parsons at that point, as opposed to the rapture I directed toward Quatermass, Atomic Rooster and the other then–and–now obscure British progressive bands that seemed, on drugs, like gods descended from on high. But gradually my circles

©1973, KIM GOTTLIEB

GP rapping with literary figure, Cameron Crowe ("Fast Times At Ridgemont High") at left

widened, my tastes changed. Tired of dope, clearing my head, the music I'd knelt down before began to seem fatuous and the stripped–down intellectual snarl of the New York Dolls a perfect antidote. I spent long hours forcing Johansen's words of wisdom down the throats of friends while they slipped Parsons and his ilk in the air around me whenever possible. Eventually, we both gave in. Unfortunately, it took Parsons' death and the surrounding brou-ha-ha to bring me completely to my senses. By the time *Grievous Angel* appeared eight months later I was ready and wowed. Parsons became and remains important to my life.

People like me have difficulty accepting Country Rock as valid and important when its pale afterbirths, groups like Poco, Pure Prairie League and the Eagles, so clogged the airwaves during the formative period in our discovery of Rock music. Like any relative impurity in any form, Country Rock can irreversably and easily be poisoned for the skeptical with an incorrect introduction. For many the term Country implies mawkishness disguised as mega–emotion as opposed to the powerful respect the word Rock commands. The lucky among us remain open–minded enough to sense and understand the purity and brilliance Parsons had in mind when he merged the two over ten years ago. Hearing his music, more than hearing work by the best of his students (mid–period Dylan, Prine, Byrds, etc.), opens the door to a style of music well worth exploration. Granted, there is only one Gram Parsons. So, sudden converts to Country Rock via Parsons who return to the Eagles' records they'd previously dismissed will probably not find new riches there. Very few artists have done top notch work in the form, as broad and developed as it has become. No one has been able to take it any further than Parsons did over his brief six disc exploration of it.

My interest in Gram Parsons has not led me to a deep interest in the form he developed. He is valuable to me for his artistry, in the same way he would have been had he decided to pursue his early inclination towards prose writing, whether he'd been a painter, a jazz musician or reveler in the pop formula from whence Billy Joel slunk. What is important to me is his skill at songwriting, at evoking emotion, his formal sense of popular music, his bold steps, his intelligently chosen lyrics and the calculation involved in his attempts at his hitting the masses' hearts. I'm fascinated by the improvements from an early version of his classic song "Hickory Wind", where he sings the words in a straightforward and heart–felt manner, to the final version on *Grievous Angel* where he lets his voice break at the conclusion of each line, causing a deeper, sadder impression than one could have previously imagined. Like any great singer, Parsons obviously thought out this new trick–of–voice in order to leave the impression of spontaneity. People tend to mistake calculation with a lack of sincerity, but here and elsewhere, as an artist, he toys with his instruments in order to find the clearest mode of expression. When he sang the song he felt the content, applied it to a form and what resulted is a best of both worlds. So the brilliance in Parsons' artistic decisions is in no way a disclaimer to the feeling in his art.

If one has an inborn appreciation of the skill involved in creating a classic song, it is easy to appreciate what Parsons has done. He was both the innovator and perfectionist of an art form, a dual accomplishment more common in popular music than in other areas of creativity. A lack of real expression in much of today's art has swung attention to and created an obsession for style, rather than the emotive qualities highly valued in other periods. This trend in popular music has existed with slight variations since The Beatles began their reign over the airwaves in the early Sixties. In their music, taking a cue from the more staid music of Broadway and moviedom, they sublimated emotion in deference to style and, in what once may have seemed a convoluted method but now is common, used the songs' form (repetition, restricted melody, bridge, instrumental texture) to flesh out the emotions (mainly love and loss) which their lyrics merely hinted at, relegated to meter and rhyme. Pop music has tried in vain to broaden that central idea ever since, always returning to that basic to begin again, like some runner who keeps overshooting the start of a race. In 1976 rock again returned, through New Wave and Punk music. The few tentative steps since are promising but we must keep in mind the doomed nature of previous forays.

Parsons has set the tone for Country Rock. He took it far enough in so many directions that, like The Beatles, his work may never be overshadowed. Since the Country and Western form is so tied to (some say mired in) the emotions, his work is touching even at its driest and most shallow. In the form he traverses, a little corniness and sentimentality are acceptable and appreciated. While Parsons rarely drifted very far in those directions, he did utilize the nostalgic and volatile to create an affecting emotional pastiche, inserting it here and there for effect, in places where he clearly understood what it would do for his songs, to his listeners. Not that Parsons wasn't a man full of deep and romantic feelings, it's just that he was also a highly intelligent man. He kept a close watch on that heart of his, as John Cale says. Parsons' unhappiness in his life was refined in his art. We may only feel the tip of the iceberg but that edge is ominous and the force behind it clear, overpowering and often frightening.

Unlike my fellow editor, I am not from where Gram was. I haven't even come close to flirting with the Christian Life and the piousness in Gram's vision is interesting to exactly and only because of its formality. Parsons' feeling of true purity coupled with a fascination with the impure is a major and immense theme not only in his music but across all art. If I had met Gram Parsons I wouldn't have wanted to shoot the shit with him, get loaded, talk the South up or down. I'd be interested in his art, how he applied himself to it, what he considered its successes and failures. In this I am a hopeless, relentless aesthete and certainly not pure in any sense that he would believe. From the few interviews done with Gram in his life, it is clear he was a mixture of both the aesthete and the honest, full–hearted man he portrayed so often across his recorded work. For this reason he is vastly important, and for that reason two people as different as Sid and myself can both have a deep love of him, his music and his achievements.

–Dennis Cooper

1973

Gram Parsons and The New Wave: Dennis Cooper

When Gram Parsons died his effect had already been deeply felt. Country–rock was a popular form, encompassing a massive amount of radio time. Never the commercial steamroller Disco had become in the late–Seventies, it nevertheless cut the course for popular music during its multi–year reign of the airwaves in the early-Seventies. In effect, all Country Rock music and its derivatives are influenced by Parsons' vision, though some of its practitioners may never have spun the albums Parsons appeared on, having learned the ropes from Poco, the Eagles and the rest of Parsons' immediate successors. It would be pointless and endless to list that multitude here.

What is probably surprising to some of you, and surely would have been to Parsons, is the admiration in the New Wave for his songs. Elvis Costello, to cite the most obvious case, has filled his interviews with praise for the Fallen Angel. Costello's songs contain a reliance on subtle irony similar to Parsons', and their construction shows the effect of many types of popular music, as did Parsons'. More clearly, in the few country songs he has written – "Stranger in the House", "Radio Sweetheart" and a couple more – he clearly imitates the Gram Parsons style. That they are fine songs is a tribute to Costello's taste more than anything else. Moreover, Costello has promised more Country ventures in the future, including an album recorded with C&W great George Jones, one of Parsons' greatest heroes.

Another New Waver, Tom Petty has named *Grievous Angel* as his favorite record. Petty hasn't come close to attempting anything in the Country vein thus far, but don't be surprised if, an album or two from now, he's stuck his nose in that area. Petty's lyrical bent, conveyed in a manner similar to Parsons', is the only clearly discernable effect GP has had on Petty's music, but the taut–yet–lanky form his hooks take is quite possibly derived from Parsons' sense of structure. But all this is speculation. The point is that Petty points to Parsons as a favorite and influence. The details are his to delineate.

Strange as it may seem, Parsons and the New Wave could have been friendly for a number of reasons. While obviously a form which has progressed far enough to include both Keith Richards and Pink Floyd among its forefathers can't be summed up under one moniker, it seems the music shares two qualities, at least, in common: honesty and a cautiously ambitious stance. Even the New Wave bands which work with pretension seem to do so to effect a simultaneous anti–pretension. From the extraordinarily clear music Johnny Rotten has created (in his Sex Pistols and Public Image bands) to the pure but synthesized sounds emitting from Wire, XTC and Human League to the Let's–put–our–cards–on–the–table fatalism of Talking Heads and Cars, there is a broadbased overwhelming of the pretensious pseudo–progressive sound rampant in the mid–decade, music Parsons hated and fought against while he was alive.

Recently, The Clash's promoting of the music of Joe Ely (the contemporary equivalent of Gram Parsons) has brought a new degree of respect to the Country form in general among at least one faction of the spike heads. More often than not Parsons and Merle Haggard are showing up on the lists of idols made up by the front line of important rock artists today. Expect a Country Rock revival in the Eighties, this time with intelligence aside its relaxation and high spirits. The bands that soiled the waters of Country with the same lackadasical drug–headedness that had raised havoc with Rock in recent times are yesterday's news. The time is right for exploration of that fusion again. Only then will we learn whether it is a true enough art form to grow beyond Parsons' grasp and whether Parsons had his eyes on the musical horizon or beyond, and how far we should follow his lead, or whether we should remain planted at GP's feet in admiration, giving up the Country Rock ghost ourselves.

–Dennis Cooper

Gram Parsons As Artist: A Selected Discography

Gram Parsons appeared as a singer and musician on the following albums. Only a few singles are mentioned since the rest of the singles containing GP work are simply cuts available on albums.

This discography does not include recordings that are re-releases on singles or albums whether they were the identical tracks, re-mixes or alternate takes.

THE INTERNATIONAL SUBMARINE BAND

Gram Parsons–vocal, guitar, piano
John Nuese–vocal, lead guitar
Ian Dunlop–vocal, bass, saxophone
Mickey Gauvin–drums

Singles: *SUM UP BROKE* (Parsons-Nuese)
ONE DAY WEEK (Parsons)
Columbia/CBS 4-43935

THE RUSSIANS ARE COMING (J. Mande)
TRUCK DRIVING MAN (Terry Fell)
Ascot 2218

Album: *THE RUSSIANS ARE COMING, THE RUSSIANS ARE COMING*
Soundtrack Album
United Artists UAL 4142 Released 1966

THE INTERNATIONAL SUBMARINE BAND

Gram Parsons–vocal, guitar
John Nuese–vocal, lead guitar
Jon Corneal–vocal, drums
Bob Buchanan–vocal, guitar
J.D. Maness–pedal steel
Earl (Les) Ball–piano
Chris Ethridge–bass

Album: *SAFE AT HOME* LHI-12001 (mono)

LHI-S-12001 (stereo)

LHI RECORDS–Recorded December 1967

Recorded December 1967

THE BYRDS

Roger McGuinn–vocal, guitar, banjo
Chris Hillman–vocal, bass, mandolin
Gram Parsons–vocal, guitar
Kevin Kelley–drums
Earl P. Ball–piano
Jon Corneal–drums
Lloyd Green–pedal steel
J.D. Maness–pedal steel
John Hartford–banjo, fiddle, guitar
Roy (Junior) Huskey–bass
Clarence White–guitar

Album: *SWEETHEART OF THE RODEO*

Columbia/CBS CS 9670

Released August 20, 1968

THE FLYING BURRITO BROTHERS

Album: *GILDED PALACE OF SIN*

A & M SP 4175

Released Feburary 1969

Gram Parsons–vocal, guitar, piano
Chris Hillman–vocal, guitar, mandolin
Sneeky Pete Kleinow–pedal steel
Chris Ethridge–bass, piano
Jon Corneal–drums
Eddie Hoh–drums
Popeye Philips–drums

THE FLYING BURRITO BROTHERS

Album: *BURRITO DELUXE*

A&M SP 4258

Released May 1970

Gram Parsons–vocal, guitar, piano
Chris Hillman-vocal, bass, mandolin
Sneeky Pete Kleinow–pedal steel
Bernie Leadon–guitar, dobro
Michael Clarke-drums

GRAM PARSONS

Album: *GP*

Reprise/Warner Bros. MS 2123
Released February 1973

Gram Parsons: vocals
John Conrad: bass
Ronnie Tutt: drums
John Guerin: drums
Sam Goldstein: drums
Glen D. Hardin: piano, organ
James Burton: guitar, dobro
Barry Tashian: guitar, vocals
Al Perkins: steel guitar
Buddy Emmons: steel guitar
Byron Berline: fiddle
Alan Munde: banjo
Hal Battiste: baritone sax
Emmylou Harris: vocals
Ron Hicklin: background vocals
Tom Bahler: background vocals "Kiss the Children"
Mitch Gordon: background vocals
Lewis Morford: background vocals

GRAM PARSONS

Album *GRIEVOUS ANGEL*

Reprise/Warner Bros. MS 2171

Released January 1974

Gram Parsons: vocals
Emmylou Harris: vocals (all songs except "Brass Buttons")
Glen D. Hardin: piano, electric piano
Emory Gordy: bass
Ronnie Tutt: drums
N.D. Smart II : drums ("Hearts on Fire" and "In My Hour of Darkness")
Herb Pedersen: acoustic rhythm guitar, electric rhythm guitar ("I Can't Dance")
Bernie Leadon: acoustic rhythm guitar ("Return of the Grievous Angel"), electric lead guitar ("Hearts on Fire"), dobro ("In My Hour of Darkness")
James Burton: electric lead guitar
Al Perkins: pedal steel guitar
Byron Berline: fiddle ("Return of the Grievous Angel," "In My Hour of Darkness" and medley "Cash on the Barrelhead/Hickory Wind") mandolin (medley "Cash on the Barrlehead/ Hickory Wind")
Linda Ronstadt: vocal ("In My Hour of Darkness")

THE FLYING BURRITO BROTHERS	Album: *CLOSE UP THE HONKY TONKS*
(contains previously unreleased recordings)	A & M SP 3631
	Released July 1974
THE FLYING BURRITO BROTHERS	Album: *HONKY TONK HEAVEN*
(contains previously unreleased recordings)	Ariola 87-585 XDT (Dutch release only)
	Released 1974
THE FLYING BURRITO BROTHERS	Album: *SLEEPLESS NIGHTS*
(contains previously unreleased recordings)	A & M SP 3190
	Released May 1976
GRAM PARSONS & THE SHILOS	Album: *THE EARLY YEARS 1963-65*
Gram Parsons–vocal, guitar Paul Surratt–vocal, banjo Joe Kelly– vocal, bass George Wrigley–vocal, guitar	Sierra/Briar SRS 8702
	Released Februrary 1979 Picture Disc May 1979
	Re-released July 1985 Sierra SP 1963 (with previous unreleased songs)
GRAM PARSONS & THE FALLEN ANGELS	Album: *LIVE 1973*
Gram Parsons–vocal, guitar Emmylou Harris–vocal, guitar Jock Bartley–lead guitar N.D. Smart II -vocal, drums Kyle Tullis–bass Neal Flanz–pedal steel	Sierra GP 1973
	Released February 1982
	EP: *MORE GRAM PARSONS & THE FALLEN ANGELS LIVE 1973*
	Sierra GP/EP 104
	Released September 1982

APPEARANCES ON RECORD OF SONGS WRITTEN OR CO-WRITTEN BY GRAM PARSONS

"A Song For You" (Gram Parsons)

Blazers STORE BOUGHT (Cream Records)

"Apple Tree" (Gram Parsons)

Johnny Rivers SLIM SLO SLIDER (Imperial LP 16001)

"Blue Eyes" (Gram Parsons)

The Flying Norwegians THIS TIME AROUND (Sonet SLP 1451)

"Brass Buttons" (Gram Parsons)

The Flying Norwegians LIVE (Sonet SLP 1451)

Poco CRAZY EYES (Epic 65631)

Johnny Rivers SLIM SLO SLIDER (Imperial LP 16001)

"Christine's Tune" (Gram Parsons/Chris Hillman)

The Flying Burrito Brothers LIVE IN AMSTERDAM (Ariola 86 439 XCT)

Country Gazette ALL THIS AND MONEY TOO (Ridgerunner RRR 001)

The Flying Burrito Brothers THE LAST OF THE RED HOT BURRITOS (A&M AMLS 64343)

"Down In the Churchyard" (Gram Parsons/Chris Hillman)

Chris Hillman SLIPPIN' AWAY (Asylum 1062)

"Drug Store Truck Drivin' Man" (Roger McGuinn/Gram Parsons)

Joan Baez WOODSTOCK (Cotillion SD 3–500)

The Byrds DR. BYRDS AND MR. HYDE (Columbia CS 9785)

"Hickory Wind" (Gram Parsons/Bob Buchannon)

Joan Baez THE CONTEMPORARY BALLAD BOOK (Vanguard VSD 49–½)

J.D. Crowe YOU CAN SHARE MY BLANKET (Rounder 096)

Var. Artists COUNTRY AND WESTERN GREATS (BBC REC 276)

"High Fashion Queen" (Gram Parsons/Chris Hillman)

The Flying Burrito Brothers LAST OF THE RED HOT BURRITOS (A&M AMLS 64343)

"Hot Burrito #1" (Gram Parsons/Chris Ethridge)

Gene Parsons MELODIES (Sierra SRS 8703)

Robb Strandlund ROBB STRANDLUND (Polydor PD–1–6085)

Country Gazette ALL THIS AND MONEY TOO (Ridgerunner RRR 001)

"Hot Burrito #2" (Gram Parsons/Chris Ethridge)

Flying Burrito Brothers LAST OF THE RED HOT BURRITOS (A&M AMLS 64343)

Flying Burrito Brothers CLOSE ENCOUNTERS TO THE WEST COAST (Nippon YX 7218)

Emmylou Harris *EVANGELINE* (Warner Bros. BSK 3508)

"Juanita" (Gram Parsons/Chris Hillman)

Phil Rosenthal INDIAN SUMMER (Flying Fish 078)

"Luxury Liner" (Gram Parsons)

Emmylou Harris LUXURY LINER (Warner Bros. BS 2998)

"My Uncle" (Gram Parsons/Chris Hillman)

Flying Burrito Brothers LIVE IN AMSTERDAM (Ariola 86 439 XCT)

"Ooh, Las Vegas" (Gram Parsons/Rick Grech)

The Crickets REMNANTS (Vertigo VEL 1020)

Emmylou Harris ELITE HOTEL (Warner Bros. MS 2236)

American Echoes 45 RPM (Phonogram)

"November Nights" (Gram Parsons)

Peter Fonda 45 RPM (Chisa 004)

"Return of the Grievous Angel" (Gram Parsons/B. Brown)

Lennie & The Hawks LENNIE & THE HAWKS (RCA PL 40025)

"She" (Gram Parsons/Chris Ethridge)

Lena Andersson DET BASTA SOM FINNS (Polar POLS 276)

David Clayton–Thomas DAVID CLAYTON–THOMAS (Columbia 31000)

Emmylou Harris LUXURY LINER (Warner BRos. BS 2998)

"Sin City" (Gram Parsons/Chris Hillman)

Flying Burrito Brothers LIVE IN AMSTERDAM (Ariola 86 439 XCT)

Emmylou Harris ELITE HOTEL (Warner Bros. MS 2236)

J.D. Crowe BLACKJACK (RAMBLIN' BOY) REBEL (King Bluegrass SLP 1583)

"Still Feeling Blue" (Gram Parsons)

Country Gazette OUT TO LUNCH (Flying Fish 027)

Cliftones DU ER DEN JEG SOKER (Country C 507)

"Wheels" (Gram Parsons/Chris Hillman)

Emmylou Harris ELITE HOTEL (Warner Bros. MS 2236)

TRIBUTES AND DEDICATIONS:

"Boulder to Birmingham" (Emmylou Harris/Bill Danoff)

Emmylou Harris PIECES OF THE SKY (Reprise 2213)

"Artists and Poets" (Johnny Rivers/Michael Georgiades)

Johnny Rivers ROAD (Atlantic SD 7301)

"Crazy Eyes" (Richie Furay)

Poco CRAZY EYES (Epic 65631)

"My Man" (Bernie Leadon)

Eagles ON THE BORDER (Asylum SYL 9016)

"Seems Like I Can't Live With You, Can't Live Without You" (Burton Cummings/Domenic Troiano)

The Guess Who FLAVOURS (RCA CPL 1–0636)

"A Wailing Goodbye" (Ian Matthews)

Ian Matthews SOMEDAYS YOU EAT THE BEARS (Elektra 75078)

SESSION CREDITS:

Gram Parsons appears on the following recordings

The Byrds	*UNTITLED*	Columbia CG 301127
Jesse Davis	*JESSE DAVIS*	Atco SD 33-346
Delaney & Bonnie	*MOTEL SHOT*	Atco SD 33-358
Fred Neil	*THE OTHER SIDE OF THIS LIFE* *(Ya Don't Miss Your Water)*	Capitol ST-657
Steve Yo'ung	*ROCK, SALT & NAILS*	A&M 4177
Rolling Stones	*EXILE ON MAIN STREET* *(Sweet Virginia)*	R.S. rec. COC-2-2900
Rick Grech	THE LAST FIVE YEARS	(RSO 50 876)

MISCELLANEOUS:

In addition THE LAST OF THE RED HOT BURRITOS by the Flying Burrito Brothers contains a GP interview for liner notes (A&M SP 4343)

The Byrds' BALLAD OF EASY RIDER has a Parsons arrangement of an old Dixie hymn called "Jesus Is Just Allright With Me" that Parsons showed McGuinn. Later the Doobie Brothers had an AM hit with the same arrangement

The Gram Parsons Memorial Foundation (GPMF)
3109 Ola Ave.
Tampa, FL 33603 U.S.A.
(813) 224-9083

The Gram Parsons Memorial Foundation (GPMF) is a worldwide non-profit organization to document and perpetuate the music of Gram Parsons. Founded three years ago by Mark Holland of Tampa Florida, The GPMF offers membership to all those interested in the music of Gram Parsons and who want to share in fellowship with others around the world in his musical legacy. The Foundation offers a continuing newsletter on its activities and maintains as well as makes available to its members discographies on songs and recordings, printed articles and other documented materials relating to Gram Parsons. Gram's vision was to bring people together through his music and the GPMF is carrying on this ideal.

Reference List

ARTICLES WRITTEN ON GRAM PARSONS

Melody Maker – England:

7/25/70 Gram Parsons Burrito Ego Man
4/7/73 Parsons Knows (Loraine Alterman)
7/27/74 Country Parsons (Allen Jones)
2/8/75 Burrito Deluxe (Allen Jones)
2/15/75 Red Hot Burrito (Allen Jones)
3/22/75 Grieving Angel (Allen Jones)
5/17/76 Intrepid Aviators
6/5/76 Parsons Death Ritual
9/25/76 Taste Makers
6/26/76 Parsons Wild In the Country

Rolling Stone – U.S.A.

8/24/68 Parsons Refuses Gig in South Africa
5/17/69 Records, The Gilded Palace of Sin (review)
3/1/73 Ex–Byrd Solos: Gram Parsons No Longer In a Hurry (Judith Sims)

3/1/73 Gram Parsons Record Review (Bud Scoppa)
3/28/74 Jim Stafford Swamps & Spiders & Snakes
10/25/74 GP Mysterious Death and Aftermath (Patrick Sullivan and Eve Babitz)
6/17/76 G.P. Sleepless Nights (Billy Altman)
4/21/77 Random Notes

Crawdaddy – U.S.A.

Oct. '76 Gram Finale (Judson Klinger, Greg Mitchell)
July '73 G.P. Sweeps Out the Ashes (Jay Ehler)
July '76 Crazy Eyes Goodbye (Greg Mitchell)

Country Music – U.S.A.

Sept. '74 The L.A. Turnabout (Bud Scoppa)

Country Music Review – U.S.A.

Dec. '74 Gram Parsons: Grievous Angel (John Firminger)

Hittin The Note – U.S.A.

Aug. '76 The Making of a Grievous Angel (Marris Johnson)

Soundings – U.S.A.

April/May '68 Gram Parsons

Zoo World – U.S.A.

7/5/73 Gram Parsons (Michael Bate)
8/15/74 Gram Parsons: A Posthumous Reunion (David W. Johnson)
4/11/74 Grievous Angel (record review)

Rock – U.S.A.

11/19/73 G.P. A Last Gesture for a Country Gentleman

Gosh! – U.S.A.

May '79 Gram Parsons (Sid Griffin)

The Thinking Person Magazine

May/June '79 The Flying Burrito Brothers (Jerry Milbauer)

U.C.L.A. Times Calendar – U.S.A.

April 14, 1968 C/W Flags Flown By Submarine Band

U.C.L.A. Summer Bruin – U.S.A.

6/22/74 Burrito Bonanza

Los Angeles Times Calendar – U.S.A.

11/2/75 Gram Parsons Straight Home to US (Robert Hillburn)

Encyclopedia of Pop, Rock & Soul – U.S.A.

(Entry) Gram Parsons
(Entry) Byrds
(Entry) Flying Burrito Brothers

Country Music Encyclopedia (Melvin Sheotack)

(Entry) Gram Parsons

This book typeset by the Assistant Editor at Newcomp Graphics Center, located at the Beyond Baroque Foundation in Venice, California

---

Born in Lake Geneva, Wisconsin in 1947, JOHN DELGATTO moved with his family to Southern California in 1954. Absorbing the varied music of the area as a youth, he performed in several folk groups in the early '60s. Playing banjo, guitar and mandolin, John appeared at such coffee houses as the Ice House, the Troubadour and the Ash Grove. His early musical influences included The Weavers, Elvis Presley, the Kingston Trio, Journeymen, The Modern Folk Quartet, Clarence White and the Kentucky Colonels and fellow high school mate, David Lindley.

In the late 1960s, while majoring in television production in college, John could be heard on the Los Angeles airwaves doing a variety of radio programs. He hosted the first "all bluegrass" radio show to be heard west of the Mississippi while working at Paramount Studios in lighting for the "Star Trek" television series.

In 1969, John produced and engineered his first record album – a local bluegrass festival. This led to his involvement in the world of bluegrass as a producer, writer and reviewer for such publications as *Bluegrass Unlimited, Sing Out* and others. After college, in 1971, John travelled to various music festivals with Doc and Merle Watson which led to his association with such music notables as Clarence White, Country Gazette and Gram Parsons. Deciding not to go with Gram Parsons as equipment manager on the Fallen Angels tour in 1973, John accepted a position as disc mastering engineer eventually cutting sides for such diverse artists as Elvis Presley, Lee Michaels, Graham Nash and Stan Kenton.

John's interest in all areas of record manufacturing led to his creation of Briar Records. Among the first albums he produced for his new label were a fiddle album by the legendary Leslie Keith, a Doc Watson Family album (never released) and an album of classic live performances by the Kentucky Colonels. This live album was a joint production effort with Clarence White. The collaboration was cut short by Clarence's death in July, 1973 yet the album, finally released in 1976, is the only fully authorized live recording of the Kentucky Colonels.

John opened new record company offices in West Los Angeles in 1978. Calling the label Sierra/Briar, he released albums by Nashville West, Scotty Stoneman, Gene Parsons, Gram Parsons and others. Closing that office in 1981, John returned to his home base of Pasadena/Sierra Madre, California. He and co-producer Marley Brant released, on Sierra Records, the GRAM PARSONS AND THE FALLEN ANGELS – LIVE, 1973 album in February, 1982. The following year, that album was honored with a Grammy nomination for "Best Country Performance By a Duo/Group" for the song "Love Hurts."

Currently John has returned to the field of television production specializing in film and videotape research of vintage television music programs. Partner Paul Surratt, business associate Ron Furmanek and John are considered among the leading authorities on televison/video music history. Production credits for their company, Research Video, include 1982-84 Emmy Awards broadcasts, "Here's Television Entertainment" (winner of two Emmy Awards) and home video projects of the Beach Boys and the Doors. Most recently John and his associates have produced and directed "The Carpenters – Yesterday Once More," a home video hits album for A&M Records.

Gram Parsons: A Music Biography is the first publication of John's newly-formed Sierra Books division of Sierra Records.

SID GRIFFIN was born in Louisville, Kentucky, where he was raised. He graduated from the University of South Carolina with a degree in Journalism in 1977 and moved to California later that year, ostensibly to attend grad school at the University of Southern California but in reality to join a rock n' roll band. He is presently ringleader of the Long Ryders, an internationally acclaimed American music band. A professional musician, he is also a freelance writer of note, contributing to *Creem, BAM* and *Musician.* This is his first book.